Gabriel Lock:

BOUND BY LAW

By: D. & H. Cancio

ISBN: 978-1-962825-27-6

This book is a work of fiction and non-fictional events based on expression. Some of the names, characters, places and incidents are products of the writer's imagination or have been used fictitiously. Any resemblance to persons, living or dead, actual events, locale or organisations is entirely coincidental.

A novel inspired by true events.

Any similarity to any specific person, occurrence or event is purely coincidental.

"The Sacred Charge of Lawyers is to give themselves to those who need them."

-Thomas Lock

Chapter 1: The Plea Deal

Miami, Florida: Late December 1980

Gabriel ran his hands under the faucet, letting the warm water run down to his wrists, just before his rolled-up sleeves, revealing his white skin. His lower back twitched and strained, as he stared into his own reflection in the mirror in front of the sink. The stress of the last twenty-four hours engulfed him, manifesting down his leg as his sciatica flared. He winced and leaned further forward, trying his best to stretch the muscles and relieve the discomfort. Gabriel held the pose and counted to thirty, listening to the ticks of his watch as the seconds passed by. Finishing the stretch, he rose and glanced down at the time as he raised his wet hands from under the faucet. *12 minutes*, he thought. As he reached to his left, he grabbed a few paper towels and dried his hands before placing them on the edges of the sink. Returning to the mirror, he saw a man out of choices.

"I'm leaving because I refused to break my promise," he whispered to himself. His lower back forced the focus from his cerulean eyes, and he lingered for a moment. He had to break the news as gently as he could. The knuckles on his hands whitened as he balled them into fists and brought his weight down on them. Still staring at the mirror, he said: "Enough, just do it."

He collected himself, brushed off a few wrinkles from his grey suit and walked out of the restroom into the hallway, as he approached a couple in their late forties.

"Mr. and Mrs. Adegboye, good to see you both."

"It is good to see you again, Gabriel, but please, we have asked you so many times to call us by our first names.

You do know them, right?" joked Mrs. Adegboye, flashing a quick smile from beneath her dark lips. Her ebony eyes fixed on his as with one graceful movement she brushed her black hair to the side with her rich milk chocolate fingertips before reaching for his outstretched hand.

"You'll have to ask me once more, Mrs. Adegboye, but I do know that your names are Sharice and Leonard, and I know them well," explained Gabriel, now taking Mr. Adegboye's outstretched hand and with firm grips, they shook. "Please, this way."

Gabriel led them down the hallway to an empty conference room with a few chairs, a table, and the fresh scent of bleach.

"The cleaning crew must have just finished," commented Leonard, flaring his mahogany nostrils, and covering his nose for a moment.

"Oh, don't fuss, Lenny," said Sharice as she waved a hand in front of her face, disregarding the smell, "Gabriel doesn't have that much time."

"Thank you," said Gabriel. He gestured to the seats on the opposite side of the table where they took their places as Gabriel took his. He did his best to conceal his deep breath by raising his briefcase from the floor to the table. The latch clicked open, and he retrieved a set of files from within. "Mr. and Mrs. Adegboye, I asked you to meet with me here today because I wanted to speak to you in person."

Sharice pointed her eyebrows inward and the thin skin between her nose and forehead wrinkled, channeling her dark eyes to an unpleasant stare.

"Mr. and Mrs. Adegboye, I wanted to let you know that I will no longer handle your case as I am leaving the State Attorney's Office."

Leonard's eyes widened and Sharice's lip quivered. Silence befell them for a moment as Gabriel opened the file. Neither Sharice nor Leonard moved. Gabriel opened to speak, but Leonard's voice sounded first as the linebacker of a man stood up.

"Eighteen months," he began, "we've worked with you for eighteen months."

Gabriel remained silent, containing his emotions.

The resonant voice continued.

"My father is in a wheelchair, bound to that limited existence for the rest of his lessened life. Do you know what pain that is?" The ashen hairs of his goatee ruffled as he pursed his lips in malevolence.

"Lenny," said Sharice, putting a hand on his, caressing the veined skin on the back of his hand.

"It's alright, Mrs. Adegboye," said Gabriel. He swallowed and began, "Mr. Adegboye," Gabriel leaned toward them, shifting his weight onto his elbows and forearms. "I am leaving you because I have no other choice, but I wanted to meet with both of you to review the case one last time and clarify the position and evidence that will work in your favor to attain the maximum penalty possible."

Lenny faced Gabriel and his huge voice began to fill the room. "You can walk away from this because you didn't run into your family store and see your father lying on the floor, shot down. You did not grab the nearest rag and try to stop the gushes of blood coming out of his wound. You did not feel the movements of his broken body desperately reaching for life on the cold hard floor. You never walk away from that, Mr. Lock. Never." Lenny glared at him with angry black eyes set in reddened eyeballs. Gabriel felt his face get hot with resentment towards the division chief. He held his composure, skin warm from the curdling blood within him, but kept his professional tone.

"I spoke with my division chief, and the attorney who will represent you is one of our very best."

"What is his name?" asked Sharice while her svelte body turned in her chair to look at Gabriel through feminine tortoise shell glasses.

"Brian Donovan. He is an outstanding attorney and he's unrelenting," said Gabriel with feigned conviction.

"Is he as clever as you?" inquired Leonard, not caring for much else.

"Yes."

"Maybe it's a blessing that we'd get a lawyer who's actually passionate about justice and does right for the victim."

"Leonard!" cried Sharice, her face aghast as her mouth lay open, "apologize, now."

Mr. Adegboye did not budge.

"Leonard, this is beneath you," continued Mrs. Adegboye.

"It's fine, Mrs. Adegboye," stated Gabriel, defusing the situation, "Mr. Donovan is as fervorous about his cases as I am."

"Just more committed to justice than you." His voice boomed.

"LEONARD, ENOUGH!" ordered Mrs. Adegboye as she pushed her chair back in her seat a bit and leaned toward him, trying to stare him down.

"My father is in a wheelchair and our lawyer decides he wants to LEAVE?!" Mr. Adegboye fumed now as his breath quickened and his broad shoulders throbbed as if they spoke for his mouth. "If your father were the one and not mine, you would act the same!"

Sharice shook her head but did not say a word.

Gabriel wanted to say so much, but he could say so little. "I understand," he said finally, surrendering to the situation.

"Do you really?"

"Yes, I do."

"And still, you walk away?" Mr. Adegboye glared at Gabriel. After a moment he broke off his anger and barked "When do we meet this, Donovan?"

"Any minute now," said Gabriel, glancing at his watch and remaining professional despite Mr. Adegboye's anger, "I asked him to speak with you at 9:30 this morning and it's almost time. He will review the file with you and go from there."

"Good, at least you did that right!" he fired. A moment passed and a knock sounded at the door.

"Come in," said Gabriel, turning to face the tall, balding man with a thick mustache and grey eyes who slid through and introduced himself.

"Mr. and Mrs. Adegboye, I am Brian Donovan, the attorney who will handle your case moving forward." The Adegboyes nodded.

"Donovan, would you let me have just a minute with them?"

"Sure, I'll wait outside," he said, stepping out.

Gabriel stood from his chair and closed the briefcase, taking it in his hand. He left the file on the table and brushed the wrinkles from his suit jacket. "It has a been a pleasure working with both of you from the beginning and even now," he said.

Mr. Adegboye scoffed at him.

Gabriel nodded and left the room. As he closed the door behind him, he found Donovan waiting for him, leaning against the opposite wall, with a hand covering part of his mustached face. His thinning hair and receding hairlines marked the evidence of the overworked state attorney.

"From what I heard; you softened them up for me."

"They're good people, Donovan, I don't fault them."

"Still noble despite the disrespect, you're really something, Lock."

"Part of the job, nothing more."

"And humble too," joked Donovan, "well, I don't care for any of that wrath, with the little time we have for each case, we do what we can with what we are given. I don't know your reasons, but now I must sell them the plea which you refused to do. So, excuse me, Lock while I do your job too." Donovan scoffed at him, opened the door, and walked through.

Gabriel stood in place for a moment, decided to shrug off the comments, and strode back toward the elevator and to his office, his muscular legs still feeling flashes from the tension concentrated in his lower back. He knew that Donovan was overtaxed like the rest of them, but he also knew that Donovan was always the first to leave at the end of the day.

When the elevator reached the correct floor, he walked down the corridor until arriving at the familiar space. He closed the door behind him when he entered and, as he shuffled toward his desk, he moved to kick the garbage can against the far wall but stopped himself before contact. He glowered at the wads of paper inside the receptacle. Exasperation nearly got the better of him, but he remained civilized. He moved back to his chair and sat, staring at his signature on the forced resignation from earlier this morning. He leaned back and closed his eyes, recalling all that had transpired that day. By late afternoon he would leave and his time as a State Attorney would come to an end. Gabriel rose from his chair and grabbed the empty boxes to pack his belongings.

"The next chapter," he said aloud.

Chapter 2: The Next Chapter

Miami, Florida: Late December 1980

Gabriel's cerulean eyes closed as he grasped at his lower back and winced. He did his best to comfort the knotted muscles, hoping to soothe them, but had little luck. As the swelling culled, the chair behind his desk appealed to him. He knew sitting would increase the pain when he stood back up but preferred the immediate relief in exchange for later agony. He turned to face the window as the sun disappeared behind the Holiday Inn next to the river.

He returned to the task at hand, knowing that he had to remove everything before he left. Glancing over to the photographs he allowed himself to display, he calculated how he would fit them into the boxes without breaking them.

Beneath his tucked elbows sat the box of his personal items on the edge of his desk. He grabbed the last picture frame and looked at Abuelo's face as he held it in his hands. Years before, they had stood together at the top of that mountain and contemplated all that his grandfather had left behind when he and Abuela decided to emigrate from Asturias to Miami. Now it was Gabriel's turn to leave. He was done at the State Attorney's Office, done with the limitations, the politics, and choosing which victims mattered most. He placed a finger on the glass, brushing away a bit of dust, and smiled weakly. *Abuelo, they told me that I didn't understand, told me that I didn't care, but they weren't there when I held your hand at the hospital. They didn't see me sleeping on the floor next to your bed, and they didn't hear my prayers when you were shot coming home from your store. I understand their anger and I know their pain, but I can't share that with them. I wanted to push this as far as it could go but was forbidden to.* Gabriel sighed as he wiped a bead of sweat from his temple. *Life would be easier if you were here, Abuelo. I miss our talks.*

He paused for a moment, valued the happier time, and lowered the frame before resting it onto the emerald towel in the box and wrapped it for safety. Pulling his sleeve from under his watch, Gabriel straightened himself up and began removing the rest of his mementos from the desktop. He glanced beyond the chair to the aged maps of Florida and Asturias beneath his diplomas from the University of Florida. *I'll save you for last,* he thought as he moved the frame to the side, protecting it.

He glanced at his watch to find the minute hand had moved to half past five. He ran his fingers through his black hair, massaging his scalp, for a few moments, attempting to lessen the tension of the day's earlier events. Gabriel paused, exhaling deeply. The muscles in his lower back tightened and his sciatica flared. "I know," he said to himself, "I'll deal with you all weekend and long after I start working with Dad." Trying to shrug the pain from his left leg, he straightened himself up, and, after checking the door was closed, he lowered his torso down and reached as far as he could toward the carpet.

He stood up and jolts surged down the back of his left leg from his lower back through his hamstring and to his toes. They numbed for a second before the second wave of pain shot through him forcing him to gasp for air. His breath shallowed and he held the position until his watch sounded for the tenth time. He bent his torso forward and inhaled slowly and deeply as his back cracked, watching the second hand click for a few more times before repeating the movement several times. Despite the pain, the tension began to give way and Gabriel wiped a few drops of sweat from his forehead with the back of his sleeve.

His mind shifted from the discomfort to the conversation with his division chief, Nikolaos Drakos, earlier that day:

"You're sure that you want to do this, Lock?" said Drakos, his smoky amber eyes focused on Gabriel's.

"Yes sir, I'm sure."

"Before you go thinking that I say this to everyone, I want you to know that you're one of the best young assistant state attorneys in this office and I hate to lose you." Drakos leaned back in his chair. "I suppose that it's no surprise given your father's reputation as a lawyer, but if you keep this up, you could be the State Attorney or even the AG by the end of your career," said the division chief, shaking his greying brown hair. Gabriel lingered on the words, trying his best to hide from the experienced litigator the fact that he had already made up his mind. He counted the ticks from his watch, determining that enough time had passed before replying.

"Thanks Nikolaos. I appreciate very much that you would think so highly of me, but honestly, I have wanted to practice with my dad ever since I was a kid."

"I understand that and respect it. Not everyone is lucky enough to have Thomas Lock as a father. You know, there're many similarities between us Mediterranean families," he said, alluding to his Greek heritage, "If I would have had any love for mechanical things when I was younger, maybe I would have been a mechanic like my old man and maybe I would have worked alongside him too. He would have loved to put *and son* on his sign."

Gabriel smiled, looking at his very sharply dressed boss and pictured him covered in grease.

"Lock, I understand that you want to work with your old man but is that your reason for leaving or is there something else?" pressed Drakos.

"No, and he really needs my help so... now seems like the best time to make the transition."

"Okay," confirmed Drakos, "Then I need you to sign here on your letter of resignation." Drakos reached into the breast pocket of his navy pinstripe suit and retrieved a pen. He stretched out his hand and slid the document across the table of the conference room toward Gabriel. Gabriel took the pen and drew the paper toward him. He read the document for a few moments before rotating it slightly and signing it next to the x at the bottom.

"I think that you're only the second person I've supervised that I have released from their 3-year commitment to the State Attorney's Office."

Gabriel offered no reply.

"Since it's Friday, you're welcome to take as long as you need to clear out the office, but should you exceed eight o'clock, you'll have to return on Monday to drop off the key when the doors open. If you need a cart, I'll have someone from maintenance bring it up to you. Do you need any boxes to pack your things?"

"I could use the cart and a few boxes; I've only got a small one."

"I'll have maintenance bring up a cart and two banker's boxes. Should you need more, just ask."

"Sure thing."

Drakos rose from his chair and reached toward Gabriel. Gabriel, seeing the outstretched hand, took it in his and shook, bidding farewell. Drakos left the office, taking the pen and the letter in his hand, while Gabriel dawdled reflecting on the last time he used this conference room.

"Another time," he said aloud returning to the present and acknowledging that he still had things to do. He rose from his chair; the swelling grew and tension in his back stiffened. He grimaced, and jolts of pain shot up and down his left leg. He leaned on the corner of his desk and, mustering his will, labored to the wall behind him.

Gabriel felt the frame unhook from the nail on the wall. Circling, he saw the emerald towel lying flat on top of his desk. He placed the last diploma on it and slowly wrapped the metal and glass frame with the cloth, inserting it next to the other frames in the bigger of the two banker's boxes covering the desktop. He placed the cardboard top on and lifted the box, positioning it on the folding cart that carried his personal items. He had loaded the smaller box in a second and was looking around the empty office, making sure he had left nothing behind. Crouching, he winced as he grabbed the end of the bungee cord and stretched it around the items, hooking it onto the handle.

As he secured the cart, he heard a slightly accented and deep voice behind him. "Have two years really worn you down so much that you're so quick to leave?"

Gabriel struggled to grin.

"I'm ready to leave the place and the job, but not the people," said Gabriel.

"That's good to hear." The taller man's espresso arm was outstretched as Gabriel stood up and met the warm hand with his own. "Sciatica flaring again?"

"Yeah, just making my last day memorable."

"It always seems to visit you when you're stressed and I must admit, I figured that today wouldn't have been one of those days. You should be carefree."

"When is a lawyer ever carefree?" said Gabriel looking up at his friend.

"When he's six under."

"Morbid."

"Truth," finished Moses. He paused for a moment and walked around the bare office. "As I was coming up the elevator, I was thinking that since you are leaving, I would have to have lunch with Rodrigo whenever he was in the building, and you know how much I hate defense attorneys," he said, grinning. "You have caught me off guard with your decision to leave. I thought you'd be here for another year at least."

"I thought about this for a long time, Mo. I was going to stick it out, but now my dad needs me at the firm earlier than he and I had calculated. New investors from South America have been investing their money in real estate in

Miami and elsewhere, so they've retained him quite a bit. The civil wars in Central America, Venezuela, and Columbia are heating up, so their need to move their investments forward has increased. He is bombarded with work, and he needs me. Besides, you know that criminal prosecution is not really satisfying work for me."

"Yeah, I do know. I've seen it change you, especially over the last few months. As you know, my parents left Congo because brothers and sisters committed too many crimes and never paid for them. Politics should never get in the way of justice. I do my best every day to help ensure that those injustices do not happen here, and though I know I fail often, it keeps my head held high. But this is not what you had in mind as a career path."

"I just want to protect the common person, not punish the uncommon one."

"There is nothing uncommon about a criminal; most of them are brutes," said Moses, raising his voice an octave. Moses cut his speech short as Gabriel raised his eyebrows. "A debate for another time."

Gabriel nodded and slipped behind his desk, grabbing his briefcase from the seat of his chair. Moses grabbed the handle of the cart and moved it toward the door. Gabriel turned off the lights with Moses tailing him. He looked through the glass pane one last time and then at his name on the right side of the frame before shutting the door. They found the elevator to the lobby and walked out into the warm Miami night.

"It's going to be a big change," said Moses softly as they walked to the attorney's parking lot. "The first year in private practice will be tough. You won't be answering to another lawyer for your work or your results. Instead, you'll be looking at the client straight in the eye and letting them know how your work has affected his or her life. It is intimate and personal, and that can be exceedingly difficult." Moses removed his spectacles and used his lower jacket to wipe them.

"Speaking from experience?" pressed Gabriel.

"No, secondhand at best, but are you ready for that level of investment?" Moses returned the glasses to his eyes after massaging between them. Gabriel stopped short of his Buick Regal and looked up at Moses's glasses, staring through to his eyes.

"I learned a lot here. I made hard choices and took hard stances on those who deserved it. I did the right thing by living it every day that I stepped into that courtroom, but, eventually, I felt empty. The only thing that felt personal was the punishment, and that's not the personal I wanted to feel."

"If you fail your clients out there, you run the risk of it being too personal, you know that, right?"

Gabriel lingered on the words, choosing his answer wisely.

"There are limits to both, Mo, but answering to clients means that they choose how long to pursue justice. It's not chosen for them."

"Is there something more than going to work with your dad at play here?"

"No, there isn't," said Gabriel, flashing to the conversation with Drakos and the non-disclosure he signed a few hours ago. "I'm just ready for the next chapter."

"Okay, Lock. It's been fun having you here. I guess that I'll have to settle for seeing you at our weekly game."

"Yeah," agreed Gabriel, chuckling, "But it'll be the five of us and we'll be people instead of lawyers."

"Yes," acknowledged Moses, sighing relief, "it's hard to turn that off when we're here, even as friends."

"And harder when the friend is a defense attorney."

Moses laughed and Gabriel changed the subject.

"Would you mind doing me a favor, Mo?"

Moses gave a blank expression.

"Sure."

"Can you turn this in on Monday for me?" asked Gabriel, reaching for the key to his office.

"I will, Lock. Not a worry."

"Thanks, Mo," replied Gabriel, deciding not to linger on the conversation, "I really appreciate it." Moses slid the cart toward him and departed back toward his own vehicle on the other side of the lot. Gabriel opened the trunk of the car, loaded his things, and closed the lid. He waited for Moses to leave before taking a moment to gather his thoughts. The conversation with Drakos returned to him:

"There are bigger cases than this, Lock. The State can't devote anymore resources than it already has." Drakos had said.

"Nik, I can win this."

"It doesn't matter that you can win because we aren't going to trial. We are going to plea this out and it is your job to convince them that this is the best option. Convince the Adegboye family that this plea deal is the best thing for them, and they won't have to sit in court and relive the horror of what happened. Besides, even if you win it is only five more years of jail and that is not relevant after the Defendant has served twenty years."

"But this plea means accepting a lesser charge and a lesser penalty. I made them a promise that I would not plea this out for anything less than what we can get in court. Nik, I can win." He finished in a whisper.

"You should know better than to make any promises. It's a done deal, Lock. We don't need their consent to offer the plea, it just looks better in the community if they do. Get the victim's family to accept the plea deal, or I'll find a lawyer who can."

"But the bond with the client. The trust they give us. How can I walk away from that?

"Lock, the victim is not your client, the victim's family is not your client; the State is your client. And right now, as your boss, I am the State, and I am telling you to convince the family to take the plea."

"I won't."

"You're a good lawyer and I don't want to lose you, so I am going to give you tonight to think about it. I want your answer tomorrow morning."

Gabriel sighed, dismissing his thoughts and everything that had transpired in the last forty-eight hours. He forgave everything that Mr. Adegboye had said to him just hours earlier. Emotion was a luxury afforded to people, but not attorneys. As he walked toward the driver's side, he glanced at the Gerstein building once more, hoping that it would be for the last time, before driving into the night and back home.

Chapter 3: The Arrest

Miami, Florida: Early March 1981

The Yankees led by one at the bottom of the ninth inning as the batter walked up from the dugout, spitting a wad of dip from between his teeth and flexing his shoulders from back to front. Swinging the bat across his body and warming up, the sun shone above him, and he seemed to look up to the sky, searching for an omen. He stared at the pitcher in his pinstripe uniform and shook his head, letting his light brown hair flow from under the helmet. Joaquín stared at the game through the grainy resolution of the large TV in his living room. The vibrant colors fluctuated as the wind blew, and the dish on the house's roof teetered from side to side. *Damn it, the picture better not go out again*, he thought in Spanish as he popped the top off a cold Budweiser and flicked the condensation from his hand on to his slight pot belly. As the batter stepped up to the plate, the doorbell rang, and Joaquín cursed. Not wanting to miss anything, he yelled to his wife.

"Rosa, can you come grab the door, honey?" He waited for a response but only got a muffled sound from the other side of the house. *Shit*, he thought. Placing the Budweiser back down on the glass pane of the coffee table, Joaquín hoisted himself up from the plastic-wrapped couch, feeling the pull of the plastic on his leg hair as he twisted with momentum. Launching himself up but not straying his eyes from the game, the doorbell rang again, and he shouted in Spanish through the door.

"Jorge, my friend, calm down you animal; I'm coming!" He turned his head to the door for a second, and, at that moment, he heard a loud crack come from the living room, the crowd roared, and heard the announcer screaming with joy. Joaquín reared his head back to the game and opened the door without taking his eyes off the screen. As the door tweaked open, he bellowed instructions to come in and grab a beer when he heard an unfamiliar voice.

"Are you Joaquín Pérez?" asked the voice in English. Joaquín shifted his eyes from the game to the door, seeing a blue uniform and a badge through the sliver of open space. Bewilderment played with him, and he wondered if he was imagining things. Rubbing his eyes for a moment, he opened them wide and swung the door fully open, revealing three Miami Dade County police officers on the front step.

"I'm sorry, officers," he said in Cuban accented English, "I thought that you were my friend, Jorge. Yes, I am Joaquín Pérez; how can I help you?" The officers nodded, and one of them removed a set of handcuffs from his belt glancing at Joaquín's curly black hair.

"Step out of the house, sir. You need to come with us." Joaquín's eyebrows rose, and the wrinkles on his tan face faded as his eyes widened anew.

"But officers, why?"

"You are under arrest," said the tall officer in the back. Joaquín retreated a step, and the officers leaned forward. The sun shone off his dark sunglasses and concealed the eyes behind them. Reading the question behind his expression, the first officer spoke.

"Mr. Pérez, you are under arrest for the incident at the park."

"What Park?" asked Joaquín, terror emanating through him as his voice broke. The bolting feet sounded from the other side of the house, growing louder as they drew closer. Rosa Pérez appeared behind him, confusion and uncertainty marking themselves on her expression.

"What is happening, Joaquín?" clamored Rosa in Spanish, panting and trying to catch her breath.

"Ma'am, please return to your bedroom; this doesn't concern you," said one of the officers. Rosa ignored the command.

"What do you mean this doesn't concern me? He's my husband!" yelled Rosa in English.

"Ma'am, please calm down and return to your bedroom. We are just here for Mr. Pérez."

"But why? What did I do?" he asked through his Fu Manchu mustache.

"Mr. Pérez, we have a witness that saw you and took down your license plate as you fled the scene of the crime. Did you really think that you could hit a child with a bat and face no consequences?"

"But I didn't hit anyone!" voiced Joaquín. His angular cheeks flushed in frustration.

"We have five witnesses and your license plate number here!" said the first officer, raising his arm and opening his hand to show the license plate number drawn on his small notepad.

"This is ridiculous," roared Joaquín, "I'm calling my lawyer."

As he turned to make his way to the phone in the kitchen, the officers dashed through the door and grabbed him. "Let go of me. What are you doing?"

"Mr. Pérez, you are under arrest. Stop resisting!"

Joaquín struggled, shifting his body weight through his short stocky body, trying to free himself. Rosa screamed and clapped her hands on her cheeks in disbelief. The four men fell to the floor, and in the tussle, the officers took hold of him and dragged him across the floor. Desperate to escape, Joaquín stretched his muscular arm toward the door frame and latched onto it. Pulling his way back into the house, Joaquín's eyes met Rosa's teary ones, but before he could surrender, the officers jerked his legs away and pulled him out of the doorway. A loud pop sounded, and

Joaquín screamed in pain and his uneven teeth froze in a grimace. No one moved and, in the second it took to process what had happened, Joaquín cried in anguish as pain ripped into his right shoulder and across his chest. He tried to grab it with his left hand but felt the firm grip of the officer take him, lifting his head off the floor and dragging his limp body across the cement stoop and into the squad car. Somewhere along the way, everything went black, and Joaquín collapsed.

Chapter 4: The Partnership

Miami, Florida: March 1981

Gabriel pulled into the parking space beneath the I-95 overpass that led downtown, cracked the window of his midnight blue Regal, and heard the passing vehicles above. He glanced at the courthouse and checked his watch before reaching into his jacket to retrieve his wallet. He flipped it open to find the photo he always carried. Emotions rushed him as he stared at her picture on the intact colored paper. Dwelling a few moments longer, he returned the wallet to his pocket and composed himself, focusing on his strategy. He reached across the seat to grab his briefcase and headed toward the courthouse.

Gabriel walked across the lobby to find his client. Florida sunshine broke through the windows, and he took it as an omen. He stopped before a large wooden door to meet his client, Ernesto Ramírez, and nudged it open.

The door opened, revealing a short husky man seated at a small table with a large manila envelope. Gabriel addressed him in Spanish. "Ernesto, thank you for agreeing to meet with me."

"No problem," said Ernesto. The pair continued in Spanish as Gabriel withdrew the chair on the opposite side of the table.

"I know that all this hurts, and I want to thank you for taking the time to gather all the evidence I requested.

"Wasn´t easy," Ernesto interrupted his green eyes glazing over momentarily.

"I know that she hurt you, but when you take the stand, the other side is going to try to take advantage of your pain. Your trauma is real, and I need you to articulate that trauma in the best way that you can."

"You can´t imagine how I feel."

"No, I can't, and I know you carry it with you and think about what happened every day. But today I need you to think, not feel. When I ask you questions where you can communicate that suffering to the court, you need to do so in an organized and thoughtful manner because we have legal requirements that we need to fulfill to prove our case."

"What about the restraining order?"

"You are requesting a restraining order, but she has also filed one against you for your alleged behavior, so, being in control of your emotions the entire time is vital not only in explaining how deeply she hurt you but in defending yourself from her accusations. Please do not give the judge any reason to think negatively of you."

Ernesto nodded and looked at his interlocked hands. Gray streaked his hair, and hard lines worked their way around his face. His expression lifted the hair of his brow, and his smooth, shaven skin was taut with tension.

"Do you think that I'll have to testify?"

"I don't know, but we have to prepare for it just in case."

Ernesto returned his eyes to his worn leathery hands.

"You know, when I left Cuba at fifteen, I was in a work camp for almost a year and had to give the *Fidelistas* everything I had before I could leave the country. Now I feel like everything has been taken away from me again."

A small tear slid down Ernesto's hardened face. He clasped his hands around his wallet and opened it up to pull out a small photograph of his son, Lucas. He stared at the boy of eight, and another tear slid down his cheek.

"That's Lucas, your son, right?" asked Gabriel.

"One of the few pictures I have left of his childhood," said Ernesto with a weak smile staring at the photograph. "He's fifteen now. He'll be driving soon." Gabriel saw the sorrow in his eyes and placed his hand on Ernesto's shoulder, lingering there for a moment.

"Ernesto, your business partner claims you're stalking her to undermine her. She's now coming after you with the restraining order to cover up her misdeeds. Despite your pain, I would like to review your testimony one last time. We have about forty minutes before the hearing begins." Gabriel looked at the manila envelope and grabbed it. Holding it in his hands, he pulled back the small metal prongs and opened the flap. He peered down into it and held his client's gaze for a moment before closing the flap and handing it back to him. "Let's begin. The office had five rooms?"

"Well, there is a reception room, a general workplace with the receptionist and two project tables, a storage and lunchroom, and two offices in the back."

"Were all of your things in the office?"

"Yes."

"That included two chairs, correct?"

"Two Spanish Jamuca chairs. Valuable antiques that have been in my family for a long time."

"Where did you put them?"

"I blended them in the reception area. I wanted to keep my furniture at the office while my house was being tented for termites. They would come in handy if we had more clients."

Gabriel nodded and made a mental note in his mind. He could see Ernesto trying his best to give every detail exactly as he remembered it.

"But furniture wasn't the only thing at the business, true?"

"Absolutely."

"How long did your belongings need to be there?"

"No more than five days."

"And it's only you, your partner, and the receptionist that work there. No temps?"

"No one else."

"Okay, let's go over this one last time."

When Gabriel was sure of Ernesto's responses and self-control, they departed the small room and left for the courtroom.

"Good morning," said Judge Jay as he looked through his thick glasses and down his hooked nose, first at the petitioner's table, and then at the respondent. "I looked through your filings this morning, and both parties have filed restraining orders against each other."

Both attorneys nodded.

"This action arose as a result of a business relationship between the parties, is that correct?" Both lawyers replied.

"Yes, Your Honor."

"According to both of your documentation, Judge Kaplan over in the Civil Circuit Court has already dissolved their partnership by judicial decree and divided the assets, is that correct?" asked the judge. Peter Hill stood up.

"He has, Your Honor."

"And so, the reason we are here today is because of acts taken by one side or the other after the entry of Judge Kaplan's order."

"Yes, Your Honor," said Gabriel, now standing.

The judge fell silent and looked at both parties. Then, running his hand through his salt and pepper hair, he asked, "Are you ready to proceed, Mr. Lock?"

"I am, Your Honor," said Gabriel.

"Mr. Hill?"

"I am, Your Honor," responded the tall and leggy thin man.

"If there is no objection, then let's dispense with opening statements and go right to the testimony. Your clients are both petitioners and defendants. I think it would be best if we started with you, Mr. Hill, as you filed first."

"No problem, Your Honor. I would like to call my client, Noelia Thompson, to the stand."

Noelia Thompson stood up and made her way to the witness chair. She wore a lavender dress on her short frame and black five-inch heels were meant to compensate for that. Against her olive skin she wore a turquoise pendant that shone as the overhead lights illuminated the courtroom. Her walk was sweet, much like her demeanor and her calmness forced Ernesto to seethe. Gabriel touched his arm. He could feel the tension in his client's body. He looked over to his right to make sure the manila envelope was still there. Hill strode over to the judge's desk and stood directly in front of the podium facing his client.

"Noelia, would you please state your name and address?" asked Hill.

"Noelia Thompson, 2341 South West 26th Road, Miami, Florida," she said, looking directly at Hill and trying not to engage Ernesto in any way.

"Tell us about your relationship with Mr. Ramírez."

"We were partners for five years in a freight forwarding business. Mr. Ramírez decided that our business relationship ran its course and wanted to separate. I told him it would be a mistake as we each have attributes that strengthen the business, but he insisted."

"Were you at the business on the 28th of March?"

"I was."

"What were you doing there?"

"By order of the judge, we were allowed to make and remove copies of all the business records, including client lists and all financial records."

"Was your partner, Mr. Ramírez there?" asked Hill turning and pointing one of his long fingers at Ernesto.

Judge Jay moved forward in his chair to listen.

"He was waiting outside when I came out. He was not supposed to be there. He was supposed to let me clear out before he arrived, but that did not happen. He was stalking me to see if I had taken anything that he wanted. I do not understand why. We both have a right to make copies of any record we want or need. He didn't have to be there or stalk me to make sure I didn't take anything. I could legally take all the information I wanted or needed, as could he. He won that in court."

Ernesto's tension rose as she spoke, and Gabriel grabbed his arm again.

"Did you and Mr. Ramírez ever have a connection other than business?"

"No, not at all." She shook her head and the beads that connected the legs of her gold glasses moved vigorously. "He has just gotten greedy and thinks that because he is the salesman and visits the clients, he knows them better than I do and can steal them all from under me. This business was my idea, my dream, and now he will try to steal it all. I told Judge Kaplan that, but he said since we were both partners, it did not matter whose dream or idea it was as we both have a right to the information."

"Had Mr. Ramírez ever stalked you before that day?" continued Hill, turning to look at Ernesto behind him. Noelia paused for a moment, met Ernesto square in the eyes, and proceeded to tell her story.

"When we left the bank after closing the business accounts and splitting the money, he followed me from the bank."

"For how long did he follow you?"

"From twelfth avenue all the way down to seventeenth avenue. I would stop, and he would stop. I would go, and he would go. It was intimidating," Noelia replied.

"Did he follow you any other time?"

"No, not that I know of...but he could have."

Ernesto looked at Gabriel as if to say, "Aren't you going to object or something?"

Gabriel did not acknowledge the look. He did not want to be distracted from the testimony.

"Were you in fear when you saw Mr. Ramírez at the office?"

"Of course I was."

"Were you frightened when he followed you from the bank?"

"Even more so."

"No further questions, Your Honor," finished Hill.

Judge Jay sat back. Gabriel stood up and approached the podium. Moving closer, he made eye contact with Noelia, staring into her pupils as he prepared to speak. The charm of those eyes deceived all who didn't know her true nature. He turned back for a moment, stared at Ernesto and the envelope on the desk to his right, and began.

"Mrs. Thompson, you have accused Ernesto, my client, of having stalked you on two occasions?"

"He was there."

"He was, no doubt," concurred Gabriel.

Hill rose from his chair in protest.

"Your Honor, if Mr. Lock is admitting that his client was stalking, you can enter the restraining order against him, and we can all go home."

Gabriel laughed and turned to see Hill grinning. He paused for a moment before turning around to face Judge Jay and Noelia.

"There is no question my client was there on both occasions, Your Honor. We would never deny the truth, but I have a few more questions to ask before we can draw any conclusions."

He walked over to the defense table where his client sat, selected a file, and opened it. Gabriel glanced at the manila envelope for a second but did not make any move to pick it up. He took papers out of the file and handed the copies to Hill. He waited as Hill inspected the contents without expression. Once Hill had finished looking at the documents, he returned them to Gabriel who walked over to the podium.

"Now, Mrs. Thompson, would you agree that the bank in question is located on the corner of Northwest Seventeenth Avenue and Second Street?"

"It is."

"The exit to the bank parking lot is located on 2nd Street, which is a one-way street?"

"Traffic can flow in only one direction."

"So, if you left at the same time, my client would have no choice but to turn the same way you did, agreed?"

"Agreed."

"The street has three lanes, but the two adjacent to the sidewalks are for parking, correct?"

"Yes."

"That leaves one lane and one lane only for traffic, right, Mrs. Thompson?"

"One lane, one way."

Gabriel did not offer as much as a grin to her admittance. He chose his next words thoughtfully.

"Would you concede that if you stopped for whatever reason, my client had no choice but to stop because your car would be blocking any advance?"

"I guess."

"Is 12th Avenue the quickest way for both of you to go home?"

"Well…"

"Mrs. Thompson, please remember the judge has lived in Miami at least as long as we have."

"It is the quickest way."

"So, if you both left the bank at the same time and were both headed home, is it logical that you would be going the same way?" She did not answer. Gabriel turned to the judge, finally grabbing the file. "May I approach the witness and hand her these documents?" Judge Jay nodded. Gabriel approached Mrs. Thompson and handed her the papers. "Do you recognize these documents?"

"I do."

"What are these?"

"Payment of fees and commissions."

"Payments from business clients?"

"Yes."

"Why are the payments deposited in an account in your husband's name and not in the business account?"

"Because my husband did some work for us, and Mr. Ramírez refused to pay him."

Gabriel turned away from the witness and looked towards the door of the courtroom before asking: "So, when you get off the stand, and your husband is sworn in, he will testify that he did this work and was not paid until you paid him, is that what you are saying?"

She stared at Gabriel in silence.

"Would you like to change your answer, Mrs. Thompson?" asked Gabriel, pausing for a moment. Hill rose to protest.

"Judge Jay, I object to all this line of questioning and move to strike. Not only is it irrelevant to the issues before us today, but it has been litigated in the civil courthouse in the dissolution for partnership action."

"Your Honor, it was not litigated there because my client asked me not to go forward with it. He didn't care that she misappropriated the money. He just wanted to end the business relationship. As to the relevancy, not only it is relevant to their petition, but it is wholly relevant to ours."

"You may continue, Mr. Lock," said the judge, "but get to the point. We have limited time for these hearings."

"I understand, Your Honor, and thank you," he said, facing Judge Jay before returning to Noelia.

"Mrs. Thompson, at what time did you leave the office on the 28th of March?"

"I did not look at my watch. I left when I was done."

"Would it surprise you to know that you left at six-nineteen?"

"Like I said, I don't know what time I left."

"Didn't the order say you had until five in the afternoon?"

"I guess it did, but I wanted to finish up and not have to come back again."

"So, if you were supposed to be gone by five, then my client could have expected you to be gone by six-nineteen, right?" Gabriel left the question suspended in the space between them.

"I guess so, but my vehicle was outside, and he should have left when he saw it there."

"But isn't it also true that your husband would, on occasion, stop by and pick you up? Whenever that happened, your car would stay at the office overnight, correct?"

"Once in a while."

"But it did happen."

"Yes, yes."

"So, the fact that your car was there was not necessarily an indication to my client that you had disregarded the judge's order and remained after five, correct?"

Hill got up to object, but Judge Jay cut him off.

"Mr. Lock is on cross-examination and can structure his questions however he wants."

"Yes, Your Honor, but can he ask two questions at the same time?"

"I'll give you that. Objection sustained. Restructure your question, Mr. Lock."

"So, the fact that your car was there was not necessarily an indication to my client that you were still there?"

"No."

"It was also not an indication that you had disregarded the judge's order, was it?"

"No."

"You came up with the idea for this business years ago, didn't you?'

"Yes," she said.

"And you had it all worked out in your mind, didn't you?"

"Yes, I did," she barked, raising her tone.

"You were even approved at a bank for a startup loan, isn't that accurate?"

"Yes, Miami Federal Credit Association," she shot back.

"But you never started the business until you mentioned it to my client, and he loved the idea, correct?"

"I thought it would be best to have a partner to share the workload and the risk."

Gabriel could see the defiance in Noelia's face and felt the anger in her voice.

"Isn't it true that, besides supplying his ability to sell, Ernesto instilled confidence in the business? Wasn't that the real element that you were missing?"

"Not true," she defied.

"That is the ingredient in the winning formula that you knew you would never have. When he wanted to dissolve the partnership, you knew then that it was something that would ruin the business, am I right?"

"You're wrong. You could not be more wrong," she protested.

Hill tried to object, and Judge Jay called for order in the courtroom. Gabriel could sense Ernesto's reaction from behind him. Noelia's anger rose, and the tone confirmed it. Noelia tried hard not to pant as the frustration rose within her. Her chest burned from his persistent questioning, and she could feel the balance shifting.

"There will be order in this courtroom, madam," said Judge Jay looking over at Noelia. "Counselor," he said, shifting to Gabriel. "You may proceed, but there will be order in my courtroom."

"Understood, Your Honor," said Gabriel lessening the heat.

"Noelia, it hurt you very deeply that he would not give you a second chance, so you decided to hurt him by taking away something that he could never recover. Isn't that a fact?"

"I would never hurt anyone."

"You came into the reception area where Ernesto had placed the antique furniture that he brought from his home, but you walked past it, didn't you?"

"I was going to my office."

"But you didn't go to your office, did you?"

"I always check everything when I arrive to make sure that nothing is out of place. I go around the workspace, the kitchen and storage room, and everywhere before I sit down to work."

"Do we agree that everywhere includes my client's office?"

"Everywhere is everywhere."

"Your Honor, would you please instruct the witness to answer the question?" asked Gabriel as he turned to face the judge.

"Please answer the question," commanded Judge Jay turning his head and addressing Noelia.

"I'm sorry, I don't remember the question." Gabriel stiffened and turned back toward Noelia. He paused, and as he did so, the people in the courtroom gazed at him. He composed himself and fixed his eyes on Noelia's face. She did her best not to show the anxiety, but Gabriel had tested witnesses long enough to know concealed displeasure. He saw her full lips twitch slightly and went for the kill.

"Everywhere includes my client's office, true?" he asked, matching his gaze to Noelia's and not breaking eye contact.

"Of course."

"So, what did you do when you went into my client's office?"

"Usually, I look around and verify that nothing has been left on, no confidential papers are left out or have fallen to the floor, and, lastly, that the cleaning people have done their job," finished Noelia.

Gabriel turned and walked toward the defense table, where Ernesto stared at him in disbelief. He grabbed the manila envelope and, holding it in his right hand, he paused and turning, looked square at Noelia.

"When you entered his office, was there anything different that day?"

"There was something different."

"His office was filled with more than his usual work furnishings, correct?"

"There were many things from his house in his office. I had to skirt around them to make sure that all the electrical equipment was off."

"In his office, you saw paintings in an open box in the corner and antiques on his desk, true?"

"True."

"You saw that he had four figurines on his desk. Is that accurate?"

"He had them in the center of his desk."

"You noticed that there was a two-foot figurine of Don Quixote among them, yes?"

"That's true."

"They are expensive figurines, aren't they?"

"They are Lladrós."

"So, expensive. Now, is it a fact that those figurines encircled a set of bronzed handprints?"

"It was in the middle."

"Those handprints belong to Ernesto's son, Lucas, from when he was a baby, don't they?"

"I assume so."

"Small handprints, aren't they?"

"They are small."

"He's sixteen now, isn't he?"

"No, he's fifteen."

"How old would you say Lucas was in the picture on Ernesto's desk, the one of him playing soccer?"

"It was taken last year when they won the tournament, so I'd have to say that he was fourteen or about to be."

"Were there any other pictures in the room?"

"No."

"I see," said Gabriel.

He walked over to Judge Jay's elevated desk. With his left hand, he pulled back the wings of the metal clasp and flipped the envelope upside down. As he turned the envelope, the contents fell, scattering little squares and triangles spread all over the judge's desk. Some of them were colorful, while others were plastic-like film.

"Aren't you forgetting these?" he asked, not looking at Noelia.

Judge Jay stared at Gabriel but did not move. Silence befell the courtroom as Judge Jay examined the fragments and mutilated pieces. Lucas had been cut down to nothing more than scraps of colored paper and bits of plastic film.

Gabriel took out a little note from the manila envelope and showed it to Noelia. She looked down at the floor.

"Is this your writing?" asked Gabriel, his index finger on the note. Noelia's eyes did not leave the floor. "Is this your writing, Ms. Thompson?"

"That is my writing," She answered, still not moving her eyes from the floor. Gabriel positioned himself in her line of sight.

"Would you read it for us?"

She did not move.

"Can I read it for you?"

She gave no reply and was perfectly still. Hill stood up to object, but Judge Jay glared at him, so he sat back down.

"Your Honor?" asked Gabriel. Judge Jay nodded and Gabriel proceeded. "You have taken from me the core of my life. This business was my child. I know I will never get it back. Now we're even." Turning, he pointed to the cuttings on the judge's desk and continued, "These are my client's pictures with his child as he changed from baby to young boy, aren't they?"

"Well..."

"You saw a photograph on his desk, which is normally at his house, didn't you?"

"Of course, I saw it," said Noelia, defiance deep in her voice.

"You thought that if he had brought this photograph from home that he might have brought others, is that accurate?"

"Maybe," answered Noelia, looking for a way out.

"You knew he had brought more, didn't you?"

"Yes!" said Noelia, snapping and raising her voice.

"You took it upon yourself to make sure that he would feel the same loss that you feel with the dissolution of your business, so you searched through his drawers until you found the photographs that he tried to save, and you cut them so that he would also lose something irreplaceable, isn't that true?"

Noelia looked at her lawyer, hoping he would do something, but Hill did not object, knowing that it would be of no use. Gabriel waited. Noelia, realizing there was no escape, surrendered and avoided Gabriel's eyes.

"This business has been my life, and I will be lost without it. He didn't need to do this."

Gabriel ignored her answer.

"You didn't shred the pictures; you cut them. You wanted him to see clearly what you destroyed, and not only that, but you also took the negatives and cut them as well so that those captured moments could never be replaced."

"Objection to the form of the question!" bellowed Hill.

"Sustained," said Judge Jay. He lowered his head toward Gabriel and asked, "Is there a question in there, counselor?"

Gabriel twisted.

"I don't believe I have anything further, Your Honor," he said.

Silence crashed through the courtroom with Gabriel's words. No party spoke, and after a moment's wait, Gabriel returned to the respondent's table. He could see the sorrow in Ernesto's eyes and felt its depth. After another moment, Judge Jay spoke.

"Do you have anything further to add, Mr. Hill?"

"No, Your Honor."

Judge Jay gave a wearied look.

"I have heard enough. In a few minutes, I will be signing two orders. Mrs. Thompson, I will be denying your petition for a restraining order. Mr. Ramírez, I will be granting yours. John," he said to the bailiff, "please escort Mrs. Thompson and Mr. Hill to your office to wait for her copy of the orders. Mr. Lock, would you and Mr. Ramírez wait here? My secretary will bring you your copy of the orders." Judge Jay turned to Noelia, offering nothing more than a blank expression, "Mrs. Thompson, you're excused."

Noelia rose from the witness stand and sauntered toward Hill and the bailiff. As she passed Gabriel and Ernesto, she glared at them but said nothing. Judge Jay rose from his desk and departed through the doors behind him to the offices beyond. Gabriel and Ernesto sat alone at the defense table for a few minutes. "All of this was unnecessary," admitted Ernesto, "It could have been resolved without so much damage."

"That's the truth about most cases," added Gabriel, nodding his head. "And I am sorry you have had to go through this." They sat in unsatisfied silence until the secretary walked in with the order and handed it to Gabriel, who rose from the table and accepted it. He opened the papers and, sitting back down next to Ernesto, read them. Finding them acceptable, he gave Ernesto his copies and put his own in his briefcase.

"Thank you for this, Gabriel," said Ernesto in Spanish.

"There is nothing I can say to make it better, so I will simply say that you have a friend here whenever you need one."

The pair of them rose from their chairs and walked together down the aisle toward the exit. As they stepped, Gabriel slowed and followed his client, touching the wallet that sat in the breast pocket of his jacket. *Ernesto may not have the photos, but at least he has the real thing. He has his son and an explanation but all I have is a picture.*

Chapter 5: The Lawyers

Miami, Florida: March 1981

Gabriel walked up the tiled steps of the Cuban restaurant. Inside, he saw the familiar white linen Guayaberas on each employee. The hostess smiled at him, beckoning him closer, but he caught an olive-toned hand waving to him in his periphery. He turned to see his friend, Rodrigo seated at a booth, sporting his signature tan linen suit and calling him over.

"I'm sorry, but my friend is just over there," he said in Spanish and gestured to the booth. She smiled with blushed cheeks and let him pass. Traversing across the waiting area, he stepped a few paces before he sat down across from his friend.

"Son of a gun, she's still looking at you," said Rodrigo, his raspy voice annoyed.

"Come on, Rod, you shouldn't be upset; take it as a blessing that girls are looking at me. It makes it easier for you to remain loyal to Arlene."

Rodrigo shifted his gaze from the host to Gabriel in displeasure.

"Yeah, I'm a one-girl kind of guy now, Lock."

"I know, Rod."

Rodrigo rolled his hazel eyes, and Gabriel snickered.

"Part of me wants to get back in the game just to remind you of how invisible you were before I met Arlene."

Gabriel leaned back in his booth, resting his shoulder against the wall.

"Nah, you wouldn't do that to Arlene, and besides, I wouldn't go out with you; I'd hang out with Mo."

"Yeah, ain't that the truth? That man's practically a model. It's a wonder that Arlene chose me when she met us."

"Settled, Rod, not chose." Rodrigo's face flushed, and Gabriel couldn't help but laugh. A waiter came to their booth and remained silent with notepad and pen drawn. Both friends ordered their lunch. The waiter left, and Rodrigo looked around to see if anyone was paying attention.

"So, what's up?" asked Rodrigo, "why did you want to meet with me today instead of just calling?"

"I've got a referral for you."

"Great, not a drug dealer, I am tired of defending those."

"I don't blame you."

"What's the catch?"

"No catch, just one of my clients who is accused of aggravated assault and battery," admitted Gabriel while rearranging his silverware.

"Aggravated assault and battery? I didn't think that Lock & Lock had clients like that?"

"We don't. I can assure you he's innocent."

"Yeah sure," scoffed Rodrigo, "all the guys I represent are innocent."

"This one is," glared Gabriel.

"Okay," said Rodrigo, giving in to Gabriel's assertion, "what's your role?"

"He's been a client of the office for a long time with minor matters here and there. I can handle the claim for excessive force while you handle the criminal defense if you want."

"Excessive force?" Rodrigo's eyebrows rose.

"Yeah, the police shattered his shoulder, splitting it in half, when dragging him from his home."

"Are you serious?" Rodrigo cringed as he processed the news. He took a hand to his shoulder and rotated it, trying to imagine the pain of a destroyed joint.

"I'm serious."

"There's a catch to this, isn't there?"

"No catch."

"Don't give me that look, Lock."

"Alright, fine," resigned Gabriel, moving the menus to the side before placing his fingers together on the table. Rodrigo pulled back the sleeves of his suit and glanced at his watch while leaning forward to pay attention.

"Listen, my client is accused by the state for allegedly beating a teenager with a wooden bat at Tropical Park. A witness swears that they saw him do it and then drive away in his black pick-up truck, leaving the kid writhing in agony. He's my client because my father has worked with him for years, and he's been coming to my dad for help. I can tell you that he's not the kind of scum bag to hit a kid and much less with a bat."

"That's some pretty serious stuff, Gabriel."

"Rod, this man deserves a good lawyer. When he called my father, I thought Dad would want me to take the case, but he didn't. I was relieved when we spoke about it, and so I recommended it to you. He thought that you'd be a great fit. What do you say?"

"To get high praise from your dad is rare, and if he believes the client, then I should too."

"Alright then, I'll give your office line to my client and his wife, Rosa, and one of them will call you."

As he finished, the waiter returned with their food. Gabriel could smell the food as it came from the kitchen and the skirt steak steamed as the waiter placed it, white rice, black beans, and plantains down in front of him.

"Palomilla for you with white rice, black beans, and plantains." The waiter then placed Rodrigo's food before him. "And one Tortilla Española with a side of sliced tomato for you. Anything else, gentleman?" asked the waiter in Spanish.

"My café con leche?" replied Gabriel.

"Yes, sir," answered the waiter, "I'll be right back." Gabriel watched him walk back down to the kitchen.

"Café con leche with a Palomilla?" The corners of Rodrigo's lips tilted downward and the crow's feet at the edges of his eyes scrunched in disbelief.

"You can joke about my culinary decisions later, but I've got to meet a client in an hour, so we've got to hurry. Don't worry, I'll cover this tab."

"Sure thing, Lock. Try not to inhale your food."

Gabriel ignored him, and they began to eat.

A few minutes passed before Rodrigo lifted his eyes from his food back to Gabriel. "When can I meet with the client?"

Gabriel swallowed his food.

"Not for a while. He's in the hospital and is sedated to deal with the pain. I'll be there to visit him soon."

"He'll call me?"

"Either he or his wife."

"Okay, so you figure a timeline of at least a few weeks?" asked Rodrigo, bringing a piece of the tortilla Española to his mouth.

"Something like that. Minimum of two weeks," answered Gabriel. Rodrigo finished chewing his morsel.

"That will give me enough time to finish up a few cases. Luckily, I won't be too busy over the next few months and the firm is big on getting referrals right now instead of chasing leads."

"Not enough bad guys in Miami?" joked Gabriel, taking a sip from his café con leche and wiping his lips with a napkin.

"Plenty of them, they've just been quiet lately or at least we're not getting them as clients."

"I forgot that low lives pay your bills."

"Alleged low lives, thank you. Every one of them is an upstanding citizen. Even your client is, right?" Gabriel laughed. "I thought so, Lock. So, how was that case this morning with the restraining order?"

"We won," answered Gabriel.

"Usually, you're happier than this when you win, why so flat?"

"He lost more than the win can repay."

"I hate those cases," said Rodrigo, empathizing. Gabriel closed his eyes for a moment and recalled Lucas's face among the mutilated pictures.

"There's nothing impersonal about business. Even when people say that it isn't personal, it always is."

"My client lost everything he had in Cuba, came over here in his mid-thirties with his two-year-old boy. He lost his wife a few years ago to pneumonia and so pictures are all that he and his son have left of her." Rodrigo suspended the next bite, holding his fork in place a few inches from his mouth. He held onto every one of Gabriel's words. Gabriel felt the cold sweat begin to pool on his back and knew that it wasn't the heat in the restaurant.

"What did she do?"

"My client had to put all his personal belongings in the office because they were fumigating his house. The business partner found their photos and cut them into pieces. She cut every photo of the boy and his mother, my client's wedding photos, and even from when they arrived in the United States." Rodrigo's eyes widened and a tinge of rage sat suppressed behind his disgusted expression. "She didn't just destroy photos; she eradicated all the memories that my client had of his wife and deprived the boy of any moments saved with his mother." Both men paused for a moment. Gabriel sat, still trying to process the gravity of Noelia's actions, while Rodrigo settled his fuming anger.

"He's not even my client and I'm pissed. You must be pretty god awful to do something like that."

"Worse than your clients?" asked Gabriel.

"Almost," admitted Rodrigo. "Most of my clients commit misdemeanor crimes or felonies of desperation. This one was premeditated."

"Yeah, it was," agreed Gabriel.

"You know, a lot of my clients have simple things like possession, or they stole cars, or they punched somebody while playing neighborhood basketball and it turned into a full-scale brawl, but they always think the same thing, that it's not that serious and it's not, compared to the bigger picture. Every now and then I get a client who's a major dealer or some guy going around stealing more than just cheap cars. Sometimes, I get guys who do serious crimes, and they don't just do them once or twice, but they have a collection of charges longer than old lady's grocery list. Those are the guys that keep me up at night, the guys who do really serious things and they always think that they won't get caught. This lady seems like one of those."

"It's worse than that, Rod," clarified Gabriel. "She wanted to get caught. She wanted him to know that it was her, that she had destroyed him for destroying her business."

"Did he?"

"No, he just parted ways to do his own thing." Rodrigo nodded, and Gabriel glanced down at his watch.

"I'm sorry, Rod, I have a hearing, and it's before Judge Rodríguez in half an hour."

"Are you the Plaintiff or the Defendant?"

"Both, we filed a counter claim."

"Good luck, then, and don't worry, I'll get this," said Rodrigo, reaching into his pocket for a twenty.

"Thanks," replied Gabriel, trying his best to scoot out of the booth.

"Lock," began Rodrigo, "I'm sorry to hear about your client and his son, but at least this win will give them some closure."

"It'll only dull the pain, Rod. It's not much of a win."

"No, it's not, but it's a start."

Gabriel nodded and rose from the booth.

"Thanks, Rod. This one got to me."

"I know, but you're allowed to let it get to you occasionally. You can't be perfect all the time."

"Sure thing."

"Now get out here and I'll call you if your client calls me."

Gabriel nodded and headed out the door. *Now I need to figure out how to explain my client's actions to Judge Rodríguez,* he thought to himself as he walked back to his vehicle and pushed Ernesto's case out of his mind.

Chapter 6: The Facts

Miami, Florida: March 1981

Gabriel arrived at the office at quarter after seven in the morning. He had spent the past few days processing all that Noelia had done to Ernesto, from making his life unbearable to destroying his memories. He recalled the colored paper and plastic film spread onto the witness stand and shuddered to himself.

He crossed the small lot to the coral building. He glanced up and hoped that today would be a cooler day than the day before. Opening the glass door, he pulled it open and moved into the hallway.

He sauntered a few paces forward before he arrived at the entranceway to the office. Seeing the Lock & Lock sign his father had just installed instilled him with a sense of pride. He brushed his hand against the oaken door and entered the office. *I never doubted that this is where I belong.* No one sat in the waiting room, but he knew that no seat would be available by nine. He crossed the waiting area to the door and placed his briefcase on the floor before removing his jacket. *I figure I've got an hour before Dad shows up, and Susana won't be here until half-past eight. The office is all mine*, he thought.

He collected his briefcase and strolled over to his office. He sat and looked at the calendar on his desk and examined the checklist of his responsibilities. *Ernesto is finished, Montalbán and Sons was last week, Carbonell vs. McCrocadoo's deposition is next Friday, and my Tuesday meeting with Mantovani looks to be set for next week. This doesn't look too bad, but that deposition is going to be rough.*

He scanned his desk, checking to see if Susana or his father had left him any note or memo on any of the cases. He relaxed in his chair and dropped his shoulders, closing his eyes for a moment. Rodrigo had accepted the case for Joaquín, so his dad didn't need to call his friend for a favor.

Gabriel decided to list his observations and notes along with his billable hours for the cases on his desk on a yellow pad and save it for his father. Thomas always needed the summary of billing before handing it over to Susana. As he jotted his notes, he heard the front door creak open and saw his father emerge from the waiting area.

"Well, you're here early," said Thomas, his cerulean eyes fixed on Gabriel, magnified behind his thick glass-es. Gabriel cocked his head a few degrees to the side and peered at his father.

"Look who's talking." Thomas shrugged his shoulders and entered Gabriel's office, choosing to sit in one of the vacant armchairs as he unbuttoned his suit jacket.

"So, yesterday's meeting went well?"

"Which one?"

"The one with Rodrigo," said Thomas candidly, moving a strand of his blonde hair from his forehead, "I know that letting go of his defense wasn't easy for you. It would have bothered me too."

"I'm fine, Dad. It's something that I'm getting used to. I'm not a criminal lawyer anymore, and I didn't defend people anyway. I think that the harder part is telling Joaquín that everything is going to be alright. I think he is innocent and should get off, but that's not always the case, as you know."

Thomas nodded as he agreed with his son. He paused for a moment, raising his suspenders with his thumbs from beneath his blue double-breasted blazer.

"The State Attorney's Office showed you some things that have given you some armor against this kind of work. Just remember that even armor must be repaired."

"My armor's just fine. The focus here is to figure out what we're going to do for Joaquín."

"Joaquín, just like any client, is dependent on you, and if he is innocent, then that dependence can be a lot to bear," answered Thomas before shifting the topic. "What do you think needs to be done?"

Gabriel leaned forward in his chair and rested his elbows on the mahogany desktop.

"At this point, we have not received the discovery so we do not really know which way we will set up the defense.

"Have you spoken to him?"

"He's still under a lot of pain and must be constantly sedated so that he can sleep. They ripped him so hard that they didn't just shatter his shoulder socket but caused severe damage to his labrum and rotator cuff. He's going to need a lot of surgery and therapy. He will probably never be able to drive an eighteen-wheeler again."

"Jesus," muttered Thomas, sighing and shaking his head and closing his eyes. "Have you spoken to Rosa at all?"

"I've spoken to her, but she's honestly just as distraught and is still traumatized."

"Everyone's been on edge since the riots last year. Police don't know what they're walking into, and citizens are on edge even in their own homes."

"Anyway, I've got the billable hours for my last couple of cases that I need to log. I can get them to you in a few hours." Thomas paused for a moment and allowed a weak smile to escape him.

"Sure thing, Son. Let's meet when Susana arrives in an hour, and we'll go from there."

"No problem, Dad." Thomas rose from the chair and exited, taking his coat and his briefcase.

Gabriel returned his neck to the comfort of the cushion and closed his eyes, thinking about the transgressions that Joaquín suffered and what it would mean if he were innocent. He checked his watch: Forty-five minutes; Looking at the pile of files he began to work fast.

Susana arrived at half-past eight, walking in with a colada in hand and offered the jolt of caffeine in her usual loud manner.

"Lario made it for me this morning, so it has a little extra sugar," she said in Spanish to both of them, "and it's hot, very hot."

The invitation to coffee summoned them to her desk and as Gabriel and Thomas joined her, she poured their servings in the usual little plastic cups and sat down at her desk. She drank a sip before raising her hand to fix her chestnut hair in an improvised bun held together with a pencil.

"Susana, thank you for the coffee, per usual, and tell Lario that I appreciate it when you see him next."

"I will," she affirmed, wiping her full lips with a napkin before smiling through her dark eyes.

"Susana, Gabriel, I wanted to talk to both of you about our billing process. I would like to get some ideas about how we can make it a little easier. Any thoughts?" Susana's cheeks turned a light shade of pink.

"I think that you should just put your hours at the end of the case note instead of separate."

"Is that really all that it would take?"

"Maybe not in the long run, but that would be a start. What I really need is for both of you to be more consistent with getting me the billing information and since you always do case notes, it'll be much more efficient."

"Okay. What about you, Gabriel?"

Gabriel had almost spaced out when he stood a little straighter.

"Yes, that would be fine."

"Okay, it's settled then. Son, can I see you in my office for a moment?" Gabriel nodded.

"Give me a minute, Dad."

Thomas returned to his office while Gabriel moved toward Susana. She looked up at him from her chair.

"What can I do for you, Gabriel?" she asked in English this time.

"Nothing much. I just need you to do me a favor concerning Mrs. Rosa Pérez."

"It's awful what happened to Joaquín."

"It is, but we'll handle it."

"I know that you will. So, what do you need?"

"When you get a chance, will you call Rosa and ask if anyone is there for her to help her with Joaquín when he returns home? I don't want her to become overwhelmed by taking care of him alone."

"Sure. Anything else?"

"Yeah, can you give me the number to a good flower place nearby? Abuela's anniversary is in May, and I want to make sure that I get her something nice."

"Look at you, taking care of your grandmother, but it's a little early for May, no?"

"Well, Mother's Day is in May so if you don't order flowers early, you don't get the ones you really want. Abuelo would order them in late February or March, and I want to keep up the tradition for her."

"No problem. I'll find one and give you the number in a bit."

"Thanks," said Gabriel. Susana nodded, and Gabriel left her to begin her work. Turning back toward his office, he took one stride before he realized that his father was waiting for him. Gabriel entered the office and stood at the doorway. Thomas lowered the file he had been analyzing.

“Close it, will you?” he requested, gesturing back toward the door.

Gabriel closed it behind him.

“I wanted to let you know that Ernesto called me yesterday and had only the highest praise for you. I know that leaving the State Attorney’s Office wasn’t easy, and it’s not easy to come and work with your father when you want to make your name as your own man, but you are doing very good work. You are further along in your transition to civil practice than I thought you would be.”

“Thanks, Dad,” said Gabriel in a hushed tone.

“I saw in your calendar that the McCrocadoo depos are coming up.”

“Finally, after they have been delaying them. I ended up filing a motion to compel and they agreed to these dates even before Judge Stone heard the motion. Those are over the next few weeks. It’s the deposition for McCrocadoo that I’m worried about.”

“Why so?” asked Thomas, peering at his son and raising his glasses as they slid down his long, crooked nose. “Have they suggested settlement at any point?”

“We have talked around it but nothing really acceptable, they always push amounts that are laughable.”

“Postponing depositions and offering an obviously low settlement, what does that tell you?”

“That there is something they need to hide and want me to go away for cheap before I find out.”

“So, who should be worried, you, or them?”

“I know what they are afraid of and that is not what bothers me. I just want to make sure that I approach taking our guy’s deposition in a way that protects McCrocadoo as much as possible so we can reach a good settlement for our guy.”

"Don't worry, just go over the facts with the client and make sure that he understands our point of view."

"I've taken criminal depositions before. Now, I'm taking a deposition from someone who wasn't a witness or victim to a traumatic robbery or crime that hurt someone. I'm concerned that I'll be too aggressive in my approach."

Thomas grinned, and the older man's skin became taut.

"You're afraid that you haven't shaken off the prosecutor side of you even though you've left criminal law, right?"

Gabriel fumbled for words, surprised by the question and its sincerity. Thomas continued.

"It's part of who you are. That's your style and it's what made you a good prosecutor. Let those experiences help shape the way that you approach things. Let them guide you."

Neither man spoke for a few moments as Gabriel absorbed the truth of his father's words.

"Any other truth you'd like to share with me?" asked Gabriel.

"It'll cost you a quarter."

Gabriel smiled and dug his hand into his pocket. He rattled the change from within his pocket and his father laughed.

"When you have your approach and questioning laid out for these depos, we will take a look at them together. This could be a big win for us because our client has a lot of work that he divides between different firms, but he's looking to consolidate, and if we win, he insinuated that he could send it all our way. For now, do you see this stack of files to my left?" he asked, pointing toward the manilla files that lay on his desk behind the lamp. "You've got these to handle. Get to them by the end of the day so we can discuss each one tomorrow morning."

Gabriel nodded his understanding, then furrowed his brows at the mountain of files on the desk. "Those look fun."

"I wanted to get them to you a little earlier, but you were tied up with Ernesto, so I organized them and gathered all the necessary paperwork for you. You will also find background notes."

"So, we'll talk tomorrow morning?"

Thomas reached across his desk to grab his red calendar book and flipped through it, "Eleven o'clock. Want me to order lunch in?"

"Good for me."

"Done."

Chapter 7: The Plans

Miami, Florida: Early April 1981

Some time had passed since Gabriel and Thomas discussed the strategy for his deposition for McCrocadoo and that had turned out well. The case settled and this morning they received the papers with the accompanying releases and non-disclosures from the other side. It was late afternoon, Rodrigo and Susana had contacted Joaquín and Rosa. Gabriel had just given Susana a few cheques from two of the bigger clients that Thomas had passed down to him. Passing quaint stores, cafés, and oak trees on Coral Way, Gabriel made his way into the office.

As he opened the door to the waiting area, he saw Susana's dark-haired head and dark eyes staring at him. Giving her a confused look, she brushed it off with a wave of her arm and beckoned him closer to her.

"What's going on?" he asked.

"You have a client waiting for you in your office. She needs to speak with you and says that it's urgent."

"Have we seen her before?"

"She is the daughter of a former client of your father's. He handled her divorce years ago, and now it seems that her daughter needs your help," answered Susana, widening her eyes slightly.

Gabriel grimaced.

"I've not done much divorce work before. Did she say anything about it?"

"Not a word."

"Does she have a name?"

"Yes, Valerie."

"Valerie what?"

"Valerie Romero."

Gabriel crossed through the door of the waiting area and into the space between it and his office. His door stood ajar, and through it, he saw a young woman staring back at him. She sat in the less-worn armchair in front of his desk. Her brown hair looked disheveled, and traces of blond highlights seemed faded. She reminded Gabriel of the victims he used to see at the prosecutor's office, ones who only came forward when exhaustion and abuse gave them no other choice. He treaded delicately.

"Mrs. Romero, good afternoon, I am Gabriel Lock," he said, outstretching his hand to formally greet her. Valerie stood and offered her hand to him, taking his and gripping it. "My secretary told me that your mother was my father's client some years ago?"

"Yes, he handled my mother's divorce some time ago, and she recommended that I come here to see him. Is he available?" she asked with a weak voice.

"I'm afraid not, Mrs. Romero, but I assure you that I can handle your divorce for you."

"When will he be available?" she asked, ignoring his offer.

Gabriel noticed her hands fidgeting as they held each other. Her knees touched, and her feet bent inwards. She held her bottom lip between her teeth, and he noticed the bruising on her arm that she tried to conceal with the sleeve of her shirt.

"Mrs. Romero, I'm sorry, my father is detained by a client who requires all his attention, but as I stated before, I assure you that I can handle your divorce."

"You look young," she answered flatly, avoiding eye contact.

"I guess so, yes."

"Have you ever handled a divorce involving a drug dealer before?" she inquired, fuming.

Gabriel paused, watching the veins in her temple bulge as the blood flowed through her skull.

"Mrs. Romero, I worked at the State Attorney's Office where I had the pleasure of sending bad people away for a very long time. Putting a lot of scumbags away was my full-time job, so helping you divorce this man will be an enjoyable experience for the both of us."

Valerie relaxed and eased in her seat.

"I'm sorry," she said, apologizing. "I just have been through a lot recently and needed some reassurance."

Gabriel gave her a stern look.

"I understand, Mrs. Romero. Why don't you tell me a little bit about what is going on so I can try and get a better picture of what we're facing?"

Valerie turned her head behind her, staring at Susana. Gabriel got up and closed the door behind them.

"I trust Susana completely, Mrs. Romero. During the divorce, she will be a constant point of contact between you and me. I am under an ethical obligation to protect what you tell me, and as our assistant, that attorney-client privilege extends to Susana. What you say to us stays between us."

"I understand," she murmured, "when you are married to a man like this, you become paranoid, and there is so much that runs through your head." Gabriel nodded and pointed to the door in the rear of his office.

"We have a conference room through there that will allow you to be more comfortable as you tell me about your situation."

Valerie agreed and grabbed her purse from her side before rising from her chair. Gabriel moved toward the door and held it for Valerie to pass through. She started slowly, deciding on every word.

"I loved Mike. I still love him, but a few years ago, he stopped loving the kids and me when he decided he wanted to make drugs more than a recreational sport. During the first years of our relationship together, it was all fun and games. We would get high and would have marathon sex on weekends. We tried everything from weed and cocaine to ecstasy. It was all just for fun until I found out that I was pregnant with Little Mike. When Marcos, my other son, arrived, the drugs were nothing more than a faded memory from that past life." Valerie took a deep breath and began recounting everything. "For Mike, it was the opposite. He hid it at first. He didn't want me to know that he was using it while I was pregnant. He supplemented our income by selling drugs so he could afford them and the additional mouths to feed. Eventually, he quit his job and became a full-time dealer. I began looking for a way out, but it became progressively more dangerous as the drugs started really messing with his brain, and he became violent." She took her left hand in her right, massaging her right palm between her index finger and thumb. "Mike was no longer the handsome man I married. He lost weight, his eyes were sunken now, and he had this weird smell about him. He even covered his body with ink and had an enormous dragon tattoo on his back. This is not the man that I married, Gabriel. He's nothing like the man that I met. I don't even want to sleep in our bed anymore. I must pretend that my kids are sick or are having nightmares because he disgusts me!"

A mixture of anger and grief washed over her as her cheeks flushed and her eyes teared up. Gabriel remained silent, choosing not to utter a word. Valerie panted for a few moments, shame venting from her as she recalled all her sufferings.

"How often does he beat you?"

"Three times a week, most weeks."

"Have you tried to leave?" Valerie burst into tears, and her voice became high-pitched.

"I can't," she wailed, her dark hair matting to her cheeks with the tears.

"The kids?"

"He'll hurt me, and then who's to say that he won't hurt them?"

"Has he ever been violent to your children?"

Valerie shook her head.

"No, but if I'm not there, who else is going to take the punches?"

She sobbed and held her head in her hands. She wept into her hands and hid her face while her body shook.

Gabriel turned and found a box of tissues in one of the room's drawers in the cabinet against the back wall, offering the box to her.

Valerie took it and wiped down her cheeks and eyes before blowing her nose a few times.

"You know what I think?" asked Gabriel after a few moments. "I think that your children are very lucky to have a mother like you. One who is willing to take a beating from an abusive husband to make sure that he doesn't beat her kids."

She lost it and sobbed anew.

"Do you have other markings of abuse?" he asked, pointing to her arm. "What else can you give me to make sure that he never has any chance of visitation for these kids until he gets better and gets clean?" She looked up, surprised.

"We will have to prove a pattern of constant abuses. The problem is that just like the parent has the right to see the children, the children have the right to see the parent.

That is why the requirements are so high to prove this," answered Gabriel, staring at her intently.

Valerie reached down for her purse and rummaged through her belongings. She withdrew a series of photographs ranging from her appearing broken but not bloodied. In others, she was bruised, but not in the face. Mike was in others, appearing impaired and possessing drugs.

"Is this all you have?"

"Yes, is this enough?"

"The pictures are disturbing, but under Florida law, it is assumed that if a man beats his wife, he will then beat his children. This is the statute in Florida. These are a start. Who took these?

"A start? Gabriel, my ribs are broken in this picture." She paused, not satisfied by his blank stare. "I took the pictures."

"Were there witnesses other than yourself?"

"No."

"Did you file a police report, and did you cite him as the cause of injury?"

"No," she admitted before lowering her head in disappointment. "But what about these pictures that I have of him snorting cocaine?"

"How do you prove to the judge that it's actually cocaine?"

"Just look at the picture."

"A judge can't rule without proof, Valerie. You must give me something more."

"I don't have anything more, Gabriel. I mean, not really anyway."

"What do you mean by that?"

"There's a chance that even without the divorce, he'll never see the kids again." Gabriel's eyebrows rose, and the muscles in his lower back tightened. Something warned him against what she was about to say, and he braced himself.

"What do you mean, Valerie?"

"It's what I did." Gabriel's lower back shot pain down his leg, and he shifted in his chair, trying to alleviate it.

"Are you okay?" she asked.

"I'm fine, just a former sports injury," he said, brushing her question off. "Valerie, what did you do?"

"I didn't have much choice, okay? I did what I thought was right for the boys and me." "We set it up with the police," she admitted finally.

"Set what up?"

"A sting to catch him."

Gabriel processed her words and saw the danger. Heat rose from within him, forcing perspiration from every pore in his body, but his face bore no expression. *Why would you set up a sting while you're still living in the same apartment with him? What if it goes wrong? What if he attacks you in front of your children? You don't want them to see that!* Worst-case scenarios ruled his mind during the moments he remained silent. *None of it matters; it's already done. There's no time for emotion; solutions, not emotions. Get the facts, Gabriel, and minimize chance,* he thought to himself. He cleared his throat, took a pen from his desk, and leaned in, ready to write on the legal pad.

"Tell me the plan, and don't leave out a *single* detail."

Chapter 8: The Calculated Risk

Miami, Florida: Early April 1981

Valerie turned the key, but the engine wouldn't start. Her blue Mazda sat behind the law office, baking in the heat of the sun. She turned the key again. The ignition clicked, but nothing came from the motor. Her head whirled. She needed to get to the school and pick up the boys. She had told them not to take the bus, and now she had car problems. "Please, not today," she prayed aloud as the drops of sweat formed on her temples. Sitting back and feeling her blouse stick to her, she inhaled and tried the ignition one last time. The engine rumbled, the motor started, and she thanked God that it did.

The air conditioning cooled her skin as she reversed the automobile from its space and left the parking lot. Maneuvering onto the street, her thoughts went back to the meeting with Gabriel. *What choice did I have? If they don't catch him, he'll probably kill me sooner or later,* she thought.

She glanced at the small scar in the palm of her hand and at the reminder of what she risked. Mike had been drunk. He had dropped his beer bottle on the kitchen floor, and it had shattered. She had made the mistake of making a comment about it, and he had responded. He had risen from his armchair, taken her by the face and thrown her against the wall of the kitchen. Then he grabbed her by the shoulders and threw her down to the floor. To break her fall, she stuck her hands out, and the shards sliced into her right palm. Shards protruded from her bloodied hands, and one had gone all the way through.

Valerie accelerated, remembering what Gabriel had said during their meeting. He had tried to talk her out of the plan, and there was no way to stop it.

Gabriel had listened to every detail in silence and with no interruptions, and when she finished, he had pleaded with her to find some other place to go to and make sure that Mike was in jail before going home. If the plan didn't work and she failed to go back to her usual time, it would confirm that she was behind his problems with the police, and they would never be safe with nowhere to run or hide.

Anguish set in as she thought of what could transpire if her plan failed. Her boys' smiling faces gripped her before the fear crashed in. She began gasping for air. If this fails, he'll find out, and if he finds out, he'll hurt me, but will he hurt them too? As she pondered the consequences, she began recounting all their history together in her mind.

Valerie snapped out of it, and her breathing steadied as she swallowed the fear and regret. The trap was set. Timing was the one thing that was out of her control. She couldn't know when Antonio would report Mike to the police nor when the police would move in on him.

She pondered about the conversation with her mother when things started to get worse. Her mother, one of the most sheltered and aloof people she had ever known, had accosted her one day and insisted that she move out.

"Tell you what, Mom; you call me every night at eight to make sure I am alright, okay?"

"No, not at eight. That is the time for my novella. Seven forty-five is better for me.

"Okay, Mom. Seven forty-five every night." She now smiled. Priorities are a strange thing.

She approached 32nd Avenue and turned right towards the kids' school. She drove to 6th Street, parked, and patiently waited for the boys in the carpool line. They would go to baseball practice and then home. She hoped that if the timing of the arrest was wrong, as Gabriel had warned her, then staying out of the house, at least until after practice, might help correct that.

When Mike got high, he would lose track of time. He would talk, revealing all kinds of information, and that's how she found out how and where he would be making his next deliveries. Until now, he had been a small-time dealer. Back then, he was the small fish in the ocean of cocaine passing through the streets and canals of Miami before hitting I-95. Now he moved greater quantities and was worthy of police attention. Mike's addiction drove him to become a mule for one of the cartels. His moniker had become Dragon, and she made sure to explain that to Antonio. Mike loved the nickname because it made him feel more important than he was.

If there were even a hint that she was the informant, his wrath would be the least of her problems. She needed to be very careful because if the cartel found out, they would kill her and the boys. She had been over the plan with Antonio more times than she cared to remember, but by the end of that night, he understood exactly what had to be accomplished and how.

A phone tip from a public phone in a far neighborhood would direct the police to the person, place, and time the drugs would be in transit. Someone would pick up a kilo of cocaine and transport it from the main house in Little Havana and take it to a specific locker in the bus station for out-of-state transport while the payment was left in a different locker. Mike's job was simple. He had to move the cocaine from the first locker to a second locker and, if no one moved in on him, he would go and pick up the money in the third locker. The cartels rotated bus and train terminals, with only a few people knowing the details of the drops. If the plan went accordingly, he'd be arrested on his way from one locker to the next.

If they couldn't catch him, she couldn't divorce him. She knew it even before Gabriel confirmed it during their meeting. Telling him would set him off, and he would kill her. Mike's record was spotless. No paper trail of drug use, violence, or offense. He didn't even have a parking ticket.

Despite driving around Miami stoned out of his mind, Mike never received a DUI, and no matter what motion she and Gabriel thought to bring before the court, she had no evidence to corroborate her story.

Someone opened the door to the car, and Valerie jumped in her seat, hitting the horn accidentally. She looked up to see the teacher's face and found her breath again. Mike Jr. and Marcos climbed into the vehicle, their backpacks hitting their calves as they hoisted themselves into the backseat.

"You guys already have your uniforms on?!"

"Yeah, Mami, we're all ready for practice!"

"I can't wait for next year, Mami. I want to play coach pitch like Mike Jr."

"Me neither, baby," she lied, "Mami will just have to figure out how to get your practice schedules to be the same." Thinking about how she would have to cut back her hours at work to fit different schedules, Valerie thought of her tightening finances.

"How was school today?" she asked after a few minutes on the road.

"Papi came by the school today." Her heart sank with his words. She paused and collected herself.

"Oh no, was there something in school that I forgot about?"

"No, Mami. You didn't forget nothing," said Mike Jr., "Papi didn't even come in; he just waved from outside the fence." Disappointment riddled his voice.

"Well, you know your dad is a busy man, and he usually doesn't have time to do anything but work during the day. At least he went by and saw you in school."

"He didn't see me!" complained Marcos, "My classroom doesn't face that part of the fence."

"Well, I am sure another day he'll go and see you." Her thoughts raced, and she stared at her boys in the rear-view mirror. Beads of sweat slithered down her face, and her blouse stuck to her skin again.

"Mike, do you remember what time Papi came to see you?"

"Before lunch, Mami." Valerie breathed a sigh of relief; the drop wasn't until two o'clock. "They got him," she said, muttering to herself. She looked at her sons and relaxed. "Who's excited for baseball?" she asked with renewed vigor.

"ME!" They both yelled with joy.

"Me too!" she answered.

Gabriel sat behind his desk chair; fingers laced with his forehead resting on his index fingers while the bridge of his nose rested on his thumbs. A small pool of sweat filtered from his back to his shirt and his shoulders ached while his left leg burned as it began its sciatica routine.

"Susana!" he called out to her, glancing over to her desk through the door.

"Yes?!" she asked, turning to face him. Her dark brown eyes grew as she raised her eyebrows.

"Can you get Sergeant González's number for me?"

"Yes, I have it right here; just a moment," answered Susana, leaning over the opposite side of her desk to search through her rolodex. Gabriel leaned back in his chair, the jolts of pain rippled through his left leg and the muscles tightened. The wrinkles at the corner of his eyes grew as he took a hand to massage his eyelids while he waited.

"Transferring to you now," continued Susana, raising her voice so he would hear.

"Thank you," answered Gabriel. He waited a few seconds as the dial tone drummed on before he heard a familiar voice.

"González?" he asked before the recipient confirmed. "I wish I had time to chat and catch up, but do you know anything about the sting earlier today concerning a woman named Valerie and her husband, Mike?" González returned with a few questions. "No, he's a suspected drug mule and she coordinated with Officer Perucci from your precinct. Their last name is Romero." The line silenced for a moment and Gabriel rose from his chair, guiding the phone cord gently to the side to avoid his things. He placed both legs shoulder width apart, tightened his knees, and slowly lowered his chest toward the ground. A slight sense of release warmed him as he felt the muscles in his lower back elongate when González returned to the line.

"What do you mean you didn't get him?!" asked Gabriel, pausing to listen. "González, Valerie didn't tell me anything about going to a motel. I'm sure she's got the boys by now or will, but she's headed home. She thinks that you guys got him." Scenarios began playing in Gabriel's head, images of previous atrocities from his work at the State Attorney's Office displayed like artwork at a gallery. "How many units can you get to her house?" Words emanated from the line to Gabriel's ear. Light sweat streamed down from his temples to his fingers before falling to the carpeted floor. He did not stand straight and remained in the stretched position fearing the tension would wreak havoc on his lower back more than it already had. As González fed Gabriel the details, Gabriel composed his tone, "You know you can't enter unless you have exigent circumstances." González confirmed. "González, one last thing. Valerie told me that Mike is heavily armed." As González peppered him with questions, Gabriel answered based on the little he knew. "I don't know what he has, but I know it's bad."

Chapter 9: The Dragon

Miami Florida, Early April 1981

The practice went longer than usual, and Valerie knew that Mike's muling would make him even more suspicious than his paranoia already did. It was twilight when they made it home. The kids ran up the stairs and down the hall to the apartment, and the fear that Valerie held since she left the law office weakened her as she labored up the stairs and gripped the black metal railing like a cane. The anxiety ailed her more than the heat as she reached the top of the stairs. She felt sick, and cold sweat sopped her from head to toe, not knowing what to expect beyond the door. The boys had knocked but received no response.

For an instant, hope ran through her. She heard the lock click, saw the door swing open, and the hope faded in an instant. A million questions appeared in her mind. The boys picked up their bats and gloves from the floor and walked in. She followed and saw Mike standing next to the door, holding it open for her with one of his strong hands as she passed. She entered the living room from the doorway and saw that Mike had one of the samurai swords sitting in the armchair next to the coffee table along with the two shorter swords in the collection.

"Hello, Sweetheart," he said.

A chilled tone penetrated his voice, and she could tell that he was high. She glanced once more at the swords and knew that this was his way of telling her what he could and would do to her. Gathering her courage and making sure her voice carried strength, she spoke.

"Mike, I've asked you not to be high when the boys are around and certainly not handling those!" She pointed to the swords.

He dropped his gaze to hers while speaking softly.

"I didn't know when you would be coming home with them. I thought maybe you would be spending the night at your mother's house with the boys."

"Not without telling you first and certainly not on a school night." Her response seemed to throw him off for a second.

"Well, there's nothing that I can do about it now, is there? Why don't you hurry up and fix their dinner and then put them to bed? I've had an interesting day that I would like to inform you about."

"They just came from baseball practice, so they need to take baths first," she answered quickly, anger tinging her voice.

"No problem, sweetheart. The truth is that I've got all the time in the world." He lingered on the last words, and she knew that something had happened today.

"Fine," she said, "I will give the kids a bath and get them fed."

She turned to the children and pointed to the bathroom. They bolted toward the bathroom door, pulling their clothes off as they raced down the hall. As she reached into their pajama drawer, she noticed her hand trembling and leaned her body against the dresser. *Just breathe. It's okay for now, take as long as you need with the kids, but just breathe,* she thought. She looked down at the scar in her palm. The boys were in the tub, playing with their toys and splashing each other. She exhaled deeply, and a smile found its way to her face. Mike was outside, ready to hurt her and maybe the boys, but here they were, worried that Batman and Robin were lost in the bubbles and soap. Valerie smiled, rolled up the sleeves of her blouse, tied her hair in a ponytail, and began to bathe Mike Jr. and Marcos.

Half an hour later, Marcos's stomach lurched, and Mike Jr. asked if they could eat. Valerie gently pulled each of them from the bathtub. Grabbing Batman and Robin from around the drain, Mike Jr. handed Robin to Marcos as Valerie patted them down, drying them.

"Do you have any homework tonight, Mike Jr.?" she questioned the boy as she wrapped him in a towel. Mike Jr. held Batman close and looked up at his mother.

"No, Mami, I did my homework at school when we were waiting for you."

"Are you sure?"

"Yes, Mami, I promise. I don't know about Marcos, though."

She turned to Marcos.

"Do you have any homework, Marcos?" She looked down at her son.

"No, Mami. I did all my homework, so I don't get pow-pow." He looked back at her, smiling. She laughed nervously.

"Okay, Marcos. Good job, no pow-pow for you today."

Children have a way of simplifying things. There she was, scared that Mike would kill her and take the boys, and all Marcos cared about was not getting a spanking for not doing his homework. He looked back up and smiled at her through the gaps in his teeth. She held onto every second with her boys before she had to face Mike again.

"Are you boys ready to eat some dinner?" she asked, hugging them both and picking them up in her arms.

"What's for dinner, Mami?" Mike Jr. asked.

"Hmmm, what do you think about Mac 'n Cheese?"

"Yeah, Mami!!!" They both roared.

"Okay, well, follow me."

They walked from the bathroom to the living room and found Mike still sitting in his armchair, focused on his collection. Valerie grabbed a pot from the cabinet and placed it on the stovetop. The boys jumped into their chairs at the table and began singing about mac 'n cheese dinner.

"Do you want a hot dog in the mac and cheese?"

"Yeah, Mami!!!" yelled Marcos, "Can we have two?!?!"

"One for each of you, or are you that hungry, Marcos?"

"One for each. I'm not that hungry, Mami."

"Mami, can we have apple juice?" asked Mike, Jr.

"Sure, do you both want apple juice?"

"Uh-huh, but can I have my apple juice in the batman cup?"

"Of course, sweetheart. I'll get you both batman cups."

About ten minutes later, she retrieved a pot from the stove and served them their mac 'n cheese and poured them both apple juice. They ate, munching away at the cheese-covered pasta and sipping their apple juice from their batman cups. Valerie shifted her attention from the boys to Mike, who had neither moved nor uttered a word to her and the boys.

Mike was too quiet, and Valerie knew that he was high. Her eyes darted around the room, searching for signs of usage, any clues possible to know how much he had used. As she looked around, she felt a tug at her arm and flinched with surprise. Seeing Marcos's smiling face, she relaxed, felt her heart slow down, and breathed deeply.

"Mami, when you tuck us in, can you tell us a story?"

"Sure, sweetheart," she said, taking his little hand in hers and helping him off the chair. She turned to Mike, Jr., "Are you all finished?"

"Not yet, Mami. Almost."

"Okay, we'll wait."

After dinner, Valerie helped them brush their teeth and then scurried them off to bed. She looked around the room and saw the plastic toys on the ground. She saw the familiar castle playset that she bought a year ago.

"Mami," said Mike Jr., "can you tell us another story about Valiant, please?"

"Yeah, Mami. Tell us about Valiant and the dragon!" said Marcos. Both boys were holding onto their favorite action figures from the castle playset. She grabbed the dragon from among the toys near the castle and sat on the edge of their bed. She tucked them in, making sure that they were warm and covered. They beamed at her with wonder, holding onto their favorite toys and readying themselves for story time.

"Okay, boys, I'm going to tell you the story about Prince Valiant, but I'm only going to tell you one story. Your dad is waiting for me."

"Okay, Mami," they said.

Before Valerie could begin, Marcos spoke.

"Mami, can you tell us about the time that Valiant fell down the hill?"

"No, Mami, tell us about when Draconius hurt Valiant's hand."

Valerie looked down at Mike Jr.'s curious face before lowering her gaze to the scar on her palm and beginning the introduction that she told them every time.

"In a kingdom far away, a long time ago, there was a prince named Valiant who was the bravest and strongest in all the land. He would train, hunt, and ride every single day, and from time to time, he would visit the people in the kingdom and bring them bread and would be kind to all. The kingdom loved him, especially his little brothers. You see, the prince loved them more than anything else in his kingdom. They would tell him how much they loved him, and he would do the same for them. They would play and go to school and would make the prince smile. To prince Valiant, they were the most important people in the kingdom, and he would do anything to protect them." They beamed, their eyes begging her to continue. "Prince Valiant lived in harmony in his kingdom until one day, the great, big dragon, Draconius, came to the kingdom, flying high above them, burning trees and villages with his fire. Prince Valiant feared for his brothers and their safety. The kingdom was in chaos, and he wondered if he could stop the dragon that was always in the clouds and would only come down to hurt the people. Then one day, the prince came up with a plan to capture Draconius and keep his kingdom safe, but he knew that if he failed, he would die, and no one would be able to stop Draconius from hurting his little brothers."

"What happened, Mami?" asked Marcos. She swallowed hard and continued, lowering her voice.

"Prince Valiant came up with a plan to have Prince Antonius, his sister's husband, help him to catch the dragon. They would work together and assemble the strongest knights to go to Draconius's lair and find the source of his power. They knew that the dragon would be too strong and would hurt them, so they assembled the men, tracked the dragon, learned his habits, and then went through with their plan...." She stopped, and the boys complained.

"Mami, is that the end?"

"It is, for now, boys."

"But Mami, that can't be the end! Did Prince Valiant and the knights find the power?"

"I don't know, boys; we'll see tomorrow."

"But Mami, why didn't Prince Valiant just use his sword to kill the monster?"

"Because he didn't have his sword, honey, he counted on his men."

"Do we have to go to bed, Mami?"

"Yes, boys."

"But we don't wanna." She waved off their protests, kissing them on their foreheads.

"It's time for bed."

Valerie turned off the light and wiped a tear from her eye as she exited their bedroom. The hallway loomed ahead of her, and with resounding determination, she marched to face her own dragon.

Mike sat in the armchair next to the coffee table, taking a cloth to one of the sword's blades. On the sofa lay his collection of knives. She knew the sets included a Bowie knife, several different hunting knives, and a traditional Japanese knife. He took the sword in his hand and put it on the table, exchanging it for the longest of the three blades. He grasped it in his hand and stared at her until she met his nut-brown eyes hidden partially behind his mashed nose. He had never hurt her while the kids were home. She turned her eyes from his and tried to stay calm.

He changed his gaze to the sword, took the white cloth, put some more oil on it, and started stroking the blade again.

"The Katana," he said, "the preferred weapon of the Samurai of feudal Japan. Sharp and strong, capable of cutting through armor, flesh, and bone." His eyes rose to meet hers again, and she tried to change the subject.

"Mike, you have told me this before, and you know how I feel about you having your weapons out with the kids here."

"I'm sorry, my love, I guess that's two strikes for me today, but I really wanted to make sure that these were clean. I've had a long day, and this calms me down. Are they asleep?"

"On their way there. Practice went really well, so they are a little excited, and it may take some time for them to nod off."

Valerie had to gain every second that she could. She would never leave the apartment without the kids because she feared that he might take out his paranoia on them or hurt them to get back at her. If something happened to her, he might end up with custody of the kids. I need to stay alive; I need to shield the kids from any of his violence.

He was high but not high enough. The phone rang, and she jumped, causing Mike to laugh as he picked up the phone.

"Nervous tonight?" He grinned, Samurai sword in hand. He focused his attention on the phone. "She's right here," he said. He extended his arm with the receiver still in his hand towards her. "It's your mother."

For a second, the lights from the numbers looked like headlights on a highway. Valerie snapped back to reality and took the phone.

"Hi, Mom...Yes, the kids are asleep. Practice was hard today, and they have a big game on Saturday."

Valerie looked at Mike while listening to her mom, asking her about a man named Gabriel.

"Yes, I will pick you up if you want to go." Valerie held the receiver tight to her ear, hoping her husband would not hear her mother telling her that the police were outside of the apartment waiting on exigent circumstances. Valerie closed her eyes in grateful prayer. "That's wonderful, Mom. You see, God gives you what you pray for. Your application finally came through. I am so glad to hear the news. Take care, Mom. Talk tomorrow." She hung up and turned to Mike. "Are you done cleaning those?"

"Nope," his long mousy brown hair swinging back and forth as he shook his head. "I've only finished with the swords. Gonna start on the knives now," he said without looking at her. He caressed the sword with the white cloth, slowly, back and forth along the blade, from the handle to the tip.

"Make sure you put all of that away. Later you forget, and, in the morning, I go nuts trying to keep the children away from them," she said sharply.

"I will," he smiled, "no hurries, but can you answer something for me?"

"Yes?"

"Was it you or Antonio?"

"Antonio?" she asked, purposely.

"The one who informed the cops," he said with an amused look.

His calm made her fear him much more than when he yelled. For an instant, she almost ran to the children's room and locked the door, but she remembered the police outside.

"You are being vague to find out if I know whatever it is you are referring to. Tell me what you want to know, and I will tell you what I know. You and I have been married long enough, so just ask me straight."

Terror froze her, but Valerie kept her composure, and he continued.

"I had my first big pick up today. I got to the place, tried to make the switch, but at the last moment, I realized that I had forgotten the key. As I walked out of the terminal, a shitload of cops from the city surrounded me. They searched my bag but found nothing, and they had to let me go. I've always been a lucky dude, but had I not forgotten the key, I would have been on my way downtown to do fifteen years. I had to report to my superiors and explain what happened, and it wasn't an easy conversation. They thought that I had stolen the stuff and was making up a story. The people I work with screw people over all the time, and it puts me in a bad situation. They know about you and the kids, so I didn't dare mention to them that my family snitched me out. I don't give a shit about you, but I do care about the kids."

"Believe me, if I were going to betray you, it would not be to the cops," she fired back, upping the ante and challenging him.

"Good to know."

He raised his slim, sinewy body from the chair and pointed the sword at her. She jumped back, and he crept towards her.

"You forget that I have been married to you for as long as you have been married to me. That mouthing off is your way of covering up your fear. Stupid bitch, I know that you gave me away." He went quiet and whispered, "I'm not going to kill you tonight. They had the perfect drop for a kilo, and you fucking blew it. If they find out that I talk when I'm high, they won't let that pass, and then you, me, and the boys are fucked." He continued advancing toward her and raised the sword, pointing the tip at her. "But, you know, in a couple of days when all of this has calmed down, a slice here and there where no one can see will teach you the price of betrayal and the safety of silence."

Her chance was slipping, but he wasn't high enough to do anything reckless. The police were outside, but they couldn't come in unless they could prove she was in real danger. He was calm, too calm. She needed to work him up and give him a reason to attack her.

"If you really thought I betrayed you, nothing would stop you. Talk about excuses; you don't have the fucking balls. That's your problem, Mike: big sword, small balls!" She was raising her voice and gesturing emphatically to cover up her slow retreat towards the front door. "I used to be so intimidated by you until I realized that you were a coward. You piece of shit! I hope the boys are like the men in my family, real men, not cowards like you." His eyes began to bulge.

"Bitch, you want me to lose it? I'll end you right here and right now. I'll smack the shit out of you, so you'll never speak to me like that again. You hear me?!"

"Yeah, that's like the guy who gets into an argument and then runs into his friends' arms and cries 'hold me back, or I'll kill him,'" she laughed at him. "You think that you're big time?! You think that you're tough with your little dragon tattoo and Samurai sword? You're the little bitch here, Mike. You're a little bitch!"

"You fucking cunt." He yelled and raised the sword above his head, moving toward her.

She didn't expect that and shrieked. Stumbling backward and slamming into the wall, she hit her head as the door crashed open, and blue uniforms filled the room.

Surprise caught Mike, and he jumped back.

"Bring him down!" yelled an officer.

Mike had the sword raised, but before he could swing it, two SWAT officers tackled him to the ground. In the struggle, another cop went for the sword. Mike gripped the sword and tried to free himself, but a SWAT officer hit him across the face, and another wrestled the sword out of his hand. A fourth officer ran into the kids' room and calmed them down as they came running out the bedroom door and into the hall. By the time it was over, an officer was standing over her, checking if she was okay. He took her by the hands and helped her up. Valerie looked and saw that Mike was standing, hands cuffed behind his back, with a little blood on the left corner of his mouth and a bloodshot eye that looked like it would bruise well. The police hauled him out of the apartment, and the kids yelled from across the hall into the room.

"Mami, are you okay?"

"Yeah, boys, I'm okay." She turned and walked toward them, hugging both boys as they escaped the officer's grip. "Let me talk to the officers, please. Go watch TV in my room."

"Okay, Mami." The boys bolted to her room and closed the door behind them. She returned to the sergeant.

"How can I thank you?"

"Don't thank us. Thank your lawyer," said the sergeant, "I know Gabriel from his days at the State Attorney's Office. He set this up with a friend of mine, Sergeant González. If you can spare a minute, I'd call him."

"I will," she answered before pausing to take in all that had transpired, "well, thanks for everything. For a while there, I didn't think I would live," she said with a small teary smile.

"I can understand that. Ma'am, but it's our job to serve and protect," said the sergeant, nodding and turning to leave.

"Wait, your name?" she asked. He turned back to her.

"Perales, Ma'am," said the stocky officer.

"Thank you, Officer Perales." He nodded again as the forensic personnel entered the room, ready to collect physical evidence. She led them to his stash, including his favorite glass tube. She knew he had enough there to qualify as possession with intent. Then, she went to check on the boys. As she checked on the boys, it occurred to her to call Gabriel. She looked up at the alarm clock next to their bunk bed.

Valerie walked back to the living room where she reached for the phone. Grabbing it from the cradle, she waited until the noise the forensic personnel made died down a little before dialing. After a few moments, an answer came.

"This is Gabriel. Are you alright, Valerie?"

"Thanks to you, I am, but how did you know that it was me?"

"Who else would I expect at this hour?" he asked rhetorically. He sensed her pause on the other side and continued "Are Mike Jr. and Marcos alright?"

"They're a little scared, but they're okay," she said, twisting in place to check that the kids weren't in the living room. "I've got them in the other room watching TV. They're exhausted and have had quite a day."

"Yeah, go figure," he said.

Valerie giggled skittishly. Composing herself, she relaxed her breathing and tried to settle her nerves. Her right hand still trembled as she held the receiver. She paused for a moment and pieced together words from raw emotion. Valerie exhaled, emptying her lungs, and expelling the nerves away.

"I feel so lucky. You told me not to risk it, but I just wanted out of this life for my boys and me."

"Sometimes we get caught up in the emotions of moments like these that we lose sight of the alternatives around us."

"What's going to happen with Mike? I've been through so much just to get here that I hadn't really thought past this point."

"You did this for your kids and your family. I would recommend spending the next couple of nights at your mom's. She'll be able to give you a hand with the kids while you and I do all the things that we need to do. Can you meet me at my office tomorrow at three?"

"I'll be there. Are we going to get a restraining order?"

"You won't need that. I don't think your husband will be getting out on bail with the attempted murder charge as well as the trafficking, but, if he does, the judge in criminal court will be issuing a stay-away order. We will file freedom papers instead for you and the boys. We now have a judicial record, so we have cause to keep him away from you and your boys for a long time."

"Thanks, Gabriel. Seriously. I am alive, and my boys still have their mom thanks to you."

"I must confess that I wasn't thrilled about a single part of this plan.

"So, you called in the extra security?"

"Yes, and I'm glad I did."

"After having a sword come at me, I am surprised I'm alive. I didn't have it all under control."

"Well, luckily the boys have a very strong mom."

"Had you not called my mom, they wouldn't have one now."

"It was the only thing that I could think of to let you know that the police were outside. Had I called, it might have changed Mike's tactics. Your mom was the only person who could have relayed that information." Valerie wrapped the phone cord around her finger, attempting to calm the nerves that wracked her for what might have been. "Did Sergeant González speak to you?"

"No," she answered, "another office spoke to me, his name was Perales."

"Okay. The officers might be a little longer going through your place, but they should finish tonight."

She a nervous chuckle escaped through her teeth, then a sad smile crossed her lips, and she thanked him again.

"Have you been at the office this whole time?" asked Valerie, realizing which number she had called.

"Yes," answered Gabriel, "it's not a problem. I wasn't going to leave until I knew that you were okay."

"Now I understand why my mother sent me to Lock & Lock."

"Thank you, Valerie," he said. "There's a chance that Officer Perales may have questions for you, but when you can, come by the office so that we can file the paperwork. Take as much time as you need."

"I'll be there tomorrow," she affirmed.

"Okay, I'll be ready."

"Thank you, Gabriel. I'll see you tomorrow." she said, closing the conversation, and placed the phone back on the cradle. As Valerie was about to return to her boys, she saw Officer Perales enter from the outside.

"Mrs. Romero, we should be done here soon, maybe half an hour at the most. Tomorrow, I will call you to arrange for questioning, but for now, everything seems to check out.

"The morning is better than the afternoon as my boys have baseball."

"Don't they all. So, will you tell them?

"Tell them what?" she asked, confused by the question.

"About their father."

"Yes, I will, but not tonight. Tomorrow," she sighed, looking from him to the floor and back. Officer Perales nodded and took that as his sign to leave. She watched him exit and turning to herself, she thought, *I'll tell them what happened to the Dragon tomorrow, but for now they'll sleep.*

Chapter 10: The Hospital

Miami, Florida: Late April 1981

April's close greeted the city with flurries of rain showers, and Gabriel arrived more than fifteen minutes overdue at Jackson Memorial from the Coral Way office. He parked in the visitor parking lot and made his way up to the third floor. He found Rosa, with puffy brown eyes reading through an Hola magazine, and Joaquín struggling with the TV remote in his left hand as he entered the ward.

"Gabriel?" asked Rosa, doing a double take as Gabriel opened the door.

"Hey there, Rosa," he responded in Spanish.

"Joaquín, look, Gabriel is here." Joaquín delicately rotated his head more to see Gabriel.

"Hey Gabriel, thank you for coming. How are you?"

"Not too bad, Joaquín, thanks. What about you, how are you feeling?"

Joaquín winced as he sat further up.

"It's better today, thanks be to God, not great, but better. I have surgery in the morning, and the doc is going to cut me up and drill into me, but it can't be worse than what I am feeling now." The hard lines in Joaquín's tan face rose and fell with each word, trying his best to speak through the pain and discomfort.

"I'm sorry that this happened."

"Me too," joked Joaquín, coughing. He twitched, wincing from pain again.

Gabriel turned to Rosa and moved further in front of Joaquín so that he wouldn't have to keep rotating his body.

"How are you feeling?" he asked the diminutive woman.

"I'm doing just fine."

"She's much stronger than I am, Gabriel. She's definitely the better half," said Joaquín through another cough. Rosa lowered her chin, her eyes watering.

"But he's sweeter than I am, Gabriel. Some advice for you in the future: if you're going to be the better half, there's got to be something on the other side."

"You've been out of luck there, sweetheart. I didn't have anything before you came along, and I won't ever again if you decide to walk out on me someday." Rosa wiped a fresh tear from her eye, giggled nervously and ran her well-kept nails through her graying black hair.

"Well," she said after a moment, "you've always worked hard to make sure that I don't, and I have never made plans to go anywhere. For some reason there seems to be something sexy in your pigheaded stubbornness."

Gabriel smiled at the couple and kept silent as they shared the moment until Joaquín spoke again.

"So, Gabriel, I have a small request to ask of you."

"Sure thing, Joaquín. What can I do for you?"

"I want you to represent me in this case."

Gabriel looked at Rosa and then back.

"Do you not trust Rodrigo?"

"I trust Mr. Vivar, but I still want you to be my lawyer."

"Did he say anything to you that you didn't like?"

"No, no. He was honest with me, but I want you to be my lawyer for this."

Gabriel heard the sincerity in Joaquín's wearied voice and decided not to argue with the man.

"Here is my worry; you need someone with a lot of experience defending people in criminal cases, and that's him."

Joaquín gave him a stern unconvinced look.

"Tell you what, Joaquín. I will speak with Rodrigo about how to best proceed. I think that he is the better fit because of his expertise and experience as a defense attorney, but I will participate where I fit in. Maybe he's game for me to assist him."

"That sounds fine. It's a good thing that my truck sold for what it did then. If not, I wouldn't be able to afford both of you."

"You sold your pickup truck to pay for this?"

"I sold the big truck, my eighteen-wheeler." Joaquín straightened up a little more despite the agony in his shoulder.

A string of questions flashed through Gabriel's mind. Remembering to be delicate, he subsided the surprise and was direct.

"But how are you going to work when you heal if you have no truck?"

Joaquín sighed and laid back in his hospital bed.

"Listen, I spoke with the surgeon, my doctor, and a second doctor here. The damage to my shoulder is so bad that I'll never be able to be a trucker again. Even if the surgery is perfect, the damage to the bones, ligaments, and tendons is so severe that I will never regain full motion. I won't be able to handle the steering wheel with the strength or the dexterity I would need for the road. A truck of that size is a dangerous thing, and I won't put my life or anyone else's at risk. I'll find something else to do to put food on the table. Besides, there's enough Cubans in Miami to look after me."

Shaking his head at the truth, Gabriel flared his nostrils as he inhaled deeply and accepted Joaquín's words.

"You're a good man, Joaquín. My father and I are proud to work with you."

"Your father is a great man, not just a great lawyer. He came to visit me yesterday and now you today, so I think that you are on the same path as him."

"That's kind of you. We'll see if I live up to him." Joaquín coughed again and winced with more pain as it shot down his arm and up his neck.

"The nurse should be coming in soon to give you more pain medicine," said Rosa, gazing up at the clock that hung above the door perpendicular to the crucifix that hung above his bed.

"Who's taking care of your kids, and how are they doing through all this?"

"Josué and Esmeralda are good, just a little shaken up, Gabriel," answered Rosa, moving to cover Joaquín up with the blanket that had fallen. "It's not every day that the police come to your house to take your father and much less as forcefully as they did."

"I can only imagine."

"You just try to put it behind you when it happens and try not to remember it when it's over. Unfortunately for us, Joaquín will be here for the next seven weeks." As Rosa grimaced with her final words, her eyes blinked more often than normal, and Gabriel could tell that she tried her best to conceal her nerves and keep herself together. Before he could ask another question, the nurse came in with the medications.

The process of administering Joaquín's medications lasted a little under fifteen minutes and involved Gabriel gently holding Joaquín as he swallowed the army of horse pills that she pushed into his mouth. It was miserable, and Gabriel wondered how Rosa had managed to keep herself together the whole time. Married people are always stronger for each other than they are for themselves, he remembered his mother saying to him when he was a boy.

It was just after sunset when Gabriel left the hospital ward. He bid Joaquín and Rosa farewell and walked down to the parking lot, lost in thought reviewing everything they had talked about and suffered. He made his way to the visitor parking lot, found his Regal, unlocked it, and cranked the engine. As he left the hospital, he looked at the rosary that his grandmother had hung from the rearview mirror and said a few prayers for Rosa, Joaquín, and their family. *God give them strength and perseverance during the long road ahead, and most of all, grant them justice at the end of the journey.*

Chapter 11: The Orders

Miami, Florida: May 1981

Gabriel spent the better part of the weekend sleeping, trying to make up for late nights and stress. As he lay in bed that Sunday night, he reflected on Ernesto's bittersweet verdict, Joaquín's traumatic experience, and Valerie's ludicrous plan that somehow had achieved its purpose. He rose from the bed and made his way over to the kitchen to fetch a glass of water. As he rounded the entrance to his bedroom, he glanced at the jalousie windows of his two-bedroom apartment. It was small, the master bedroom was decent, but the second bedroom was more like a den.

Reaching for a glass from the cabinet, he opened the tap. He lingered a moment as he filled the glass three quarters up before taking a few gulps. The week had drained him. As he took a few more sips, he turned the tap back on and filled it anew.

He checked the clock on the microwave and saw the time as half-past nine. Shifting his thoughts to his responsibilities, he double-checked his clothes for the next day. Seeing a few scuff marks on the right shoe, just below the laces, he debated polishing them but opted to save it for the morning.

Gabriel took his glass of water and crossed to where the den was. Examining the novels on the bookshelf, he browsed through Wilde, Dickens, Bolaños, Machado, Baudelaire, Lorca, and Hemingway, among others, before selecting Antonio Machado's collection of poetry *Campos de Castilla*.

Walking back to the bedroom from the kitchen, Gabriel glanced up at the microwave to see that it was nearly ten. Shrugging his shoulders and yawning, he turned off the lights in the apartment and made his way to bed. Analyzing the cases and the work for the week, he closed his eyes and then faded off to sleep.

The next morning, Gabriel heard the questions and answers for two hours and then the attorney for Armand said, "I have no further questions, this deposition is adjourned."

As they walked out of McClintock's deposition the attorney asked Gabriel, "Lock, can we settle this?"

McClintock turned beet red, but he took a breath and, before Gabriel could stop him, responded, "Your client signed a lease for thirty years and has space in one of my properties. For the last five years the economy has been wonderful, and they paid the correct amount on time every month. They, however, did not send me the share of their profits which they kept to themselves every month. Now the economy is a little rough and they expect me to give them a share of my profits by reducing their rent. You can dress it up however you wish and tie it with a bow, but your client and I will not agree, and I will see you all in court." The old man talked to himself all the way to the parking lot with Gabriel more like a spectator to the drama than a participant. He chuckled to himself as bid farewell to his client. McClintock had been great in the depo, Valerie's paperwork had been filed, and Mike had been carted off to jail, where he would remain without bail until the trial and then be sent to prison for what Gabriel hoped would be twenty years. *Life is good,* he thought.

He arrived at this office a little later and to his surprise, Susana was still there, but his father was nowhere to be found.

"Did my father just leave?" asked Gabriel as he entered the office.

"Your father's been gone since a little after three. He had a meeting with Santiago Alemán at his headquarters and told me that he wouldn't be coming back to the office."

"So why are you still here? Just love to work?"

Susana smiled playfully.

"No, as much as I love working here, I prefer not to stay longer than I have to. I stayed to catch up on some work, but also to tell you that you received this order from the court," she said, extending her arm out to him through the opening in her window.

Gabriel furrowed his eyebrows and scrunched his cheeks. He extended his arm, grasping the documents in his hand, and opened them.

"This couldn't wait until tomorrow?"

"No, the court representative was adamant that this had to be handled urgently. You have until Thursday to comply with the court's demand."

"Did you read it?" he asked, flipping through the unfamiliar paperwork.

"No."

"I have to be honest with you," he said, flipping the contents and moving from page to page. "I saw a lot of documents at the State Attorney's Office, but I never saw anything like this. This seems to be an order naming me Attorney ad Litem in a petition to determine competency for a certain Mrs. Rozália Kovačević. I think this is asking me to defend her."

"Defend her from what?" asked Susana, intrigued.

"I'm not sure, but I'm sure that my dad will know. Also, before I forget, did you get a chance to speak with Rosa Pérez?"

"Yes, I did. She and Joaquín are doing as well as they can. He is still in a lot of pain and will be in surgery once again in the final procedure to repair his shoulder. She didn't request it, but I think that it would mean a lot to her if you went and saw them at the hospital."

"I already visited him." Gabriel raised his eyes from the order to Susana. The lights above them reflected against her dark eyes, and for a moment, Gabriel could see himself in them.

"How does he feel?"

"In pain but recovering."

"I'll say a prayer for him and Rosa tonight."

"We all will," added Gabriel, "I'll just set these documents down in my office, and then probably leave soon."

"By the way," she said, twisting in her chair and disappearing for a moment. She reappeared with a large vase and a full bouquet of Hyacinth, Freesia, Rose, and Peony flowers. "These are for your grandmother."

"Well, they're certainly not for me," joked Gabriel.

Susana ignored his comment and beckoned him to grab them. Gabriel popped into the secretarial area, put the documents down, and grabbed the vase from Susana. As he took them in hand, he smelled them, and the sweet aroma of freshly picked flowers trickled into him.

"Abuela will love these," he admitted, "thank you, Susana."

"My pleasure, Gabriel."

Gabriel walked over to his office and placed both the vase and the order on his desk as he unlocked the credenza. He turned back to the documents, grabbed them, and placed them neatly in the drawer before pushing it back in, closing the credenza. He glanced at the frames above it, admiring the old maps of the constellations and the old world that had come as a gift to his father from the family in Asturias. He marveled at the detail for a few moments before his thoughts drifted to Abuelo. *Another time*, he thought to himself as he decided not to linger on his grandfather's memory and turned back to the flowers on the mahogany tabletop. Abuela really is going to love these. Making sure that everything was in order and secure, he grabbed his briefcase and the extra jacket he had forgotten on Friday and left.

Chapter 12: The Lost Soul

Miami, Florida: May 1981

Gabriel stared at the court order on his desk, reading the lines over again before letting out a sigh. He put a hand to his temples. It was early morning, and the gray overcast sky left him with little light. He pulled the lamp on the corner of his desk and reread the lines.

It was an order from the court to defend a client, Mrs. Rozália Kovačević, in a petition for the determination of competency. Gabriel read through the details and picked up the phone to call his father.

"Hey Dad, I just got this notice from the court. I know that it's good to do pro-bono work, but I didn't see this type of order much at the State Attorney's Office. Would you mind coming and looking at this?"

He placed the receiver back in the cradle and looked around the office. He gazed at his old mahogany desk. It had been Thomas's years before, but it looked different now. He remembered watching his old man sitting behind it when he was a boy. As his eyes rose and fell with the wonders of his childhood, the door opened, and Thomas entered. He sat across the desk and took the notice that Gabriel handed him.

"So, what are we looking at here?" asked Thomas more to himself than Gabriel.

"It's a notice to determine competency, and I just want to be sure that I understand what I am supposed to do."

Thomas chuckled and looked at his son. He was not sporting his signature black-rimmed glasses and instead wore a pair of reading glasses.

"What happened to your glasses?" inquired Gabriel.

"I'm getting the lenses checked out. I dropped them off a few days ago, so I've got a friend repairing them."

"I almost didn't recognize you," joked Gabriel.

Thomas lowered his head, tilting it forward and glaring at Gabriel from over the glasses.

"I'm grateful to have gotten your blue eyes but more grateful to have gotten mom's vision."

"Okay, so what you are asked is to represent the client, Mrs. Kovačević, in a petition for competency. By court order, you can't tell this is a pro-bono case, but we both know this client will not have any funds with which to pay for your services. For the first time, you will be responsible for investigating someone to determine their competency. You will have to decide whether to contest the doctors' decision, which is that she is incompetent and unable to take care of herself.

"Yes, but why is this determined by a lawyer and not a psychologist?"

"That analysis has already been finished, but there has to be a hearing for it, and you have to defend her before the court."

"It comes down to me to decide if I opposed the doctors believing she can live freely without someone watching over her constantly or if I choose not to defend her because she will be institutionalized and watched continuously and lose all her freedoms?"

Thomas stared at his son. Measuring Gabriel's words, he chose his own carefully before responding.

"Should you find that there is reasonable evidence through her behavior, physical capacity, and living conditions, to believe that she is incapable of taking care of herself, then you may use that evidence to determine if the assessment by the doctors and psychologists was conclusive. If you find that in your opinion, they are wrong then you are her last line of defense. It is a lot of responsibility."

"I don't know that I want to be the instrument that takes this person's freedom away," admitted Gabriel.

Thomas removed his glasses and massaged his eyelids.

"You are not. You are one more layer in the protection of her freedoms. You are the ad litem, the court's appointee, to do what is reasonable to protect her. Remember that life is one of her inalienable rights and if she cannot take care of herself, she may hurt herself and die. So, the fundamental question remains: Is doing what's better for a person more important than their right to free will? More importantly, does that person even have free will left because of his or her mental or physical state? We all ask ourselves that, and now it's being asked of you."

"How will I know the answer?"

Thomas rose from his chair and walked over to his son. He placed a hand on Gabriel's shoulder and eased the tension building in him.

"You'll know the answer when you see Mrs. Kovačević."

Gabriel nodded and leaned back in his chair. They both held a moment of silence before Gabriel grabbed his files, packed his briefcase, and snatched his coat from behind his chair.

"By the way, dinner at your grandmother's tonight will start at seven. Don't forget to bring those flowers with you." Thomas pointed at the arrangement that Gabriel had earlier moved to the floor on the far side of his desk.

"Almost forgot, Dad. I'll make sure to come back and grab them when I finish up with Mrs. Kovačević. Thanks."

"Son, one more thing. I spoke with Walter Buendía earlier today. They had another accident, and he needs to see you. I'll have Susana put it in your calendar for next week."

"Okay, brief me on it later, Dad. I've got to go."

Thomas nodded and Gabriel bolted out the door.

It was a short drive to the pale yellow and cream-colored two-story building where Mrs. Kovačević lived. Gabriel parked in the parking lot before her building. The area was older, and he could see the exterior had been neglected for some time. The original white trim along the roofs had faded and dirtied to become a light shade of gray. He could hear the unnatural rattling from old air-conditioning units. As he looked at the building looming over him, he began to climb the stairs to Mrs. Kovačević's floor.

Gabriel walked down the corridor toward the apartment. The lights flickered as he walked, and a musty smell snaked its way through his nose. He reached into his pocket and grabbed the card where the address lay. Apartment 9, he read. He looked around the breezeway, searching for the correct number, but none of the doors were marked. As he was about to return to the auto, a door opened, and a petite, silver-haired woman stepped through it. She stared at Gabriel, and neither of them spoke for a moment. She pulled the zipper higher on her flowered robe and turned to leave.

"Are you, Mrs. Kovačević?" asked Gabriel. The woman continued on as if she didn't hear him. "Are you Mrs. Kovačević?" He tried again, but a little louder.

The woman paused and turned to him.

"Yes, I am Mrs. Kovačević," she responded in accented English, "what do you want?"

There was an aloof and hollow tone to her voice, making it harder for him to discern her origin. Gabriel looked at her wrinkled face. Her eyes were a faded brown, and her veins shone through her thin skin.

"I have come on behalf of the court, and I would like to speak with you for a while," said Gabriel.

"Ah, come in."

As he stepped through the doorway, Gabriel left the musty smell of the breezeway behind, only to be greeted by a faint smell of bleach. Mrs. Kovačević continued through the apartment. He noticed that he was in the living room and that it was connected to the kitchen. It was a modest apartment, and everything looked in order.

White covered all the walls, and Gabriel saw the faded, dusty remains of picture frames and paintings that had been removed. He looked around at the furniture. There were two couches with a small table between them, hugging the corner of the living room on the far side. The floor beneath him was linoleum of an off-white hue that hadn't been cleaned for some time. Gabriel tried to take it all in, but the smell of bleach grew, and he found his breathing restricted.

"Would you like some water?" she continued.

Gabriel wrestled with being rude, but in the end, manners won.

"Sure," he said.

Mrs. Kovačević reached for a cupboard nob and grabbed it. She pulled the door open and grabbed a small glass from within. Turning with it in hand, she lowered it to the adjacent sink, opened the tap, and filled the glass.

Mrs. Kovačević seemed to float as her movements were slow and gentle. She handed it to him, and he thanked her, but she did not acknowledge him.

"Mrs. Kovačević, I am here on behalf of the court to assess that you are capable of independent living."

"Oh," she said without a care.

Gabriel stared at her and then looked at the glass. It was filthy, and the water had a hint of brown in it. He gulped the air in his throat and laid the cup on the kitchen counter.

"Mrs. Kovačević, I want to ask you a few questions, and I promise that it will be short." She nodded.

"Mrs. Kovačević, can you explain what happened with some of the things in your apartment? What happened to your paintings and photographs?"

"Nothing has happened," she said, turning to face him with a stern look, "I moved them to clean them."

Gabriel glanced around the apartment. He noticed the door at the end of the kitchen and wondered what lay beyond. He looked back down at his glass and saw swirls of light brown whisking their way in the liquid. Dust whirled and danced in the air as he rested his arm and leaned on the kitchen bar countertop.

"Mrs. Kovačević, when was the last time your maid came to clean?"

"Pernilla?" she asked, raising her gaze to his, "Pernilla comes every first Tuesday of the month."

"Pernilla Montague?" asked Gabriel.

"Yes, Pernilla Montague."

Gabriel lowered his head.

"Mrs. Kovačević, I'm afraid to tell you that Pernilla Montague died seven years ago."

Mrs. Kovačević's wrinkled face made new lines, and sliding down them were lone tears.

"How can this be? I only saw her just a couple of days ago. She greeted me when she came to clean. She even wore her favorite black blouse with white roses."

"Mrs. Kovačević, I'm sorry, but Pernilla Montague died seven years ago in a crash on the 14th of September of 1974. It was a little more than a week from the last time that she cleaned for you."

"I don't believe you. We only took this photograph together a year ago at her son's high school graduation."

She reached into her purse and grabbed her wallet, pulling out a photograph of her, Pernilla, and what Gabriel assumed to be Pernilla's son. The photograph was faded, and Mrs. Kovačević still had streaks of black and gray hair instead of silver.

"May I see the photograph?" asked Gabriel.

"The handsome young man is her son Clifton. But he hated Clifton, so I called him by his middle name, James."

Gabriel took the photograph in his hands and analyzed it. Clifton was in the middle, flanked by Pernilla and the younger version of Mrs. Kovačević. Gabriel stared at the monochromatic lines and shades, watching the three younger faces smiling at him. He turned the photograph over and found cursive handwriting.

Dearest Rozália,

This hope for Clifton's future is only possible because of the love, kindness, and generosity you showed to both of us. Much love, life, and smiles.

–Pernilla

15-5-1973

"What did she mean by the love, kindness, and generosity that you showed to both of them?" asked Gabriel.

"When my husband passed, Pernilla came to clean for me and did so for the next two places that I lived. After a short while, she became my family and is always with me every Tuesday. James needed tutoring in school. He was a bright boy, just had difficulty with a few subjects, especially Mathematics and reading."

Something had changed in Mrs. Kovačević's tone. She was sharp and clear. The aloof air about her cleared, and she was focused. Keep her talking about the past, thought Gabriel.

"Did you tutor him?" he asked.

"Only in reading, but I paid for all the tutoring that he needed. I had more than enough money, and Pernilla had become my friend." She took the aged photograph back from Gabriel and stared at the three smiling faces. "Pernilla saved my life ten years ago. I was driving back from the bank as I had forgotten to get the cash that I needed to pay her, and I wasn't paying attention to the road. I tried to take a shortcut through a remote area, and I didn't see the bend in the road. I tried to overcorrect and lost control. I hit the tree, and an old wreck like mine didn't stand a chance. I blacked out, and when I woke, I had a sharp pain in my abdomen and my left side. I couldn't move, and there wasn't a payphone in sight on that road. Pernilla somehow sensed it and called the police. A police officer in the area was driving back to the station and got the message. He gave the coordinates on the radio, and an ambulance arrived shortly." She lingered, and Gabriel saw her muscles tighten. Her expression changed as she struggled with the last words. "She saved my life that day."

Mrs. Kovačević wiped a tear from her cheek.

"I would have been a lost soul had it not been for her, and now you're telling me that the woman who saved me from a crash was lost to one?"

Gabriel saw the sorrow in her eyes. Her pain echoed through him, and he felt the sting of regret as if it were his.

"I'm sorry for your loss, Mrs. Kovačević," said Gabriel meeting her eyes, "I'm sure that James is grateful for the good that you did for both of them. Do you have any other photographs of him?"

She was lost in time and was having trouble coming back. Gabriel knew as much from the file. The state of the apartment and the news of Pernilla confirmed it. Her memories and feelings of the past were sharp, but she was still living in them.

"I have an album that Pernilla gave me. My husband and I never had children. James was like a son to me." She chuckled to herself. "Well, more like a grandson, Pernilla could have been my daughter."

"Mrs. Kovačević, in the accident, did you hit your head?"

"Not at all. It was just my side."

Gabriel remembered the file and knew that it wasn't true. In his mind, he ran through and scanned the records he had read and recollected the medical report describing the blunt trauma to her head and the subsequent assessment performed by the recommended psychologist.

Gabriel decided not to provoke any unwanted memories and anger. She was still processing the news of Pernilla, and Gabriel saw her pain. He straightened himself and left the countertop to examine the rest of the apartment. He walked over to the far wall and stared at the missing accessories. He looked at the space to find squared and rectangular dust and grime lines that had outlined where frames had been.

He walked over to a grayed chest of drawers next to the front door. Nicks and knocks lined the edges of the furniture, and the knobs lacked shine. He nonchalantly opened the drawers, and they were all empty. He examined the top and noticed small lines where dust had parted.

"What happened to the photographs and frames that you had here?"

Mrs. Kovačević looked over at the noise. She shifted her body in his direction and ambled over to him.

"Oh, I hid those away for safekeeping."

Gabriel doubted her resolve.

"Where did you put them?" he questioned. "In your bedroom?"

"No, they're over here." Mrs. Kovačević trotted over to the kitchen and headed toward the bedroom door adjacent to the refrigerator. Uneasiness filled Gabriel as he watched her stroll and, as he wondered what lay beyond the door, Mrs. Kovačević stopped. The bedroom door before her remained closed, and she turned to him.

"What's wrong?" asked Gabriel.

"It just takes a second with everything I have in there."

Gabriel didn't know what to expect from beyond the bedroom door, but he never got the chance. Mrs. Kovačević leaned against the refrigerator and put one hand on the bedroom door frame. She readjusted her body and leaned toward the doorframe before taking her leg and leaning it against the refrigerator door.

"Mrs. Kovačević, what are you doing?"

"I am just preparing myself. There is a lot behind the door, and I don't want anything to break or fall."

Fear gripped Gabriel, wrestling with him as he didn't know what to expect from a woman who had lost all touch with reality. She braced herself and began to open the door.

"I forget how cold it is," she said, laughing.

The refrigerator door began to open. With one hand on the bedroom door frame, she used her leg and opposite arm to guide it, opening it slowly as a large sack began to slide from within. Still wrestling with the refrigerator door, Mrs. Kovačević placed all her weight on her standing leg and used both hands to handle the door and the sack.

"What is in the sack?" he asked.

"Everything," she beamed back, "I have everything in here." She lowered the sack to the floor and grasped at the strings that kept it closed.

Gabriel looked into the refrigerator and noticed trays missing.

"What happened to the trays?" asked Gabriel.

"What trays?" She shot back. Gabriel pointed to the open refrigerator. Her silver hair whipped about as she turned her face to see. "Oh, those trays...they're in here also."

Gabriel crept toward her. Everything that he had read about in her file could not have prepared him for this. *Degenerated*, he thought. *She's completely lost.* Mrs. Kovačević had undone the hold on the sack and began to open it. As she pulled back the cloth with her hands, Gabriel saw where the painting and memories had gone. Knick-knacks and odds and ends filled the sack, and Gabriel tried to make sense of it.

"Mrs. Kovačević, why do you have everything in the fridge?"

"I put everything in here for safekeeping. It's the only place that they'd never expect."

"Who are they?" asked Gabriel.

"The voices. They're the ones that visit me during the day. Sometimes they're here when Pernilla comes."

"Do they leave with Pernilla?"

"Sometimes. They tend to keep me company after she's gone."

"How interesting! Are they your friends?"

"Only some of them. The others want to take my things. I can't let them do that; those things help me remember who I am and who I was. What would I do without them?"

"I understand."

"Did you see the President's speech yesterday? I don't like President Ford."

Gabriel went to the kitchen sink and washed the glass. He dried it and began to open the kitchen cabinets to inspect the contents while pretending to put the glass back.

"I don't think they've taken anything from here," he said, knowing there was nothing in the cabinets except the dirty glass he hadn't used, "have you had lunch?" asked Gabriel.

"Yes, I just finished washing the dishes before you came."

"Can I buy you something for later? My treat."

"Oh no, I don't eat past lunch. I eat enough to be full for the rest of the day."

He looked at the way her skin stuck to her bones and did not want to guess the last time she had eaten anything.

"I would love to go with you for a walk. Would you show me a grocery store around here?

She looked at him suddenly and something connected behind her eyes.

"Oh no, it's too cold outside. As you can see, I must have my house robe zipped all the way up."

"Yes, I had to wear my suit today because of the cold." Gabriel smiled.

"And I have felt it since last night," she said.

Gabriel turned and walked toward the bedroom door.

"Is this the way out?" He opened the door before she could react. As soon as he opened it, he covered his nose and mouth. A foul smell ripped through him, and he felt his eyes water. He stared at the room. The bed was unclothed, and streaks of yellow stained it. The smell confirmed the stains were urine, and it forced Gabriel to cough. He deduced that the bed sheets were the sack from the refrigerator, holding all her possessions. He turned to her and saw her staring at the floor. Shame ripped through her and ate at her like cancer. Her eyes lingered on the floor, and Gabriel realized the pain of solitude.

"You know, this apartment is charming, and it's amazing what you've done with the place," he voiced.

She looked up at him and saw him smiling. Her own weak smile began curling into a wide one.

"Mrs. Kovačević, it takes a lot of courage to live alone, and I am going to tell the court about what you did for Pernilla and James."

Mrs. Kovačević stared at him, still smiling and listening.

"I want to tell you that I want what's best for you, just like you did for Pernilla and James."

Mrs. Kovačević held onto his every word.

"And because of all that, I want to tell you that we can move you to a better apartment and better place where you can inspire and care for people just like you did for Pernilla and James."

Mrs. Kovačević nodded. He knew that she didn't completely understand, but she was smiling and knew that he had made the right decision. He shook his head and raised it to see her beaming at him.

"Thank you for coming to visit me. I can't wait to tell Pernilla the next time I see her!" Gabriel closed his eyes and forced a smile, playing along.

"I'm sure that she'll be delighted to hear the news."

Gabriel bid farewell and walked out. Walking down the corridor, he grabbed at the cross hanging from his neck. Gabriel recalled Abuela and remembered how differently she had lived since Abuelo died. He hung his head, closed his eyes, and thought about Mrs. Kovačević.

Thomas's words echoed in his thoughts. "Is doing what's better for a person more important than their right to free will? We all ask ourselves that, and now it's being asked of you."

After a moment, he opened his eyes. He would deliver the report to the judge's assistant before the end of the day. He would mention to the bailiff that this case would not be contested, that it was an emergency, and Mrs. Kovačević should be taken care of right away.

As he descended the steps from the building, he took one more look at the building, one more look at apartment 9, and smiled to himself, understanding that no matter what happened, or where she was, Rozália would always look forward to Tuesdays.

Chapter 13: The Dinner

Miami, Florida: May 1981

Gabriel arrived at the office later than he wanted. The encounter with Rozália left him unsure of himself and of his decision even though he knew that her mental state was unsavable. The bitter taste was knowing that it had been left up to him to defend her in court, and he had chosen not to, concurring with the psychologist's evaluation. He decided that her safety was more important than her freedom, a choice he hoped to never make again. Unbuckling his seat belt, Gabriel shrugged off his thoughts, exited the car, and made his way to the office to grab the arrangement of flowers for Abuela's dinner.

As he departed, he glanced at his watch and knew that little time remained for him to be acceptably late. Spanish time allowed him an extra fifteen minutes, but anything more and Abuela would scorn him. As he floored it down Coral Way, he saw the rosary begin to sway from side to side and took it as an omen to slow down, doing so with enough time to see a squad car on the other side of the intersection.

A loud horn blared from behind him and interrupted his thoughts. He looked up to realize that the stoplight was green, and judging from the sounds and swearing behind him, knew that it had been green for longer than a second. He roared the Buick to life, and the wheels of the Regal whirled him down the street and onto the expressway.

Focusing on the traffic, the drive to Abuela's house lasted a little more than ten minutes. After leaving the expressway, Gabriel found himself staring at the familiar sights that came with Abuela's neighborhood. He saw the usual older men wearing straw hats selling water bottles and *mamoncillos* on the sides of the road, relishing red lights, and stopped vehicles. He passed the familiar *Sedanos* grocery store and passed the *Delicias de España,* where he got her *chorizo* and occasional *fabada* beans when she was in the mood. *La casa de Abuela*, he thought.

Gabriel parked and grabbed Abuela's arrangement before walking over to the staircase to ascend the three flights to Abuela's apartment. As he climbed, he heard neighbors cooking and laughing as the aroma of familiar foods reached his nostrils. The garlic and onion powders wafted with the steam of the white rice that accompanied the black beans typical of the humbler Cuban community. He looked down one of the breezeways to see a pair of elderly men arguing over which domino tile ruined the flow of their game and granted victory to the others. He saw children playing ball and heard babies cry. In the chaos of late afternoon commotion, he saw life and knew that the surrounding life kept Abuela sane when Abuelo died. *Now it makes sense as to why she didn't want to leave*. He thought of Rozália, her isolation, and her frailty. *I hope I never see Abuela that way*. Gabriel reached for the door and paused. He inspected the flowers and adjusted them to perfection for his grandmother. He raised his hand and knocked.

Abuela opened it and greeted him with a flurry of kisses and a strong hug. She nearly pulled him to the floor, ruining the perfection of the flowers, but didn't care, and he hunched over so that her arms could reach around his neck. The smell of peppermint and incense floated over to him from within the home, and behind Abuela, he saw his mother, Laura, waiting to greet him.

"Oh Gabriel, it's been so long." began Abuela in Spanish, standing on her tippy toes, her plump fingers almost entwined behind his bent neck.

"Abuela, I saw you last Monday," chuckled Gabriel, setting the flowers down to better hug his grandmother.

"Yes, now I remember. You brought my TV up all those stairs."

"Yeah, I did," said Gabriel, rolling his eyes, "that was fun." He moved from his grandmother over to his mother, who held her arms outstretched, waiting for him to hug her. "Hi, Mom."

"Hello, my son," replied Laura in Spanish, squeezing her son and giving him a kiss on both cheeks. Gabriel rested his chin on her shoulder atop her jet-black hair as he returned her embrace.

"You should be thankful that the elevator was broken. Hoofing that TV up all those stairs will only help with your muscles and boost your testosterone which will make the girls fawn over you like I used to fawn over Abuelo."

"I don't want to hear how you used to fawn over Abuelo."

"So, your father tells me that you have been doing really well." Interrupted Laura.

"I've been really lucky with the results of some of these cases. Speaking of which, where's Dad?"

Abuela came out of the kitchen, fixing her grayed hair back into place and placing a bottle of Rioja on the table. Gabriel shrugged.

"Well," she said, clapping her hands together as they gathered around the dining room table, "we'll pray, and then we'll eat."

"It looks wonderful," said Thomas from behind Gabriel.

"Hey, Dad, how long have you been here?"

"Since before you arrived." The family took their places, held hands, and bowed their heads to pray. Finishing his plate of paella, Gabriel debated getting fresh air.

"Is everyone finished? If so, then I'll start clearing the table." Everyone nodded and Abuela rose from her seat and made her way to the kitchen, empty plates in hand.

"I'm going to get some air on the balcony," said Gabriel, rising from the chair and making his way to the balcony terrace beyond the kitchen.

"I think I'll join you," said Thomas.

Gabriel slid the glass door to the side and allowed his father to join him on the terrace. The balcony was small, barely wider than the two glass doors behind them, and only a few feet deep. Hearing the faint sound of trumpets, bongos, and salsa music, Gabriel took a moment to appreciate it and the smells that came from the restaurants below.

"You can smell it too, huh?" asked Thomas, inhaling deeply through his nose. He reached inside his coat pocket for the pipe he seldom used.

"Some of the best food is down there. Pointing with the mouthpiece of the pipe. Those small hole-in-the-wall places are the real magic in this city."

"If you had seen this town when I was growing up, we didn't really have all of this. Miami was nothing more than a southern beach town back then. Henry Flagler and Julia Tuttle built this place, but Miami became what it is now because of the Cubans that got here."

"It's crazy how many times I get asked if I'm Cuban, especially when I'm with Rod and the guys." Gabriel leaned against the wall just next to the railing while Thomas stood with his weight on his back leg.

"So, how did it go today with Mrs. Kovačević?" Gabriel half-smiled, pausing to formulate his thoughts, and Thomas waited with the pipe in hand.

"Dad, today was single-handedly the hardest day that I've ever had as a lawyer." Gabriel moved from the wall and rolled his shoulders back. "I never thought that I would ever have a case like this. I saw a lot of things at the State Attorney's Office that showed me the worst in people, but my client was the state. Twelve other people would give their verdict, and the judge would punish accordingly. Whenever the state won, I never had an issue with taking anyone's freedom away, but today, I decided not to protect her freedom and protected her welfare instead. Today, I decided that her security was more important than her freedom and I thought I would never do that. And, independent of a jury, judge, or even counsel to fight against, I made that decision." Gabriel stumbled as he finished.

Returning the pipe to his coat pocket, Thomas moved to his side and placed his hand on his shoulder, squeezing it as he pulled his son in close.

"Son, I know that at the office, I am your senior partner and outside of it, I am your father, but now after you've been through this, I need to speak to you as your senior partner instead of your father. There was a reason I didn't tell you much about this kind of case when we spoke about it earlier. I wanted you to experience this without my input. What has occurred to Mrs. Kovačević is not your fault. You went to investigate the accuracy of the initial assessment by the appointed psychologists, and you determined that they were correct in stating that she was incapable of living on her own. You agreed with that assessment because the evidence was either overwhelming or in accordance with what had already been determined. Now, she can get the help she needs. If she had broken her back, there would be no question that she would receive treatment in a hospital and there would be no doubt that the doctors would decide the best course of action to take. In this case, she has broken her mind, so she will be placed in an assisted living facility where she will receive the treatment she needs, and, most of all, she will have human contact again."

Gabriel lowered his head as he listened to Thomas's words.

"This was an important case because, for the first time, you saw the degree to which a client depends on you. By the end of your time as a prosecutor, you handled robberies and aided in one murder case, and you always requested a denial of freedom by imprisonment. You never had to deal with a case in which it was up to you to impose the depravation of freedom."

"But I didn't even defend her."

"Do you think that Mrs. Kovačević could live on her own?"

"No."

"Then stop beating yourself up. She probably has no concept of what happened, nor will she realize the change in her life. If anything, you stopped her from hurting herself or possibly something worse."

"So why do I feel this way, then?"

"Lawyers don't always have a way to win. Sometimes all we can do is limit the damage of our charge, and often, that is a victory unto itself."

Gabriel nodded, and Thomas held his son a little tighter. Gabriel could feel the clip of his father's suspenders digging into his side from beneath the sports coat as his father squeezed.

"Now, don't worry about this case too much. Don't let it get to you, and don't let it make you think that you were a bad lawyer. It's one more step in the learning process. Now you know that sometimes, you lose, and sometimes there is nothing to fight for. Let's get back inside."

"I'll join you in a minute, Dad." Accepting his father's words and feeling the weight lift from his shoulders, entered the apartment, and returned to his family.

Chapter 14: The Patient

Miami, Florida: May 1981

Gabriel sat behind his desk, taking a few moments to look over some of the case files Susana organized for him. He ruffled through the pages, searching for facts among the handwritten notes and arguments from past thoughts and reviews. He flipped a folder shut as the intercom sounded, and Gabriel picked up the handset. "Yes?"

"Your two o'clock is here," replied Susana.

"Thank you. Please bring in the client and the file." Gabriel placed a clean yellow pad on his desk and waited. Within seconds, the door swung open, and Joaquín was in his office sporting a blue sling on his right arm over his white button-down shirt. Gabriel stood up and came around his desk, patting him on the uninjured shoulder.

"Good to see you, Joaquín."

"Good to see you too, Gabriel."

"My dad wanted to be here to say hello, but his closing is running late, and he can't leave until the money is wired into the title company."

"Please tell him I appreciate the thought."

"Of course."

"I came by to talk to you about several things."

"Let's sit down and talk then." Just then, the intercom rang. Gabriel pressed the button and waited.

"Are you and Joaquín interested in a little Cuban coffee?" asked Susana.

"Absolutely," responded Gabriel, walking around his desk while Joaquín nodded his head behind him. Susana walked in with two large plastic thimbles of a black liquid. Both men grabbed one, and Gabriel sipped his, but Joaquín, feeling through the thin plastic that the liquid was only warm, drank it like a shot of whiskey in a western.

"Thank you, Susana." Joaquín smiled at her as he handed the little plastic cup to her outstretched hand.

"Yes, thank you." Susana left, and both men took a seat. "I have sold my truck, and I should have your fee paid by next week." The response caught Gabriel off guard.

"Joaquín, you didn't have to do that; we would have given you credit."

"That isn't the way you pay a criminal lawyer, and I do not want special treatment."

"But your truck was your living."

"It was, but at my age, other things become important. This injury is painful, but it has given me a lot of time to think. I missed too many family occasions and times with my kids because I was always on the road. Rosa never liked the danger of me driving too many hours. I was readier to give it up than I thought."

"How will you make a living?"

"I know I am not entitled to any worker's compensation, but do I have a civil lawsuit against the officers who mistreated me this way?"

"I had already thought about that. So, if you allow me to, I can consult someone I know that does this type of work."

"Please."

"You realize that before you have an action for this damage you must be declared not guilty in the criminal trial." Joaquín nodded slowly. "Okay, I prepared this letter for you to sign, giving us permission to give the civil attorney copies of your case so that he can give us an evaluation. Still, no matter what, you should look for a new job."

"Maybe I can find a job as a dispatcher or something that doesn't require much hard labor."

"Makes sense. When do you start your outpatient physical therapy?"

"Tomorrow," whispered Joaquín. A tinge of pain filtered through his voice. "It hurts more than I expected."

"What about the medicines?"

"They have their limits." Joaquín smiled weakly at Gabriel, and the two men kept silent for a few moments. "When do I see you again?"

"Our focus right now is your criminal case. We need to resolve that before we can think of compensation or filing for an award of damages of any kind. The criminal case is moving ahead slowly. As soon as our discovery and investigation start bearing fruit, we will begin to meet with you to plan our defense depending on what we find in the evidence that the state gives us and the facts we find independently," responded Gabriel, raising his left hand to shake Joaquín's. Joaquín's breath sounded, and his weak smile widened, and he glanced from his slung arm to Gabriel's outstretched one. He reached with his left hand, and they shook.

"Then I hope it is soon," replied Joaquín, nodding his head before turning to leave."

Chapter 15: The Arrival

Miami, Florida: September 1960

The plane had been circling for fifteen minutes above the Miami airport. Joaquín felt a mixture of fear and excitement. He left his parents behind in Cuba for the chance at a new life in the US. When the teachers told the children that they did not need to obey their parents, only the Communist party, his parents decided to sneak him out of the country. Now he sat, fourteen, unaccompanied and curious, staring out the window, watching the Florida coast appear from above the clouds. Joaquín leaned back in his chair and tried to relax.

Just before the stewardess came for him, he remembered his mother's words, "My sister Cárola will take care of you as though you were her own. She will be your mother until I get there." The stewardess checked his seatbelt and asked him for his empty cup of water. Tossing it, he tried to hold down his wonder at being in a new country and placed both of his arms on the armrests. A few minutes later he felt the jolt of the wheels touching the runway. He had made it to freedom.

When Joaquín reached the exit at customs and immigration, he saw his aunt, Cárola, smiling and waving slightly at him. He walked toward her with his suitcase in hand, and she hugged him warmly. "Was everything okay on the plane?" she asked in Spanish. Joaquín nodded, but his focus dwelled on the scenery around him. This airport was different than at the American base at Guantanamo's. "Come on, let's get out of here," she said, pulling him slightly toward the exit. "Your uncle, Osvaldo, is driving around with Ciro and should pick us up in a minute."

Ciro? Who's Ciro? He thought.

They moved toward the exit and, finding their way through the crowd of people, stepped out into the Miami sun. A green 1955 Chevy Impala entered the covered roadway between the airport building and the parking lot. He saw two heads in the car, his uncle's and a shorter figure with curly black hair like his.

"You have a son?"

"Yes, Ciro, your cousin."

"I never knew."

They approached the Chevy and he saw Uncle Osvaldo exit the vehicle. He walked over to them, hugged his nephew quickly, and ushered him into the car on the driver's side. When he entered, he saw wide dark eyes fixed on him. His cousin Ciro stared at him blankly. Joaquín outstretched his hand. Ciro stared at it for a moment. Aunt Cárola looked back at them.

"Go on, Ciro," she said. Ciro met her eyes and obeyed. He took Joaquín's hand and squeezed hard. They released and Joaquín sat back against the seat, turning his head, and staring out the window. Anger had surged through the handshake, and he felt an inner rage in Ciro, something unnatural.

"Ciro, Joaquín is your new brother now." Joaquín turned to see her smiling and saw the grimace on Ciro's face.

"Where will he live?" he asked.

"With us, you'll share a room now."

"But Mom, we don't have enough to eat, how will he eat too?"

Aunt Cárola smiled weakly and opened her mouth to speak, but Uncle Osvaldo spoke first.

"We will be just fine, Ciro. We are family and we have each other. We take care of one another, and we will be fine. You will always have a bed and will always have food. I promise. Joaquín," he said and stared at him through the rear-view mirror, "we will always have enough to eat, and you are family. Family is always first. Do you understand?" Joaquín nodded. "Do you understand?" he asked again.

"Yes, Uncle!"

"Good. We'll be home in twenty minutes, and we'll have rice and beans for dinner. Do you like rice and beans?"

"They are my favorite," he answered.

"Excellent. We eat rice, beans, and salad almost every day."

"But not meat," jibed Ciro.

"We have meat once in a while and for now, it's enough," smiled Aunt Cárola.

"Now that Joaquín is here we'll have meat, rice, beans, and salad every day from now on," corrected Uncle Osvaldo, realizing that they would no longer have to choose between getting family to freedom and eating meat. "Neither of my boys will go without. Is that clear, Ciro?"

"Yes," said Ciro, begrudgingly.

"Now, let's sit back and enjoy the ride," said Uncle Osvaldo, turning up the radio and taking a deep breath. Joaquín returned to staring out the window. He marveled at all the cars and breathed in the scenery. Finally, he leaned back, closed his eyes, and waited until they made it home.

Chapter 16: The Family Business

Miami, Florida: Late May 1981

The rest of the week flew by, and as the midweek of the following week reached him, Gabriel looked over at the enormous teardrop parking lot from within Walter Buendía's industrial office. From the ground level, it was hard to tell how big the property was, but from the second floor, the blacktop stretched like a football stadium. A small group of buildings stood on the other side, and Gabriel stared at them, reflecting on the size of the trucking operation. There's enough room for 100 cabs and their trailers over there, thought Gabriel. The buildings across the way had three signs. A larger one bore the company's name: *Miami Truck and Cargo*. Then the two beneath read *Parts Department* and *Maintenance and Repairs*.

"I've never been able to see those two buildings from this view before. Did you sell some of your trucks?" asked Gabriel, pointing with his finger at the buildings.

"No. Why?" questioned Walter Buendía from behind. The client sat at his desk some fifteen feet behind Gabriel with a business casual look that was more appropriate for an accountant than an owner of a small trucking company.

"I have been here quite a few times through the years," he turned but pointed towards the lot, "and I have never been able to see the buildings on the far side from this window. You've always had a row of trucks in the way."

"We have been extraordinarily busy." He moved a long arm across his lean body. "All our trucks are on the road, and I have been able to open a good deal of spaces here for trucks. If you look to your left, you will see a line of them waiting to be weighed on the scale. They're coming from the port. Each one of them must make sure that they are carrying no more than their maximum weight before hitting the road. Everything is growing in this town, Gabriel, and as the town grows, we must grow with it."

Gabriel turned to look at this elegant man and saw the clump of white strands invading the rest of his light brown hair. "When I started following my dad to court in high school, everything was handled in the courthouse downtown. There's been so much growth that they just rented seven floors of a building down the street to house the family division. If you've been so busy, how many employees are you at now?"

"One-hundred and fifty-three employees. One-hundred and fifty-three jobs, One-hundred and fourteen families, and four-hundred and ninety-five mouths to feed. It's a lot of work."

"Wow, I remember when my dad brought me here for the first time as a kid. You only had about twenty-five or thirty employees back then, and that was only sixteen years ago."

Walter said, rising from behind the chair and walking to the front. He leaned against it and crossed his feet as he sat on the edge of the desk.

"Gabriel, I must be honest with you, I've been a long-time client of your dad's, and even though you and I only started working together recently, we have been on the same page, and I'm appreciative of the work that you've accomplished. I'll be out of this business soon."

As Walter finished, Gabriel took a moment to process the statement. Unsure of what to respond, he kept silent. Walter sensed the confusion and clarified.

"I am putting this business up for sale, together with the property," he said, gesturing his open palm toward the window and signifying the lot, the office building, and the warehouse. "I'm going to retire to the west coast. Maybe

Cape Coral, Port Charlotte, or Sarasota. Whichever one strikes my wife's fancy."

"I'm surprised, to say the least, but I'm confused; you're still a young man, and you and I were speaking about the plans to grow this business not that long ago."

"I appreciate that, Gabriel," began Buendía, taking a hand to his goatee, "maybe in age, but not in experience. I have been through a lot. My father, Aurelio, built this company before he died at sixty-two. When I think about the stress in his life and how it affected him, I wonder if I, too, want to leave this life before seventy. That leads me to ponder about these two and question how they'd feel without me," he said, pointing at a picture of his two children, Antonella and Luciano, wrapped up in his arms on the grass of their front yard and laughing. "I'm selling the company right away. Those mouths that my father fed and I now feed deserve the best. They give me their best efforts. I've started looking at who could come in and run the company, who would have the heart and soul to keep building on what my father and I built. We're looking for someone who's going to run this business well but treats their employees like family. It's not going to be easy, but I'm confident that I'll find someone who'll do this place justice."

"What brought this on, Walter?"

"Gabriel, the last two years have been especially rough. The first accident took a lot out of me, and when I thought that I had recovered and was doing better, this one happened. I don't have enough insurance left to really cover the damages she suffered if they blame my truck in court."

"We will never get to court. I can promise you that," assured Gabriel, offering a stern look of defiance.

"Logic would say we won't, but these things sometimes defy logic, don't they? Thirty-seven days ago, after I thought that I'd never have another accident, I got a phone call about this girl, and everything changed."

"Logic can be defied, Walter, but much less than people think." Walter smiled and walked over to the mini fridge that he had in the corner of his office.

"I'm going to have some water. Would you care for some?"

"No, thank you," responded Gabriel, using his facial expressions more than his voice to decline.

"Suit yourself," said Walter, leaning over and dropping to a squat. He opened the mini fridge, grabbed a bottle of water and a small glass, and closed the door before walking back to his desk to serve himself. As he poured the water, he spoke. "Having this business puts my whole life's work and my family's future at risk. There are much safer investments I can make with my money. Trust me when I tell you that I never looked at things this way, but after these two major accidents, I realize that whatever I'm making from this place, it's simply not worth it." He turned slowly to look at Gabriel. "I can't sleep. I toss, roll over and close my eyes, but once I'm awake, I can't find my way back to any type of regular sleep. He stood up. "My truck did not do anything wrong and had no part in causing the accident, and yet, I'm on the verge of losing it all."

He closed his eyes. The weight on him had been great, and Gabriel noticed the light shades of purple beneath his eyelids. Walter silently processed all the years, wins, and losses that he had lived through. As he recounted them, Gabriel cut in.

"In Florida, all the participants in an accident are thrown in a pot, and the jury gets to decide the culpability of each one," said Gabriel, walking toward the closer of the two chairs in front of Walter's desk, and sat down. "They decide three things. First, if there is anyone to blame. Second, what constitutes the total damage caused to the plaintiff. And third, if there are defendants to blame, how many of them are to blame, and what percentage of guilt or blame does each have."

"See, that's the problem, Gabriel. My truck did nothing wrong. The driver stayed in his lane, and the black car caused everything. The jury should come back with zero for us."

"When the jury looks at your company and realizes that you have insurance, they will decide that Katerina, the young lady did nothing wrong, but is really hurt, and they will give her the insurance money and maybe some of your money. No one can be sure of how much, but she will receive something because jurors will think that they are serving justice, though each one of them may realize deep down that they are not following the law."

"You can't argue with emotion," admitted Walter, sighing, and opening his watering eyes.

"This is why the insurance company has agreed to talk to the young woman's attorney."

"Gabriel, I can't go to this meeting. I need you to sit in for me. The first accident was enough, and I can't take another one. Can I give you a power of attorney or some other document, for you to be there in my place?" asked Walter before taking a sip of his glass.

"You can give me the power to settle within the policy limits and no higher," answered Gabriel, "I should be able to come to an agreement with the plaintiff and the insurance company." Regaining his composure, he began again in a serious businesslike manner.

"Prepare the document and get this settled at the conference. I do not want to sit through a trial listening to a lawyer talk about how negligent my company was and what terrible men my drivers and I are."

"I understand," confirmed Gabriel, rising from the chair, and turning toward the small table where the window was, to grab his briefcase.

"I know what you might be thinking. How can this man not want to go and defend his own company? But I just can't. Not because I don't want to, but I can't see what happened to her. If I had the money, I'd pay anything to help her through this even though it wasn't our fault. No one should have to go through what she'll go through."

"You still see them, don't you?"

"Every night, burned to a crisp, all eight of them."

"None of this is your fault."

"That doesn't mean that I sleep at night." Walter ran a hand through his curly black hair before using it to massage his eyes. "Not a single night."

Gabriel looked at Walter square in the eyes. Smiling weakly, he walked up to his client and outstretched his hand.

"I promise, Walter, that I'll handle this. And no, I don't think that you are less of a man for not wanting to see the photos and feel her pain. You've got a family to think about, and your health and wellbeing are important to them and to your employees. Don't worry about it. I've got this."

"Thank you, Gabriel. I'm sorry that I won't be working with you guys for much longer."

"Sometimes, the best thing to do is to walk away, but would you consider taking on an assistant or an operations chief that might share some of the burdens and lighten your load?"

They released their grips, "It's a thought," said Walter, "but it would have to be an experienced person who could have my full confidence. That's not easy to find."

He nodded as Gabriel bid farewell, grabbed his things, and left. As he walked back toward his car, Gabriel thought to himself. *Our legal responsibility may be simple in this case, but the human one is not simple at all.* He looked around the parking lot and at the buildings and figured that at least one hundred families lived off this business and it was on the brink of closing. It was up to him to prevent it.

Chapter 17: The Daughter

Miami, Florida: June 1981

Her foot strained as she smashed it into the brake pedal, praying not to crash. Glass shattered around her as metal scraped and bent into the other car. Her hands gripped the steering wheel as it collapsed into the speedometers and the bones in her hands splintered. Tendons tore and ligaments frayed as the pain overwhelmed her. Her torso rammed the steering wheel and twisted around it like licorice. Everything shuddered as she came to a standstill. In the distance, she recognized a truck stop, and two men jump out. Then the pain overwhelmed her, and everything went dark. Katerina's eyes blinked and she was in her living room. She thought she had only been sitting in the wheelchair for a few minutes, but she was too stiff and uncomfortable. It must have been longer. She looked down at her hands, stared at the scars and the crooked fingers, and tried to make a fist. Electricity shot up her right arm. Clenching her left fist, she held it there for ten seconds before wincing in anguish. Her left thumb protruded beyond the rest of her knuckles, and once again, she knew that she would never be the same. Her mother, Darja, walked back into the room.

"Do you have everything you need?" she asked, looking around the room and checking to make sure that nothing would be left behind.

"Yes, Mom. You packed everything perfectly, and everything is in place," she finally said in a horse whisper. Pain emanated from her lungs and chest with each syllable as Katerina forced herself to speak.

"It's so nice to hear your voice, sweetheart. I know that it hurts, but it's a step in the right direction." Katerina smiled weakly.

"Thanks, Mom. It doesn't hurt as bad today."

"Did you take your medicine this morning?"

"My next set of pills will be in an hour or so," she said, gazing up at the clock and taking note of the time. "Did you bring my brush?"

"Yes, sweetheart. I have it right here." She rummaged through her purse, unhinging one of the black straps from her arm and opening the bag wide to spread the contents. When she found the brush, she took the purse from her arm and placed it on the bed. Katerina stared at it in her hand. "Do you want me to brush it, or do you want to try?"

"Would you mind if I tried?"

"Only if you promise to let me do it if the pain in your hands becomes too much."

"I promise, Mom." Katerina took the brush from Darja's outstretched hand and clasped it in her hand. Little jolts of pain surged from her fingertips through her wrist and up her arm to her shoulder, but she didn't care. As she retracted her elbow and bent it, drawing the brush closer to her red hair, more pain shot up her arm, and a tingle spread through her fingers. Her nerves were on fire, but she ignored them. Taking the brush to her head she began at the ends. She moved it down through her hair slowly until it met her other hand, brushing slowly and moving upward until she reached her scalp. Again, she thought as she raised the brush to her scalp, powering through the pain. Again.

The agony heightened with each attempt and sweat began to pump through her frail body. Her arms shook from the pain, jolt after jolt, stroke after stroke, but Katerina took a deep breath, not wanting to surrender to it. She looked up from the sink at the mirror in front of her and saw Darja's face. Red and teary-eyed, she had not said a word as Katerina fought through the pain. Seeing the tears, Katerina resigned her efforts.

"Would you brush my hair for me, Mom?" she asked, droplets of pain, anguish, and acceptance forming in her green eyes.

"Let me help you with that." Darja hid her face for a moment to dry the tears. "I hope you never get tired of me, Sweetheart."

"I won't, Mom," she said, taking her mother's hand in hers and placing it on her cheek, "not everyone is as lucky as I am."

Chapter 18: The Prosecutor

Miami, Florida: June 1981

"Mr. Vivar, we will take a plea on Mr. Dixon's case on...." Judge Fernandez paused and seemingly asked the air, "when is the next available date, please?" A clerk to his right consulted the big, 17 inches wide stack of computer paper held together by perforated lines and answered.

"Wednesday, September 23rd, at 9:00 o'clock."

"Thank you," Responded the judge, "we will take the plea at that time. Have a good day, Mr. Vivar."

"Thank you, Your Honor," said Rodrigo, who nodded at the judge, picked up his file from the podium, and turned to walk out the door after also nodding to his client who sat in the jury box with several other prisoners, shackled at the wrist, around the waist, and down to the ankles. He looked up and saw a mat of curly dirty blond hair on a guy a little over six feet tall. He sped up, recognizing the figure as Brian Donovan, the prosecutor in Joaquín's case. Rodrigo caught up to him.

"Donovan." Rodrigo watched him spin around.

"Vivar, good morning. How are you doing?"

"Good and you?"

"Well. What can I do for you? I'm in a hurry?"

"I am still missing a bunch of discovery in the Joaquín Pérez case."

"Well, the victim is still in New York seeing his family and the family doctor. He is also recuperating. Your client really did a number on him."

"My client did not do this."

"You've received enough discovery to know I not only have the victim but another independent witness identifying him as the perpetrator."

"They're mistaken."

"Yeah, all the witnesses are wrong, the evidence is lying, and your guy's the angel sitting next to Mother Theresa. Is that about right?"

"You should listen to me. Do a lineup."

"Don't need one, so why waste time?"

"Because you have the wrong guy."

"Tell you what, bring me the right guy, and I'll drop all the charges against your guy. How's that?"

"Now we have to do your job for you to be fair with an innocent man?"

"No, I'm convinced I have the right man. You're the one insisting he is not, but then again, he's your client, what motive would you have to defend him? All I said was to prove me wrong, but you can't."

"I don't know how you sleep at night."

"I sleep just fine Vivar, you're the one I wonder about. How many sleeping pills do you have to take every night to stop your conscience?" Donavan whirled and walked away with determination. Rodrigo felt the case closing in. Finally giving up, he took the escalators down to his next hearing.

Chapter 19: The Choice

Miami, Florida: July 1981

The stack of pending cases waiting on his desk occupied Gabriel's mind as he took the elevator from the lobby to the fourth floor of Rodrigo's office building. So much had happened that he felt as if a year had gone by since he was last there. Checking the day, he could not believe that June was ending and that the scorch of July was only a few days away. He wiped his brow as the doors to the elevator parted. Tables strategically occupied the spaces near the corners of the room and were flanked on either side by uncomfortable-looking chairs. He crossed the room to the receptionist, who was hiding behind a strong piece of glass sporting an unamused look.

"Good morning," smiled Gabriel, "I am here to see Mr. Vivar. We have a ten-thirty appointment."

"Are you, Mr. Lock?" she asked, not raising her eyes from the magazine in front of her.

"Yes, I am."

"He is expecting you. Mr. and Mrs. Pérez are also in the conference room, so please, follow me." She rose from her chair, walked around her desk, and unlocked the door. As the door swung, she signaled him to follow. As he walked through the front door, he caught Rodrigo's nameplate on the door of an office in the back corner that did not seem to have either much size or a view. Low man on the totem pole, thought Gabriel, smiling to himself.

The receptionist moved to the side and allowed Gabriel through the door. The conference room was large and only a few steps away from the entrance and the exterior glass that covered the building. The tint of the glass gave the room a slight blue tinge as the morning sun permeated the room. He thanked her and walked to the other end where Joaquín stood holding a Louisville Slugger in his good hand. Gabriel was about to admonish Joaquín for touching the evidence when a voice behind him spoke.

"That's not *the* bat." Gabriel whirled around to find Rodrigo. "I found an exact duplicate of the one allegedly used to hit the victim, and I thought I would bring it to show our client."

Rodrigo walked across the room past Gabriel and straight up to Joaquín.

"Have you ever owned a bat like this?" Rodrigo's tone was aggressive and caught Joaquín off guard. Startled, Joaquín looked from Gabriel to Rodrigo, then to the floor and back to Rodrigo again.

"No," he answered.

"Have you ever had one like this one in your hands or borrowed one? Did you pick one up on your way to pummel the victim?"

"What the hell is this?!" asked Joaquín, becoming defensive.

Rodrigo reached into his pocket and took out a stack of pictures and, throwing them on the table, he scattered them in front of Joaquín.

"Did you use a bat like that to make him look like that?" Rodrigo almost yelled with his question as he first got very close to Joaquín, only to pull away and point at the photographs.

Gabriel stared at the pictures, seeing a bloodied face with wide puffy eyes.

"I didn't do this. What the hell is wrong with you?" asked Joaquín, stepping forward and placing his face an inch away from Rodrigo's.

Gabriel stepped forward, placing his hand on Rodrigo's shoulder.

"Hey, Rod."

Rodrigo did not move. Rodrigo and Joaquín stared at each other without so much as blinking. Seconds clicked on the clock above the door, and eventually, Rodrigo pulled away.

"I had to be sure."

"Sure of what?" asked Joaquín, his eyes still fixated on Rodrigo while his tan face burned with anger.

"That you would hold up under cross-examination by the State Attorney if it ever came to that. You may be innocent, but there's a difference when you get called up to the stand. It's not about being innocent. It's about making sure that the jury knows that you are. When you do what I do, it's black and white, so I had to be sure." He paused for a moment and exhaled deeply.

"Did I pass the test?" Joaquín asked sourly.

"For now," responded Rodrigo. "Let's get to work. All of them took seats around the table, and when they were seated, Rodrigo began, "I have spoken to almost all the individuals on the list of attendees that your daughter gave me. I need you both to give me your timelines. Please include the description of each activity and the place where it occurred to rebuild your movements throughout the day right up until the time you woke up in the hospital," he said, pointing to Joaquín.

Joaquín and Rosa spent the next hour telling Rodrigo and Gabriel in detail about their movements on that day. Occasionally, one or the other would interrupt the narrative to ask a question.

"Then, I woke up in the hospital to find that my left arm was handcuffed to the bed.

"Did everyone else remain at the picnic?" inquired Rodrigo.

"Yes, as far as I know."

"Who was in charge of taking Carla and Charlie home?"

"My cousin, Ciro."

"Who did you leave your car keys to?"

"To Ciro. I left with Rosa in her car."

Rodrigo's eyebrows rose, and Gabriel knew he did the math in his head.

"Describe him to me, please."

"Is this necessary?" asked Joaquín, evading the question.

"Answer him, Joaquín," snarled Rosa, glaring at him.

All three men stared at Rosa, surprised by her tone and demeanor. Joaquín lingered on her for a moment, shocked. His eyes fell to the floor before rising again to answer Rodrigo.

"He's broader than I am and has a wider face, but he's an inch or so shorter with the same facial features."

"Does he also have wild curly black hair like yours?" Joaquín nodded.

"And he stayed behind when you went to Walgreens, didn't he?" asked Gabriel.

"Yes, and he drove the car home," finished Rosa.

Rodrigo's risen eyebrows almost reached his hairline as he processed the new information. Careful not to lose the moment, he lowered his voice to almost a whisper.

"Ciro is your closest cousin, isn't he?"

"Yes," answered Joaquín, "we grew up in the same house." Rodrigo glanced at Gabriel, and he knew to take the lead.

"What do you mean?" Joaquín lowered himself in his chair, sinking into the cushion with his arms on his lap.

"When my family began our exile from Cuba, Ciro and his parents came to the USA first. They found an apartment in Hialeah and settled in for about six months. Six months later, I swam across Guantanamo Bay with two other boys to get to the American military base. The Cuban Army shot at us while we swam. Arnaldo and I made it, but Hernán did not. They shot him, and he drowned. I was taken from the base and was flown to Miami to live with my closest relatives."

"And that was with Ciro, wasn't it?" asked Rodrigo. Joaquín nodded.

"My parents could never come to Miami. They were punished because my father revolted against the communist government, and I escaped from Cuba, so my sister and mother were denied exit visas repeatedly. During all that time, Aunt Cárola and Uncle Osvaldo raised me and cared for me. Knowing her son well, my aunt, on her deathbed, asked me to take care of Ciro. I've kept that promise ever since."

"Yes," began Gabriel in a soft tone, "but if you do, you might spend ten years away from your family."

"His parents gave me ten years."

"They did, and you'll never be able to pay that back, but when your aunt made you swear that promise, I'm sure that she didn't want you to trade your life for his."

"My word is my word, Gabriel. I am an innocent man; nothing will happen to me. Ciro must be left out of this." Rosa buried her face in her hands. Gabriel and Rodrigo attempted to protest, but Joaquín cut them off.

"Okay," said Rodrigo, accepting Joaquín's demand.

Gabriel looked up at the clock to see that an hour had passed in what felt like a few moments. Rodrigo eyed Joaquín, surveying his panting breath and uneasy demeanor.

"Let's all go home. It's been a long hard day." Rodrigo relaxed his shoulders a bit, cutting the tension in the room. Joaquín nodded and exhaled.

"Yes, my shoulder is already starting to hurt," signaled Joaquín to Rosa, who agreed and rose from her chair.

"Go get some rest," said Gabriel, giving Joaquín and Rosa an approving look. "I'm going to speak with Rodrigo for a bit. I'll call you both later. They nodded in agreement. Gabriel waited until the couple entered the elevator and the doors closed behind them. He counted to five and then turned to Rodrigo. "I wasn't expecting that, Rod."

"Neither was I," replied Rodrigo, inhaling slightly.

"Where do we go from here?"

"Well, we have the evidence to clear him, but we can't use it. So, we're going to have to get creative," mused Rodrigo, taking a hand to his temple and massaging it.

"Do you think that it is a good strategy not to take the victim's deposition for a second time?"

"I already showed you the transcript, and the victim admitted he was shown a line-up of six pictures, took a long time staring at the pictures, his finger moved toward our client's picture but then he hesitated and would not pick Joaquín out. A different State Attorney attended that Deposition, not Brian Donovan, despite it being his case. We will be taking the deposition of the other state witness soon, and we will make the final decision then. I'll talk to the prosecutor again about the misidentification if the time comes. You know that prosecutors have so many cases that they basically depend on the officers for identification. If that reliance is misplaced, it's to our advantage."

"Our chances are thin," admitted Gabriel, taking a seat at the conference table. Rodrigo followed suit before answering.

"They are, but they're still there." Gabriel examined the table surface and chuckled to himself. Rodrigo stared at him, not sure if he had missed a joke somewhere. "Did I miss something?"

Gabriel leaned back in his chair and brushed a few strands of his jet-black hair from his face, it ached from thinking almost as much as his head did and he found small release in nervous laughter.

"I left the State Attorney's Office because my boss would not let me take a case to trial. I had promised the victim's family that I would not plead the case out for anything less than what we could get at trial. They knew the risk and I explained that the Defendant could get off with much less time if the jury misinterpreted certain evidence. They were okay with that because the only thing they wanted was for a jury to hear the evidence, to have their day in court. Then, the division chief ordered me to convince the family to accept a lesser plea and close the case. I left the State Attorney's Office because I wanted my clients, not the state, to tell me when to stop, to pursue justice to end, but now it's my client forbidding us to do what is necessary to achieve that justice."

"Yeah, but at least your client's deciding. That's all you can do, Gabriel."

"I suppose," replied Gabriel, agreeing reluctantly.

"So, you left the State Attorney's Office because you wouldn't do it? That's why you left so suddenly?" Inquired Rodrigo. Gabriel nodded before answering.

"Yeah. He gave me a choice and well..." He responded looking at his friend and shrugging his shoulders.

"You didn't tell me that. Why?"

"Because I signed an agreement that stated that I would tell no one," he said, opening his palms.

"And that's why you would avoid the question."

"I hadn't told anyone, not you or even my father."

"Well, you're telling me now."

"No, I'm revealing my feelings about a case that we are trying together, as your co-counsel," circumvented Gabriel, grinning. Rodrigo chuckled. The pair of them thought for a moment before Rodrigo pressed on.

"Do you think he might change his mind before the trial?"

"I hope so, if not, it might take a miracle to get him off."

Chapter 20: The Letter

Miami, Florida: December 1960

Joaquín ran home and slammed the front door. He heard Uncle Osvaldo's voice yell from the garage. "Don't slam the front door!"

"Sorry, Uncle!"

"When the door falls off, sorry won't be enough." Joaquín popped his head back through the door frame and back into the garage.

"I got a B, Uncle. I got a B on my English final! Where's Aunt Cárola? I need to tell her."

"She's in our bedroom," he said without looking up from his work, "but good job." Joaquín's lips curled into a smile. He closed the garage door behind him and walked from the kitchen through the dining room and into the little hall that connected all the bedrooms. He contained his enthusiasm and knocked softly on the last door on the left. A broken voice responded, "Yes...?" asked his aunt. He knew immediately that something was wrong.

"Aunt Cárola?" he murmured as though afraid to ask. "Is everything okay?"

"Come here and sit next to me for a minute, son." Joaquín walked over to the bed and sat next to her. The curtains were drawn, and the rug and bed cover were darker than ever. He felt the bed shake with her body, and turning to her, he asked,

"Are you crying?"

"Yes," she said softly, "Your mother sent me a letter." Her thin hand trembled, forcing the paper in her hand to sway back and forth. Joaquín stared at the paper, waiting for Aunt Cárola to speak. After a few moments, he lost patience.

"Are they alright?!"

"They are okay," she admitted reluctantly, handing him the letter. "You should read it and hear it from her." Wrinkles formed at the corners of Joaquín's eyes and disbelief riddled his mind.

"No, you read it. Please," he begged. She swallowed hard, nodded, and began to read.

"Dear Cárola, I just received a visit from officials from the ministry of the interior. They have informed me that Lisandro has been tried, found guilty of conspiring against the people of Cuba, and sentenced to 30 years in jail. As for me and Lesis, we are prohibited from ever leaving the country. I will immediately be removed from my job at the ministry of tourism if I do not shun my husband and become part of the Communist party. Lesis will receive no schooling, career, or official job for the rest of her life. I don't know what to do. I had hoped that we would all be together in Miami. At every turn, I knew that this punishment was a possibility, but now it's real. Please watch over Joaquín, Cárola. He's a good boy." Cárola's voice broke as she read the last line. The tears felt hot then cold as they made their paths down Joaquín's face and onto his shirt. He crumbled his test in his hand. The B no longer mattered.

Chapter 21: The Friendly Neighbors

Miami, Florida: July 1981

Gabriel sat in his midnight blue Buick Regal, looking at the one-story white ranch house that used to be Richard Nixon's. He remembered the secret servicemen and the Metro Dade police officers surrounding the house as the President and Kissinger discussed the fate of the world, but that was years ago. A flock of seagulls flew overhead, chirping as they glided with the wind, and Gabriel took it as a sign to move.

He turned the key, and the engine roared into life as he pressed on the accelerator. Palm trees swayed as the ocean breeze blew inland from the water. The smell of salty air relaxed him and calmed his nerves. *Reaganomics,* he thought, I wonder how much the economy will grow with the tax cuts. Refocusing on the road, he knew that the client's building was somewhere on his right but was unsure of how far he'd have to drive.

Gabriel drove up to the guardhouse and gave his name and identification to the guard together with the number of the apartment where Janine Gustafson waited for him.

"It's the second building on your right, Mr. Lock," said the guard, handing Gabriel back his license and pointing toward the apartment homes. He left the automobile with the valet and walked into a luxurious lobby. He could see the ocean through a big window at the end as he found his way to the elevators and pressed the button for the eighth floor. When the elevator stopped, and the doors opened, he tightened his grip around the handle of his briefcase and read the sign on the wall in front of him. He saw that the brass numbers, 801 – 809, and departed down the corridor toward 809. When he reached the door, he looked for the bell. After hearing a low ding, shoes scuffled from behind the door, and the scuffles sounded louder until the peephole became dark.

"Are you Mr. Lock?" asked a petite, blonde-haired young woman.

"Yes, I am Gabriel Lock, and I presume that you are Ms. Janine Gustafson?"

"I am Janine. Would you like to come in?"

Gabriel noticed her overcast sky eyes as Janine opened the door fully and stepped to the side, allowing Gabriel entry. When he stepped through the doorway, light reflected off a crystal and gold chandelier that hung in the center of the room. Ivory tile lined the floor, and the countertops were made of black granite. As Gabriel looked around to see the unit, he noticed several post-impressionist paintings in gold-colored frames lining the walls.

"This apartment is beautiful, Ms. Gustafson. Truly beautiful."

"Please, call me Janine," she began. Gabriel nodded and raised his gaze toward the windows at the far end. Just the ocean was visible, no beach from his view, only blue waves crossed the still horizon. "May I offer you anything to drink?"

"A glass of water would be great."

Janine smiled and walked over to the refrigerator, where she grabbed a small ice tray and removed a few cubes from the top freezer. She placed them in the glass that she retrieved from the cupboard, grabbed a pitcher of water from the lower door, and poured it into his glass.

"So, how do you know my friend, Edward, Edward Rapkins?"

"I've only spoken to him once, and as soon as I explained the situation, he told me to call you. I just moved here and don't really know anybody in town yet, but I overheard two of the residents talking about his firm in the elevator, and so I called, looking for anyone to help me. When I called, I was directed to Edward, and when he heard my story, he said I would be in better hands with you, so that's when I decided to give you a call. Thank you for meeting me all the way out here. I can't afford to leave my father alone for longer than half an hour, so it makes most things a little more difficult."

Gabriel scanned around but did not see anyone else.

"Do you want your father to join us?" Janine shook her head and extended her hand toward him with his glass of water.

"He's with the nurse that comes to see him once a week. They meet in one of the private rooms downstairs, and when she's finished, she's kind enough to take him for a walk around the neighborhood. He says it's good for his lungs." A tear slid down her cheek.

"How long has he been ill?"

"Nine years," she said dryly, "there was an accident at work twenty-one years ago that caused a fire. Dad had served on a destroyer during World War II. When the fire caught people inside the building, he ran back and rescued someone trapped on the third floor," she continued, raising her eyebrows and allowing a half-smile to escape her. Janine walked over to the main room with the large windows overlooking the ocean. "He saved her, but the fire and smoke took their toll on his body; we just didn't know it then. Nine years ago, Dad started having issues with his lungs. It was a lot worse than the asthma he got after the incident, and his lungs really started failing. It got so bad that six and a half years ago, he couldn't walk anymore, so that's what pushed him into the chair."

"I see," said Gabriel, looking around the apartment. "How did you both end up here?"

"My mother died just after he couldn't walk anymore. She caught a bad pneumonia and was gone in two weeks.

You'd think that after seeing what smoke did to Dad's lungs that she would have given up on it, but she smoked a pack a day up until the day she died. Her lungs probably looked worse than his do, but what can you do?"

"I see."

"I'm sorry, let me get back to my story," she said with a sad smile, "We moved down here because my aunt, Sharon. Sharon bequeathed me this condo when she passed away. She died two years ago from a massive heart attack. I guess the hard work, incessant coffee, and the back-to-back cigarettes were too much. I was so surprised when she passed over the rest of the family and left me this unit. I packed up everything that I could, sold the house, and moved down here. It was just what my dad needed."

"It sounds to me like you've been through a lot with your parents and their health."

"I was their miracle baby, and my older siblings have their own kids to worry about."

"Have they been able to help much?"

"Not really. Gary and Paul moved to Detroit to work in the auto industry and never really came back too often. My older sister Nancy moved to St. Paul with her husband, and they've got three kids, so it was a hassle for them. Don't get me wrong, my brothers and sister have helped me a lot financially, but if it wouldn't have been for Aunt Share, we'd be in a much bigger mess."

"What did your aunt Sharon do?" asked Gabriel.

"She was the assistant to a hedge fund manager in New York. She couldn't have kids, so she never bothered getting married. She used to tell me that men were only good for their toys and that only kids would make her want to settle down. I'm sorry, Mr. Lock, I feel so rude. Did you want to sit?" asked Janine, pointing to the table and chairs. "Or do you prefer to sit on the couch?" Janine raised her arm slightly, signaling to the couch and two armchairs at the end of the room. "There's also a terrace if you want to sit outside?"

"It's your place, so I'll let you decide."

"The breeze is nice. My father sits out there for hours, but it's probably still a little too warm to sit out there." She walked across the living room and signaled Gabriel to take a seat in the armchair on the opposite side of the sofa.

"Thank you," said Gabriel, taking his seat and pulling his briefcase onto his lap. "I would like to go over the details of what you told Edward. He sketched out the problem, but I wanted to make sure that nothing was overlooked or had changed from what he told me. Could you get into what you explained to him on the phone from the beginning and what is happening now?"

"Nothing has changed since we spoke."

She fell silent thinking and did not seem to know how to start.

"When Edward spoke to me about the case, he was unable to be specific about much, but he explained that the mess surrounding the lawsuit would be greater than the actual lawsuit. Can you elaborate on the events?"

"You already know about my dad's health problems but let me grab the documents. I've got them in a file in my room. Give me just a sec."

"Sure thing," said Gabriel, withdrawing his own notes and documents from the briefcase.

As Janine retreated to her room, Gabriel laid the documents on a corner of the coffee table. He shifted his eyes from the table to search for the fading sun.

"Sorry about that. I should have been more prepared," admitted Janine. She spread the files out on the opposite side of the coffee table and began presenting them to him in the same order that she had received them.

Gabriel glanced at each one, the Deeds, the closing statements, and pages with scribbles and reminders, noting all the documents in front of him. He began to put things together in his head based on what he already knew.

"You know, coffee would be a great idea right now," said Janine as she raised herself up from the table and walked over to the kitchen. "I only make Cor-ta-di-tos now. That's how you say it, right?"

"Oh, they'll understand," said Gabriel, smiling. They both laughed.

Janine disappeared for a few minutes. Gabriel used the time to study her documentation and notes in detail. He reached for his own documents and compared them to hers. He was limited to the records he had found in the courthouse but the ones he had matched hers. She walked in with a tray and placed the Cuban coffee in front of Gabriel. Then, grabbing the remaining cup, she placed the tray on a chair nearby and sat back down.

"For a procedure like this, I usually start with the documents, but this time I think I want you to tell me from the beginning how all of this got started," he said, pointing at the files and smiling.

"It's not the easiest story. My full-time job is managing my father's ailing health." She stuttered on the last words. "He's dying, and there's nothing that I can do to save him, but I don't have enough money to really support him. He's got about two years left, according to the docs, and he knows that. It kills me every time that I think about it, but the problem is that while my aunt left me this place and a little money, his medical bills have gone up. If I go out and find a job, then I'll put his health at risk. If I don't get a job, then the money is going to run out really quickly...."

Gabriel cut her off.

"Why can't you sell this place?" he inquired, looking around the apartment.

"Dad won't let me. Aunt Share left it to me, but I couldn't just leave my dad in Wabasha. I was her favorite, probably because I was so much younger than my siblings, and she looked out for me," she said, raising her chin and eyes over toward the stovetop where the Cafetera whistled. Janine rose from the couch and walked over to the kitchen.

As she did so, Gabriel noticed the slight change in color on the wall behind her. He focused on the change and then on the two paintings, equidistant from the edges. *Those frames are too small to have just two on the wall*, he thought. As he looked around the condo, he noticed that the dining table didn't really match the same wood as the rest of the furniture, but it was close.

"So, I see that you noticed a few things are missing," said Janine, inviting the question Gabriel had in his mind.

"You didn't really have much choice, did you?"

"I didn't," she said, taking two small Espresso cups from the cupboard and placing them on the countertop, "I sold what I could until it hurt Dad too much. The truth is that we could barely afford to live here when we moved. Aunt Share had left enough money for me to live comfortably for a long time, but I don't think that she counted on dying before Dad did. She was younger, in better health, and living in warmer weather, so no one expected it. Luckily, I got a lot of money for the paintings and for the dining room set, but it's not enough, and it won't be. I can't sell the place or any more of Aunt Share's things because Dad won't let me. He's too attached to them." Gabriel sat back in his chair, pondering all the information that Janine had just given him.

"So, you wanted me to meet you here not only because of your father's health but also because of your business dealings. You wanted me to come at this time because he still doesn't know."

"Yeah," she said, closing her eyes and nodding. She opened them and looked down at the floor. She rubbed her eyes, and, taking a deep breath, she raised her head and grabbed the two cups and their saucers. As she took them back to the kitchen, Gabriel sensed a renewed vigor in her step.

"Everything that I did, I did for my dad, for him and his health. I want to make this right, and I want to make sure that there isn't another thing weighing on him," she said, her voice breaking slightly.

"I understand what you have done, and I can't say I would not have done the same. What you did for your dad, moving here all the way from Minnesota, and what you're still doing, is the right thing. Your business deals and these papers are just a part of the experience. Let's go over this now, and please, tell me everything. I will decide what's important and what is not, so don't leave out any details."

"Okay," she took a deep breath and began, "I didn't know anybody in Miami, let alone here in Key Biscayne. I don't really speak any Spanish except for what I learned in high school, but most of that was gone by the time we moved here. When Dad's bills started adding up, I met a neighbor from the next building named Stella Agüero. I met her while working out at the gym in building two, and she seemed nice enough. I guess she could tell that I wasn't from around here." "Anyway, we began to work out together and go to the pool. She would see me take Dad down and work with him so that he could dip his feet in. Stella was nice enough to help me with him and, with enough time, she and I would talk about personal things. Eventually, I asked her if she worked with anybody in finance or knew anybody who could help me out. She told me that her husband, Heriberto, was a realtor specializing in investment properties and that perhaps I should talk to him. When we left the pool that morning, I felt like this was a chance to make things a little easier and decided I had ought to give Heriberto a shot."

"So, what was his plan?"

"With the money that Aunt Share gave me, I was getting just over four percent, which was barely enough to cover our expenses. As Dad's condition worsened, I sold the paintings and the dining room set to give us a little more liquidity in case something came up. Heriberto's plan was different, though. He told me that I had to be more aggressive in the market and that if I took some of the money out of the account that Aunt Share gave me, that we could invest it and get a better return."

Gabriel took a sip of the cortadito and returned it to the saucer.

"So, what did you do?"

"I didn't give him the money that my aunt left me. I gave him the money that my mom gave me."

"What do you mean? You have a second source of money?"

"My Mom invested some money for me when I was a kid just in case she died while I was still young. I didn't even know that it existed until a little while ago. I got a notice in the mail from our local bank in Wabasha saying that my mother's government bonds came due, and I could now touch the money. Since we live off what Aunt Share saved for me, I figured that mom's money was better to invest. If things went south, then it wouldn't affect Dad."

"How did you come to understand that there was something wrong with your relationship with Heriberto?"

"I liked the idea of buying and selling properties and got a real estate license. I enjoyed selecting the investments, fixing the properties, and renting them out. Not only that, but the hours were flexible, so I could work around my dad's needs. I signed up and started taking the required courses. One day after class, I talked to my teacher and explained my situation concerning Heriberto's investments with the money I had given him. She suggested that I see an attorney to help get my investments in order. She did not say there was anything wrong, but she implied it with her concern for the situation. That was last week, and now this week, I get this." she pointed at the complaint.

Gabriel reached for it and took a pen and a small notepad from his briefcase. He opened the pad and began jotting down notes as he read the Summons. He looked for the names and found José Ignacio Montes, Plaintiff vs. Heriberto Agüero, Stella Agüero, and Janine Gustafson, Defendants. He began to go through it, reading every page.

"Is this property in danger?" she asked when she thought he was finished.

"It might be."

"I understood that paper to say that my friend's husband, Heriberto, took $225,000.00 from the man who is suing, promising to buy a property for both of them and instead bought two properties and put them in my name and his wife's."

"That's what it says. It also says that you and Stella are Heriberto's partners in stealing this money because the properties Heriberto told him he was buying are now in your name and hers."

"I've never been dishonest in my life. I can't believe that they did this to me."

"Unfortunately, because Miami attracts a lot of wealthy people," said Gabriel, not raising his eyes from the document, "it also attracts others that make a living, separating those people from their money." He opened his notepad and began jotting notes as his eyes read the information from the summons.

"Look, Janine, I understand that you're nervous about the situation, and with good reason, but Edward asked me to help you. I'm here to get you out of this mess. Why don't we slow down just a little? Take a deep breath and let me ask you some questions." He put down the lawsuit.

"Okay."

"Did you ever meet the man who says Heriberto stole the money from him?"

"No."

"Did you pay Heriberto for the properties?"

"Yes, I paid him full price, $200,000.00 for both."

"Why is Stella on the titles?"

"Because I didn't have the money to pay Heriberto for the investment advice he gave me. I spent all the money on the properties. He said I could pay him later, and as collateral, Stella would have to be on the title to make sure he got paid."

"I need to investigate this matter a little more," said Gabriel, reaching for the rest of the documents on the coffee table. "Notice that the other investor, Mr. Montes, has also sued Heriberto and his wife. All of you are co-conspirators, according to this man. Once we prove that you paid full price for the houses, that will go a long way toward proving you are not part of the conspiracy. Can you get copies of the checks you gave him and the statements from the account where you took the money?"

"Yes, of course."

"How many properties, counting these two, did you buy with Heriberto's help?"

"Six. And that's not counting another property we bought, fixed, and sold." Gabriel jotted down the number.

"How many of them are in your name alone?"

"None."

"All of them are in both your name and Stella's?"

"That's right, I still haven't paid for the so-called investment advice." Janine tapped her fingers on the table.

"Did you also pay for these?"

"The only money used was mine. They put up no money." Gabriel again jotted down notes.

"Do you have the deeds?"

"He kept the originals," admitted Janine, scoffing as she spoke. Gabriel took his pen and placed it under his lower lip, allowing his head to rest on the cap as he thought.

"Do you have copies?"

"Yes, photocopies."

"May I see them?"

"I have those right over there," she said, rising from the chair again and walking over to a secretaire near the terrace.

"Here it is," she said, handing it to Gabriel and finding her seat again. He reviewed the file, scouring through it with his eyes.

"The pattern is clear. Now that you know a little about real estate, do you understand what is going on?"

"I understand that I have bought six properties, two of which were twenty-five thousand dollars above market price. Heriberto gave me false comparables for those properties and even showed me properties that he said were other deals he had made with other clients like me. I mean, we both know that they're probably scams too, but the others may not have been overpriced. He did not own them, so there was no money made in selling them at a higher price. The cheaper I bought the others, the more houses I could buy and the more commission he made. The crazy thing is that he kept Stella on the deed to secure payment for the investment advice that he shouldn't even get, but, in reality, she is the owner of 50% of the properties bought with my money."

"You learn fast. The properties he showed you, do you have the addresses? Write them down for me. I will investigate them."

As Gabriel handed her his yellow pad, he saw her eyes swell, but she wouldn't let them overflow.

"If he got good buys on those two houses, which I suspect he might have, and then perhaps those two houses may not be the full $25,000 overpriced."

"I can't think of that," she said, wiping her eyes. Her voice cracked again and became tense. "What I need to concentrate on is that the houses are giving me a way to do more than stay afloat. Aunt Share's money in the bank isn't enough to work with Dad's increasing expenses. I need those houses, and I need this market to boom, so I can sell them. I messed up and trusted Stella because I didn't have much choice, and she was so nice to me with Dad. How can I get her off my titles, and how do I deal with Mr. Montes's lawsuit?"

"We will put pressure on him through the lawsuit," answered Gabriel in a steady voice.

"Should we take him to court and expose him before the judge?"

"One thing about Miami that you need to know is that it's all about saving face and perception. If we do that, then Stella will swear that there was a partnership because to admit that there wasn't one would be admitting they committed fraud, and it would cause a scandal."

"But I paid them for the properties."

"Yes, but people saw you at the closing together. To everyone, you were partners, and you signed as partners. You didn't know that they were swindling you, but they didn't force you to do it either. They can try to claim that you were just fronting the money in the form of a loan, and they were going to pay them back later plus profit, but then the lawsuit came along, and you betrayed them, and on and on."

Janine stood up from her chair and walked over to the windows. She stared at the sea but was fixated on the scam.

"We actually did a transaction just like this one right at the beginning," she disclosed, breaking her gaze from the sea and looking down at the windowsill and the tile beneath her feet. "We bought the property, it went into both names and, when we sold it, we split the money as we had agreed. I got most of it."

"That's how they hooked you in, Janine. That transaction worries me because it creates a pattern. The other side could claim that all these transactions are supposed to follow that same pattern."

"But none of that is true."

"And you would be able to prove that in court, and it might lead to costly litigation which you neither want nor can afford. In the end, you might be forced to settle to avoid it."

"I can't ship my dad back to Wabasha. I can't just pick up and leave from here. It'll hurt him too much, and I'll never forgive myself if I must sell all of this to cover his bills." She began cracking her knuckles. "Sorry if this is rude. I just do this when I get nervous."

Gabriel raised his head toward her and saw the blue sky behind her.

"How old are you, Janine?"

"I'm twenty-three. I'll be twenty-four next month. Why do you ask?"

"I've had a lot of clients, and a lot of them have had tough situations. We move forward, and the circumstances get resolved." Janine smiled and wiped her cheeks. "You're twenty-three, taking care of your dad all by yourself, moved him from Minnesota to Key Biscayne all by yourself, have given up part of your life to take care of his, and I see in you a lot of the same strength and resolve that my client had. You won't have to ship your dad back to Wabasha or anywhere else. You won't have to sell all this, and your dad will continue to stare at the ocean from that balcony because I think I have enough information. We'll answer the complaint and go from there. A conman's career is all about saving face, avoiding scandals, and solving little inconveniences quietly. He needs to be keeping up with the Joneses to continue with his cons. Let me go back to the office, review the documents, prepare an answer to the lawsuit, and figure out what we are going to do with the other properties."

"I need to solve this quietly too. If my father even suspected I find myself in this mess, he would take a turn for the worst." She took a deep breath and met Gabriel's eyes. "I feel better now about this whole thing."

"Do you mind if I take some of these files with me?"

"Go ahead; I've got other copies of all the originals." Gabriel took the files and documents from the coffee table and put them in the briefcase.

"Janine, I really think that there's a lot that we can do, but I will need to review all of this first. Let me get back to you in a few days. Don't hesitate to call if you need anything. In the meantime, I will file our response to their claim."

Gabriel went to reach for his glass, cup, and saucer when Janine interrupted him.

"Don't worry about those. I've got it," she said, smiling and waving him off. "Dad isn't expected back for another twenty minutes, so I have plenty of time to clean up."

Gabriel nodded, said goodbye, and walked down the hallway; briefcase held tightly in his hand.

Chapter 22: The Leverage

Miami, Florida: July 1981

Janine rested her forearms on the balcony's railing as she looked out at the ocean in the fading sun. It was almost 5:00 PM, and Gabriel would arrive at any moment. The breeze from the ocean felt a bit cooler today. The constant waves stroked the sand as the moon drove the sun from the sky. Stella sat in the chair next to her, drinking Perrier and enjoying the view.

"As nice as our unit is, your view is much nicer," she admitted, taking another sip of the bubbly water. "When Heriberto and I bought the unit, we wanted another one a few floors up that had an incredible view. We got into a bidding war and lost the unit to a couple from Boston who wanted a place down near the water. We've always been fortunate, but they were high-ranking corporate people. I think that he was the Vice-President of a big engineering firm, and we just couldn't compete, so we got ours instead."

Janine smiled weakly, remembering what Gabriel told her mid-week as she listened to Stella's story. As they enjoyed the scenery, the doorbell rang, and Janine moved from the railing to the glass door.

"I'll just be a second, Stella," she said, sliding the door back and entering the apartment. Janine made her way to the front door and stared through the peephole. Seeing Gabriel, she unlocked the door and let him in.

"Is she here?" he asked, and Janine nodded in reply.

She raised a finger toward the balcony door and gestured her head toward it. Gabriel pointed at the dining table, and Janine nodded again. He sat in the chair closest to the door while Janine made her way back to the terrace. She exited through the door and found Stella finishing her Perrier.

"Stella, there's somebody I'd like you to meet. He's just inside."

"Is he cute?"

"Very, but he doesn't know it yet."

"So, he's sexy. Why haven't you mentioned him before? Is he your little secret? When did you meet him?"

"A little while ago, but yeah, he's just the guy I needed," she said, taking Stella by the hand and leading her inside.

Janine and Stella emerged through the glass door, and Gabriel rose from his chair.

"Stella, this is Gabriel," she said, turning to him. Gabriel moved toward them, leaned forward, and extended his hand.

"It's a pleasure to meet you, Stella. Janine has told me so much about you." He said to the curvy, peroxide blonde.

"Oh, he's really cute, Janine," began Stella, scanning all of Gabriel, from his shoes and watch to his eyes and jet-black hair. Stella expected him to blush or give a small smile but received only a small nod. "He's a bit stiff, though, Janine. Well, nobody's perfect." She said turning and the low-cut blouse showed a line of ivory skin where there used to be a bikini.

"Stella, can we sit?" asked Janine, raising her pitch slightly.

Stella's gaze shifted from disappointment to inquiry.

"Why?" she began, "I thought that this was you introducing me to your new man? Your voice has gotten a bit more serious, and he's dressed a little too nicely for an introduction," she continued, looking at Gabriel again, examining his attire, "So what's the play, Janine? Why are you so serious?"

Janine stared at Stella for a moment, taking in the questions and processing her next course of action. After a deep sigh, she opened up.

"Stella, Gabriel is not my new man, he's my attorney, and I think that you should listen to what he has to say concerning the lawsuit and how it's going to affect you."

"Oh no, I'm out of here. Heriberto told me not to talk to any lawyers. Not a single one."

"So, you're representing yourself then, right?" asked Gabriel, focusing on Stella.

"Representing myself? For what?"

"For this, Stella," began Janine, taking the documents that she had placed on the counter when Gabriel arrived and laying them on the dining room table.

Stella paused, her almond shaped eyes looking from Gabriel to Janine and back again.

"Why should I listen to what you have to say when my husband is telling me something different?"

"Because his name isn't on the properties in this lawsuit, yours is."

Pointing, Stella began, "So is your name, Janine. We're all getting sued."

"Yeah, but Gabriel has assured me that he can prove that you and Heriberto defrauded me when I paid for those properties. You have no way to explain that, but they can't go after your husband. His name isn't on any of those documents. Only yours is. You're the one that will be responsible, and you will have everything to lose."

The words hit Stella like an egg on the sidewalk, throttling her and forcing her to pause.

"Listen, I don't think that you really understand everything that Heriberto has done," continued Janine. "That unit you were talking about, you don't own it. Heriberto rents it, and Gabriel can prove it."

"Stella," began Gabriel, "before I start, I need you to answer these questions."

Nodding in affirmation, she turned and found a seat at the dining room table.

"Ask your questions."

"Do you have counsel representing you for this lawsuit of Montes vs. Agüero, Agüero, and Gustafson?"

"No," she replied flatly.

"May I speak with you concerning the contents of this case?"

"Why should I?"

Gabriel remained quiet for a moment.

"I represent Janine, and I am prohibited from giving you legal advice. What I can do is to point out certain facts that you may not be aware of. May I do that?"

"Yeah, whatever."

"Thank you." Gabriel raised his briefcase and placed it on the dining room table, opened it, and removed the files from within. "I want to start by telling you a little bit about what I found out about your husband's business. It turns out that the condominium that you live in belongs to a foreign company in Aruba, so Heriberto never bought it. It's a rental."

He flipped open one of the files and retrieved the deed pertaining to the unit. He handed it to Stella, who examined it. Her eyes widened as she read through the document.

"I'm guessing, based on your reaction, that Heriberto doesn't own the company in Aruba, and you've never heard of it, correct?" Stella shook her head slightly, and Gabriel continued. "Concerning your furniture, your Mercedes, your luxuries, and your comforts, everything is leased, and you don't own any of it."

"I trade in my car every two years. Heriberto prefers a new vehicle instead of driving around some hunk of junk."

"You're right, but except for the furniture, all the leases are in your name, right? Didn't you ever wonder why everything was always in your name?"

"Heriberto and I have been married for ten years. We've been together for fourteen years. He's had health problems since before we got married, and he always told me that it would be easier for me, if anything ever happened to him, to deal with the attorneys and taxes if it was already in my name instead of his."

"Leases in both names do the same thing, Stella. It's not my place to ask if Heriberto loves you, but my job is to look at the evidence. All the evidence points to him being able to leave you, free of any and all responsibility, if anything ever went wrong with his business," as he finished, Gabriel slid all the documents toward Stella. The list of items was long, and the paperwork was thorough. Stella concentrated on the pages before her.

"If he left, this is the last thing he would be leaving you with," he reached for the last file in his briefcase, opened it, and placed it on the table. "This lawsuit says that he borrowed the money, but it also says that you and Janine took it, converted it for your own use, and kept it. That is why your name and Janine's name appear on the titles of those two properties. Heriberto has not responded to the lawsuit because he would rather not answer than expose the truth," he said as he took the subpoena for deposition out of the folder and laid it on the table.

Stella's eyebrows slanted as she zeroed in on the documents before her. She read them attentively, checking the contents and surmising that Gabriel's assertion was correct. Stella reached for the subpoena, scanned it, and Gabriel saw a slight twitch in her left eyelid. Her breathing maintained its cadence, but a rosy color flushed her cheeks, and her knuckles fleshed white as she pressed her free hand on the table, a mixture of enmity and irritation circulating through her with each processed word.

Stella lifted her eyes from the papers and let them fall to the table before retreating her hands from the top of the table.

Gabriel wondered what she would do next and, after a moment's pause, realized that she was waiting on their next move.

"Tell me what you want me to do about this paper," Janine said, eyeing Stella and composing herself. "You are going to tell the truth, aren't you?"

"Yes, I am."

Stella's eyes shifted from each document as she answered. Scanning each set of papers, she knew that there was no escape and that Heriberto had set her up to take the fall. Stella's eyebrows slanted, sighing slightly; she raised her eyes from the facts and looked back at Janine.

"What guarantee do I have that you're going to leave me out of this and let me play the victim? How much of the truth are you going to tell?"

Janine leaned forward, calculating her next move and formulating her words meticulously in accordance with what Gabriel had coached her to do.

"If you sign all six deeds and deliver them to me before the deposition, then I will only say what I need to defend myself." Stella mused and opened her eyes a little wider, the twitch in her eye ceasing as she began to speak.

"So, what are you going to say if they ask you about me?"

"That you were a victim, just like she was. That's why both of you were on the deeds, and he wasn't," said Gabriel, interjecting before Janine could respond. Janine brushed her hair from her face and pushed it behind her ears.

"Gabriel, Stella has told me repeatedly that she's afraid of Heriberto, telling her to shut up about the properties and the lawsuits and not say a word to anyone." Stella nodded and turned to Gabriel. Gabriel measured his next words purposefully, making sure to articulate the objectives without threatening her.

"Stella, either Montes or Janine will keep the properties. Heriberto has no plans to go to court and engage in this litigation, but his name isn't attached to anything, and yours is. Montes and Janine will testify against Heriberto and this con, leaving you to be the only one whose name is on the deeds. At this point, if you don't go to court, you may be found in contempt, and the judge may issue a writ of bodily attachment, which means that you will have an arrest order against you. So, you either cooperate with us by signing the deeds, or I'll ask the court to have you appear in court. I know that you might be thinking that only two of these six are directly involved in this lawsuit, which is correct, but we can very easily include the other four in a crossclaim, and then we will have no choice but to further investigate all of Heriberto's real estate transactions where you appear on a title." Stella was silent again. Janine focused on Stella, not breaking eye contact or even blinking.

"How much truth do you want me to tell, Stella?"

"Enough to explain how I'm a victim too." Gabriel reached into his briefcase and took out the six deeds that he had prepared and handed them to Janine. She took them and slid them across the table over to Stella.

"You have twenty-four hours to get them back to me signed, witnessed, and notarized."

Stella gave a defiant look as she took the papers.

"Don't forget that he had everything set up to be able to walk out on you at any moment. The real question you should ask is, does he love you or the scam more? Either way, this is the right thing to do," said Gabriel, "Janine will be testifying on Friday. Please sign these deeds and leave the fully executed documents with Facundo at the reception desk tomorrow before five."

Janine walked over to Stella and stood behind her chair. Stella remained still for what seemed a long time.

"They will be at the reception desk by five in the afternoon." She did not wait for Janine to respond or show her out, did not need to look at Gabriel as she walked to the door, and did not care to say goodbye before the lock fell into place as the door closed behind her.

Gabriel smiled to himself as the door clicked. Janine sat down in her chair and cried. As she wiped the tears from her face, Gabriel handed her a paper towel from the kitchen. She laughed and smiled back at him.

"With the rental income from these properties, I'll be able to make ends meet and even a little more. Thank you, Gabriel. Thank you so much."

Gabriel nodded and gathered his things. As he finished, he turned to Janine and bid farewell, nodding in acknowledgement and buttoning his jacket as he left.

As he strode down the hall to exit the building, he remembered why he had become a lawyer, and seeing he had made a difference in his client's life, he grinned as he stepped into the elevator.

Chapter 23: The Design

Miami, Florida: August 1981

Katerina held her breath as she saw the consultant cross the lawn from behind the large window of her house. As the consultant approached the front door, Katerina saw her father cross the front porch to greet him. The two men shook hands before her father moved to the side and allowed him in. The consultant entered and noticed Katerina immediately, turning to her and offering a quick smile.

"Katerina," began her father, "this is Mr. Oliver Mason, the contractor that I was telling you about."

"Nice to meet you," said Oliver, offering his hand as he moved toward her. Miloš was about to protest from behind him, but Katerina waved him off with her eyes. With dogged determination, she wriggled the blanket from atop her and outstretched her frail arm, hiding the sharp pain she bore within the firmest grip she could give. Pain shot up to her shoulder and down her side as their arms shook, but Katerina did not wince once.

"Nice to meet you too, Mr. Mason."

"Please, all of you can call me Oliver."

They released their grips, and as Oliver was about to speak, footsteps sounded from the other room.

"Miloš, is the consultant here?" asked Katerina's mother.

"Yes, Darja, Oliver is here." Darja entered the room with her blonde hair whipping just above her shoulders as she rounded the corner.

"Oliver, nice to meet you," she said, moving toward him and shaking his hand.

"It is a pleasure to meet you all," replied Oliver, "Miloš, before we begin, would you mind if we all sat and spoke for a bit? I'd like to make sure that we are all agreed on what is best for Katerina."

"Of course," answered Miloš. Darja and Miloš sat on the couch while Katerina moved her wheelchair closer, and Oliver took the seat across from them.

"The biggest thing for me in the process is making sure that what you want is what's best for Katerina," said Oliver to Miloš and Darja before turning his attention to Katerina. "For you, this is your house and will be your house for some time at least. I want to make sure that everything is as comfortable as it can be. Your father told me that the surgeries and the procedures were successful and that you will walk again." Katerina nodded. "Okay, great. With that in mind, I wanted to make sure that the plan to add on to the house to create a second bedroom area is still what you want to do." Katerina nodded again. "Okay, none of this is easy, but it can be made easier if we all work together to find a solution and a design that best fits."

"Yes," answered Katerina. Oliver turned his attention back to her parents.

"Yes," answered Miloš and Darja.

"Now that that's settled, Miloš, do you mind giving me a quick tour of the house, both upstairs and downstairs, please?"

"You need to see upstairs?" asked Miloš.

"Yes, since we'll be adding onto the house, I'll need to see all of the house to see what the most efficient place to add on would be, where the plumbing is, et cetera, so please, if you don't mind."

"Not at all," answered Miloš.

The two men departed from the family room and maneuvered past the couches and toward the stairs. After a few seconds, Katerina turned to her mother.

"You know, you guys don't have to do this."

"Yes, we do," answered Darja, "there's no question."

"It's going to be expensive, Mom."

"So was your prom dress, but you didn't care then."

"I was useful then." Darja's face changed as Katerina finished her sentence. It became red and flushed, but she contained the anger within.

"What makes you think that you're useless?" Katerina's face reddened also; her scarred knuckles glistened white as the blood rushed within them.

"Look at me, Mom! I'm in a wheelchair. The doctors don't know if I'll be able to practice physical therapy, let alone ever walk again! I studied and worked so hard for what?

Katerina's chestnut hair whipped as she looked down at her body and spread her arms. Pain shot through her sides and arms and then through her, but she didn't care.

"Look at me!!!" she screamed and fumed. The rage reverberated, and the adrenaline drowned the pain but couldn't remove the anguish.

Miloš came back downstairs, but Darja waved her husband off.

"Are you finished yet?" asked Darja, looking Katerina straight in the eyes. Katerina didn't answer. The fumes within her burned, and she exerted herself as she inhaled and exhaled with large breaths. "I'll take that as a yes." Darja rose and moved to within a foot of Katerina's face. Kat made no reply. "Well, you're down, that's for sure. I can understand your anger, your frustration, your pain, and agony, but I won't accept that as a reason for defeat." Darja bent over and placed both hands on the armrests of Katerina's wheelchair. Katerina tucked her arms closer to her body and wouldn't meet her mother's eyes. "No, child, you look at me now." Katerina refused, but Darja took her hand to Katerina's face and pulled it straight, forcing Katerina to meet her gaze. Katerina winced in pain, flinching from the unexpected grip of her mother. "I don't care how much pain you're in. I don't care how sorry you want to feel for yourself. I don't care if every bone in your body is broken, and you are in excruciating pain. You are not worthless. You are not broken. And no daughter of mine will ever tell me that she is useless. You may not ever be able to practice physical therapy again but can still help people. You may not be able to use your hands. That's fine; use your mind. You, Katerina Nováková Danek, are my daughter, and you will not pity yourself." Darja never changed her expression, but Katerina's rage subsided.

A few moments later, Miloš and Oliver returned to the family room where Katerina and Darja waited for them.

"Well, in inspecting the house, looking through the support walls, plumbing, and slight incline outside, we should be fine to add the extra bedroom to the house. Would you like to see what I'm thinking, Katerina?"

Katerina nodded. Oliver rose, and Miloš moved over to Katerina, taking the handles of the wheelchair, and turning her to follow Oliver. They moved through the kitchen and beyond the staircase until they reached the dining room where Katerina's makeshift room was.

"So, the garage is here," Oliver said, pointing to the far wall, "and above us is your room. Over here," he said, changing his point from the ceiling to the far corner. "Here is the main plumbing line for your bathroom, so," he turned back to the far wall, "I would like to build your bedroom here, behind the garage, and tucked away so that you can have some privacy. I know that in the summertime, it gets hot, so instead of installing a door to the garage and a door in here, we can have the door to the back like your father told me you wanted, and you can be connected to the house."

"How much will it cost to do all this?"

"This is actually the cheapest solution, Katerina."

"Sure, but how much will it cost?"

"No more than remodeling the kitchen was," joked Miloš, grinning.

"Katerina, whatever it costs, my job is to make sure that everything from your personal bathroom, the ramps, and anything else is as cost-effective as possible."

"And we won't spare a penny if it means sacrificing your comfort, Kat." Katerina looked up at her father, tears lining her eyelids. She held them back and looked at her mother and father before returning her gaze to Oliver. "How long will it be before you can begin, Oliver?"

"I've got to double-check at the office, but I believe that we can get to work in two weeks. I would need to get the architect and the engineer to look at the property and the plans, and then, if all goes well, we can start construction. The only thing is that you'd have to move out of this room, Katerina, until construction ends."

Katerina looked at the medical bed that had replaced the formal table in the middle of the dining room.

"How long would construction last?"

"Six weeks if everything goes perfectly. Hopefully, there won't be a hurricane or too much rain in these summer months, and we can work efficiently. After all, we must build a bathroom, bedroom, and basically a deck on the outside of the house so that you can have your entranceway."

"From the dining room to the family room, I guess." Katerina pulled her hair back and tucked it behind her ears.

"You've endured worse," declared Darja.

"Okay, it's all settled then."

"Perfect," spoke Oliver, "I'm going to get going now that we've agreed, and I will be in touch with you very soon. Nice to meet you both." He shook Darja and Katerina's hands before turning back to Miloš and following him back through the house to the front door, where the two men spoke for a few minutes.

Katerina sighed, and Darja challenged her.

"You will get through this, Kat. It will not be easy, it will be costly, and it will hurt, but so help me, God, you will get through this, even if your father and I have to carry you until you can walk on your own."

"I know, Mom. I know."

Darja moved over to Katerina, attempting to grab the wheelchair, but Katerina refused.

"No, Mom. I'll push myself. Just walk with me." Darja submitted to Katerina's wish and only walked behind her as Katerina grabbed hold of the wheels and pushed forward, not daring to show weakness.

Chapter 24: The Deposition

Miami, Florida: August 1981

Gabriel entered the building and met Rodrigo in the lobby. The usual mob of people was not there, and the remaining lingerers in the entrance hall seemed too preoccupied with their duties to even move. For the first time in a long time, Gabriel appreciated the floor. He glanced at the time. The watch was a present from his uncle Hendry, his father's first cousin when he graduated from law school. He looked up to see Rodrigo across the way. Rodrigo moved to him from across the hall, and the pair greeted each other.

"Are you ready for this thing?" asked Rodrigo, straightening his tie.

"I am. You?"

"I'm ready. Let's just pray that this guy's story is what we expected it to be."

The pair of them departed the hall and headed for a corridor on the right after ascending the escalator. Gabriel's lower back tensed when the stress mounted. He didn't know if it was the gravity of the situation or the idea that he wasn't the one leading the deposition. Either way, it was too late for him to stretch his back, and he knew that the proceeding would be less than splendid for him.

The witness, Jeff Johnson, sat at the oaken table in front of them as they entered the room. Flanking Jeff to the left sat Brian Donovan, the prosecuting attorney, and to his right the court reporter, Eda.

"Gentlemen," he said, rising from his chair and offering his hand to them. Rodrigo shook first, and Gabriel followed. Johnson remained seated. Behind him, brushing her hair out of her face and focused on a stenotype, sat a blonde woman of no more than twenty-five.

"Nice to see you again, Brian," said Rodrigo, placing his briefcase down and taking his chair in front of Johnson.

"It's always a pleasure to see you, Rodrigo. Always."

"It's nice to see you again too, Eda."

Eda nodded and gave Rodrigo a warm smile. Gabriel kept silent as he met Eda's eyes and nodded, and she acknowledged him. Gabriel gave her his card so she could extract his information and record his presence at the deposition. Rodrigo exhaled aloud.

"Shall we begin?"

"Yes, go right ahead." Rodrigo sat, opened his briefcase, withdrew his notes, and the deposition began. "Please swear in the witness."

She raised her left hand and the witness followed suit. After she concluded, Rodrigo began his questioning.

"So, let me make sure I understand. You never saw the accused up close, is that correct?"

"No, he was about fifty feet away."

"Was he looking down?"

"Yes."

"Did he ever look up in your direction?"

"Nope, he didn't, not once," retorted Jeff, snorting and clearing his nasal passages as he answered. Rodrigo pulled out a yellow duplicate police report and skimmed it.

"You looked away for a second to see if anyone else was there to help you stop the incident, and by the time you looked back, the person was running away from you and never looked back, correct?

"Yes."

"Did there come a time when you saw a person that looked like the individual that you claim to have seen hitting the victim driving out of the park?"

"Yes."

"You saw him from behind?"

"Yes."

"He never turned around to face you?"

"No."

"And you wrote down the tag of the car?"

"Yes."

"But you weren't sure it was the same guy, were you?"

"I didn't really get a good look at the man in the car."

"So, you weren't sure."

"No, I was not, but I told the police that."

"What else did you tell the officers when you gave them the tag number?"

"What do you mean?"

"What words did you utter when you gave them the tag number."

"Here is the tag number of the car I saw driving away."

"How did you identify the driver of the car?"

"He looked like the man that was hitting the victim with the bat."

"Was the bat recovered?"

"I don't know."

"Did the police ever ask you to identify the bat?"

"No, but I told them that it looked like a long wooden bat."

"Did the man walk away with the bat, or did the bat stay with the victim?

"I don't know, and I can't remember."

"Is there anything that would help you remember?"

"Not that I know of."

"Is there anything else that you know about this incident that I have not asked you?"

"No."

"There is nothing else that you could be testifying in court?"

"No."

"Thank you, Mr. Johnson. I have no further questions."

Eda, the thin, blond court reporter that always transcribed all of Rodrigo's depositions and his hearings, punched her middle finger into the keyboard in a final decisive stroke.

"You have the right to have this transcript delivered to you for your review, and if you do not agree with all, or parts, of your answers as I have transcribed them, you can request that those be changed, or you can accept my transcription as is. Do you wish to read the transcript of your testimony before I do the final transcription, or do you waive the reading?" Jeff looked over to Donovan, who nodded back at him. Jeff paused for a moment.

"Yeah, sure, I'll read it." Rodrigo waited until Jeff and Eda had left the room before turning to Donovan.

"Is the victim still out of town?"

"Yes, but from what I understand, he will be back next week. You can take a second deposition then."

"You realize you have accused the wrong guy, right? Your independent witness never got a look at the perpetrator's face. Your cops got the tag from this witness and then showed up to arrest him. You have the wrong guy, and, deep down, you know it."

Donovan paused, and the tips of his nostrils flared upward slightly as he calculated how to best respond. The piercing stare that Gabriel saw earlier revealed itself, and he could tell that Donovan was playing chess in his head.

"You know I can't dismiss this case, Rodrigo; my superior believes that we have the right guy."

"Does she know that your ID is so dubious?" Asked Gabriel looking at his old colleague now turned opponent.

"You boys keep telling yourselves that, but it's not."

"That's one hell of an answer," said Rodrigo, fuming on the inside. "Don't be difficult. Joaquín doesn't deserve this."

Donovan bobbed his head for a second, measuring Rodrigo's words and doing his best to display empathy.

"The kid didn't deserve to be hit with a bat either, but now he deserves the chance to face his assailant."

"There, we can agree, but my guy didn't do it."

"If you know that your guy didn't do it, then bring me the one who did," said Donovan, rising from his seat and offering his hand to Rodrigo and Gabriel.

Rodrigo paused but shook Donovan's hand. He scowled inside, and Gabriel could tell only because he had known Rodrigo for a long time, but like all lawyers, he couldn't give Donovan an inch. As the prosecutor exited the room, Rodrigo slumped back down into his chair. The muscles in Gabriel's back rippled with tension, and the throbbing was beginning to shoot pain down his legs.

"I really don't know how you do this job, Rod," said Gabriel after a moment's silence.

Rodrigo raised his eyes and tilted his slumped head toward him.

"Some days, I don't either." He exhaled again and slowly gathered his papers. "You know, Gabriel, I thought that trying to save my clients who appear guilty would get to me, you know? I kept thinking to myself, 'how can I help a guy who attacked someone, raped someone, or killed someone get free and put them back on the streets, back into a warm bed at someone else's expense. I thought about that for a long time, but you know, I can live with that." He reached beneath his shirt and retrieved a small crucifix that hung around his neck. "I can sleep at night because, while some of my clients may get away with it, they will one day all be judged and get what they have earned or they deserve, but what keeps me up at night, what wrestles with my mind and never gives me peace, is the men like Joaquín who are good men, innocent men who don't deserve to have their freedom taken from them, but it is. It is now up to me to keep our client from this outcome, and he won't help me."

Gabriel sat down next to his friend.

"You know, Abuela gave me this when Abuelo died," he said, retrieving his cross from beneath his shirt, "I always wondered why he died the way that he did, but you know what comforts me about the way he lost his life?" Rodrigo raised his eyes. "It's knowing that beyond this world, and this existence is a kingdom that is just, and it is God who renders the ultimate judgement, and it is he who is merciful. Abuelo got his justice even though we never really did. The prosecution won't drop this, there's too much at stake for them, but in the end, the final judgment comes in a different place at another time."

Rodrigo nodded, and the frustration seeped from his eyes.

"I hope that you're right, Gabriel. I just know that Joaquín, Rosa, and their kids don't deserve to go through all this, and it is up to us to stop the injustice."

"No innocent person does, Rod, but it's not for us to decide if they deserve it; it's for us to help them and protect them for as long as we can."

Donovan walked down the hall, went into the elevator, and pressed the seventh-floor button. *Vivar's a good lawyer. Gabriel's a straight shooter and they both keep coming back to the same thing. We've got the wrong guy.* The elevator stopped and broke his concentration. He made his way to his office and unlocked the door, picked up the phone, and dialed.

"Good morning, Sergeant Heller. I need to speak with Officer Herrera about the Joaquín Pérez case."

"With all due respect, Donovan, we went to the hospital right after it happened and showed the victim pictures of six different people and the one he chose was Mr. Pérez's. Herrera is busy on patrol so I'm not going to interrupt him now. We stand by our actions in the case. Let me know when it goes to trial, and I'll have my people there."

"So, he identified Mr. Pérez?" Insisted Donovan, refusing to be blown off.

"Yeah, he said he looked like the guy."

"How convinced was he?" insisted Donovan running his long fingers through his thinning hair.

"How convinced would anyone be when you get hit from behind and then with a bat. It's remarkable the kid remembers anything at all!"

"Yeah, in that we got lucky," agreed Donovan.

"How many cases have you seen where we can't get a match on anything? Here we have the right photo, the right car, the witnesses, the bat, the motive, and he resisted arrest. What more do we need? This is airtight, counselor."

"Okay Sergeant," said Donovan, surrendering and exhaling.

"Don't overthink it!"

"I won't," said Donovan looking at the stack of cases on his desk and on both visitor's chairs. "Thanks."

Chapter 25: The Hard Truth

Miami, Florida: August 1981

Rain trickled down from the gutters of the house and poured onto the lawn as Katerina stared out toward the darkened sky. She sat in an armchair, cozied up in long pajamas and a blanket. In one hand, she held a novel, and in the other, she held the last letter she had received from him.

As her eyes fixed on the water, her mind wandered off with the dark clouds above her. A crash sounded in the distance, and she knew that the thunder was at least a few miles away.

"A penny for your thoughts?" asked a familiar voice.

Katerina did not turn her head from the horizon. She gazed for a few moments as the raindrops tapped the windowpanes.

"What are you thinking about?"

Katerina sighed and struggled to turn herself around. The pain in her body had dulled since she left the hospital but was still there like an unwanted companion. As she moved the chair and twisted her torso in her seat, she raised her squinted eyes to meet her father's.

"I was just thinking about the rain."

"How do your hands feel?"

"Weak, shaky, my left hand is still the more painful."

"What about your right one?"

Katerina examined her father as he asked the question. His gray hair still had a few brown specks in it, and his eyes, while carrying bags under them, still had their fierceness from her childhood.

"Still on course for a full recovery, but what about you, Dad? Are you going to recover?"

She noticed the outline of a pack of cigarettes in his breast pocket, and she raised her eyebrows, lifted her chin toward him, and used her eyes to point.

Noticing her line of sight, he raised a hand to his pocket and grasped at the box of cigarettes before opening his pocket and removing it.

"Sorry, Kiddo. It's a bad habit of mine," he said, looking down at the floor, "I promise you that I'll quit, Sweetheart. This was my last pack."

She knew that this was not the last time he would say that. Katerina always knew when her father lied.

"You know, Dad, I always know when you're lying because your eye twitches. To someone who doesn't know you, it's not a big deal, and they don't notice, but to someone who does, it's a dead giveaway." The grayed man looked down at the floorboards beneath him. He kept silent, and Katerina continued. "I won't tell Mom that you've been smoking again, but I want you to know that even though you've never quit anything before, it's okay to quit this one little thing."

She used her arms to straighten herself in the chair, and pain burned through her nerves and body. Wincing as she maneuvered, he moved forward to aid her, but she raised her right hand to signal him down.

"I'm eventually going to have to learn to handle the pain, Dad. The doctors said that it'll be there for the rest of my life, and it's not going to go away. With enough time, it'll lessen, but it's going to be some time before it does. I don't know how long that's going to be, but what I can say is that I'd like to have you around as long as I can," she said, "so those need to go." She focused back on her father, who stood empty and hollow.

"You know that I would trade places with you, Sweetheart. You know that, right?"

"I know. Both you and Mom would, and I appreciate that. I really do." Katerina looked up at the crucifix hanging above the doorway of the living room. Next to it, she saw the little sign her mother bought when she was a child that said *God bless this home*. Smiling, she readjusted herself in her chair. "You know, Dad. The doctors said that in a few months, I would be walking with just a cane and a small limp."

Her father moved to the couch opposite her and sat down. He cupped one hand in the other and thought about her words before asking his own.

"What did the physical therapist say?"

"She said that I may one day be able to walk steadily again if the limp isn't too severe, and the pain is enough to handle."

"Well, your mother and I are going to be right here for you every step of the way, and I promise you that you will get through this."

"You, Mom, and Brandon are the only ones that I can count on." As she finished her sentence, he noticed the book and letter in her hand.

"You know that reading that isn't going to make this any easier," he explained, using his eyes to point at the letter.

"I think that he was incapable of being my husband. It's easy to love when things are going well, but that is not the measure. It is certainly not the one I must look for."

She took the letter and placed it on her lap. Without saying another word, she leaned back in the armchair and covered her legs again with the blanket.

"Your mother and I were thinking about putting on a movie. What do you think?"

"I want to finish my book. I've only got about ninety pages left."

"Alright, well, I'll leave you be. If you need anything, just holler."

He moved closer to her, gently leaning in to kiss her on the cheek. She kissed him back, and as he pulled away, she cleared her throat.

"Ahem," she began, "aren't you forgetting something?" He gave her a quizzical look and did not know what to say. She extended her hand and opened her palm.

He smiled, nodded his head, and surrendered the cigarettes. As he placed them in her palm, she smiled too and thanked him. He pulled back, turned, and made his way into the other room. Katerina, stretching her neck and leaning forward to check that she was alone, leaned back against the chair and lowered her eyes to the note in front of her.

Kat,

There's no easy way to do this, but after seeing you in the full body cast, I realized that you have a strength that I don't have. I always knew that you would be the better of the halves. You always fought for every one of your dreams and still had the tenacity to push me to chase mine. I promised you once that I'd always be there for you, and I always will, but knowing that you'll always be in pain is too much for me. I don't have the strength to carry us both. I'm sorry, but I need to say goodbye. As for the wedding, I have taken care of everything and have covered any losses so that you don't have anything more to worry about. I understand if you think of this as selfish or lacking empathy,

```
but know I still love you and will al-
ways love you. Good luck.

    Nick
```

Four years of my life wasted on this guy. Unbelievable, she thought as she took the letter and folded it gently. As she bent the letter, his words sunk in. The damage was done, and there was no way around it. *Maybe it's better this way.* She looked up at the two pictures on the mantle. The first was of her mother, father, brother, and herself, while the second was of her brother, his wife, and their little girl, Shianne. Katerina smiled to herself gently.

Chapter 26: The Strategies

Miami, Florida: September 1981

They met on a neutral field in one of the many conference rooms offered in the mediation center. Gabriel sat very quietly near the far end of the table, glancing at the notes on his yellow notepad. The first hour and a half of positioning by the two sides was predictable and followed the usual script. On one side stood the plaintiff's attorney, Julius Hamilton. On the other sat Rupert W. Jackson, the attorney for Northwestern Truck and Heavy Equipment insurance company. To his right sat the adjuster for the insurance company, Cornelius Wrightly. Hamilton was finishing his argument for damages based on the income that Katerina would lose during her lifetime, and Gabriel listened intently. He could tell, the now middle-age, heavy man had once been an athlete, but that guy was gone.

"Look, guys, I have a client who is a physical therapist." He continued "She will never be able to practice her profession again. The impact of the accident was such that I think the doctors may spend a lifetime looking for that one bone in her body that was not affected in some way by the accident. There is no chance that she will ever have the physical capacity to do the things her profession requires. She will never be able to go through the rigors of leading a patient through their exercises. She does not have enough experience to teach, and again, if she did, she would be incapable of teaching her students the techniques involved."

Gabriel had reviewed the medical records. There was no doubt that what Hamilton was saying was accurate.

"We understand that Hamilton, but you need to understand that our client's involvement in the accident was minimal, and the responsibility for it was again minimal, if any," said Jackson, glancing toward Wrightly. He raised the volume and pitch of his voice to make his point. "Our client's truck was coming down the ramp to merge into the expressway. The rig wasn't even on I-95 yet. It was the black car that came from I-95 into the merge lane and hit our client's truck." He changed his body language as he rose, pausing for a moment, and continued in a measured voice, complimenting the smooth movements of his deep brown hands. He opened his palms and stretched his arms out to the sides. "So, why should Northwestern Truck and Heavy Equipment Insurance Company pay for the negligence of the black car's actions?" he asked as though the opposing counsel were a jury in a courtroom. "It was that absolute negligence that caused this mess," he concluded.

Hamilton was ready for the rebuttal. He took off his black glasses and smiled slightly acting like he was composing himself. He plunged forward.

"Yes, but then that car, because it hit your client's truck, went on to hit my client's vehicle. In this state, there will be some guilt assigned to the truck, and so the money will be paid out. It is in the interest of your client, as the insurance company, to pay enough money to Katerina, now, at this settlement, to cover itself from a bigger liability and to comply with its responsibility to protect the truck owner," responded Hamilton, looking at Gabriel and expecting him to jump into the fray.

It's not time yet, Hamilton. I'm here to protect Miami Truck and Cargo, and it's not time for me to jump in yet. Gabriel turned his eyes to Jackson, examining the attorney. *Oh, Jackson, you represent Miami Truck and Cargo in name only. In this litigation, everyone knows whose skin you're here to defend.* Gabriel glanced over to Wrightly, sitting next to Jackson. *Their money pays for your office, your salary, and your kids' futures. The law says that if Northwestern acts in good faith, it can handle and settle the litigation however it wants. You're doing two things with your strategy, you're going to settle this for as little as possible, and you're going to delay the payout for as long as possible without acting in bad faith so that the insurance company can keep investing the money and increase its worth. When this is over, you won't remember Walter or Miami Truck and Cargo. Hamilton is going to do everything that he can to get his client the most money possible, and by his presentation, which will far exceed the limit of the policy if you are not careful. He also wants to get the money as soon as possible because Katerina is running out of medical insurance coverage. My job is to make sure that Northwestern does its job and settles within the limits of the policy. They've got to pay for this as soon as possible so that Walter can sleep at night.* Gabriel finished his thoughts and looked at the other lawyers. Both had their priorities, and he was right in the middle. He remained quiet, choosing not to speak and instead analyzed their strategies, body language, and resolve. Observing the rotating strategies, it was often two against one, but not always the same two or the same one.

"Lock," began Hamilton, turning his complete attention to Gabriel and interrupting his thoughts, "you know that my claim against Miami Trucking and Cargo is worth more than the one million dollars of the insurance that your client has. Your client's assets will be responsible for any difference if we go to trial. You really don't want it to get there, do you?"

Hamilton baited him in, but Gabriel didn't take it. He was there because of that danger but elected not to respond to the attack. Instead, he nodded his head and turned to Jackson, looking at him without saying a word, deferring to his superior position and knowledge in silence. Jackson responded to Hamilton.

"I'll grant you that a Florida jury would give Miami Truck and Cargo some responsibility for the accident. They always give the injured something from the pocket of the bigger guy, just because they feel a company has more money than an individual, but, at best, they would grant ten percent."

For the first time, Jackson accepted that the truck might have some responsibility in the eyes of a jury and offered a concrete number. The true negotiations begin, thought Gabriel, leaning back in his chair. With Jackson's admission of possible responsibility, the new duel began in earnest.

"Ten percent? Come on, Jackson! You know it's more than that in trial," riposted Hamilton. Jackson, very calmly, took a sip of his tea.

"That is the keyword, isn't it, Hamilton? Trial. Jackson put his cup down gently on the polished wood surface. "We are not in trial right now," he said evenly. "We are at a pre-filing settlement conference. We are doing this because you do not want to go through the expense of litigation. You and I both know that the individual driving the black car has disappeared. Mr. Wrightly," he said, turning and extending an arm toward Wrightly, "came with me today because he has been the adjuster on this matter since day one when the insurance company was notified. As a matter of fact, all the folks in the black car are nowhere to be found. He has looked for them everywhere. Not only that, but they were probably uninsured, so you are looking to us and your client's underinsured policy as your only sources of revenue."

Hamilton stood up.

"Even if you offer the policy limits here, it's simply not enough." He walked to the end of the table, and he asked Gabriel sharply. "Are you sure there isn't another policy covering this accident?"

"Yes," he said while exhaling. "As I told you in response to your original letter to my client, at the time of the accident, there was no coverage other than this one." Gabriel's mind wandered off.

"My client is in her mid-twenties," said Hamilton, interrupting Gabriel's thoughts. "She was going to get married, but the accident happened two months before the date. Not only is it that she cannot work, but she will never be able to have children, and she lost her relationship. As her counsel, I need to be very careful because the money from this case is the only thing that stands between her and a lifetime of unfulfilled needs and untreated medical problems that we all know she will have in the future."

Hamilton removed his briefcase from the table and placed it on the floor. He took the file sitting in front of his chair from the beginning of the meeting and opened it. Taking the contents in his hands, he began to lay them in front of Jackson and Wrightly.

Wrightly removed his glasses, took a handkerchief from his jacket pocket, and cleaned them determinedly. Jackson did his best to look only at Hamilton, who now spread the series of pictures in front of their view.

"Hamilton, I've seen them before. No need to show them again."

Gabriel remained quiet, controlling the expression on his face, but inside struggled with managing the compassion for Hamilton and his client. Walter had given Gabriel full authority to settle the case because he did not want to face the pictures, drawings, and illustrations that he knew Hamilton would bring and were now spread on the conference table for effect during the meeting. Gabriel raised his head from the photographs to stare at Jackson. Jackson delayed a moment before meeting Gabriel's eyes. Resolve it, Jackson, thought Gabriel. Jackson averted his eyes and peeked at his watch.

"As I explained this morning, gentlemen, I need to take the break that we all agreed on. I need to return to the office to take a deposition in an unrelated case."

He collected his files and prepared to leave the room with Wrightly, who rose from his place and tugged at his crooked tie, adjusting it as he followed behind. Just before they exited, Jackson turned.

"We are set to continue in three weeks, correct?"

"Yes, that's right," affirmed Hamilton as he collected all the materials that he had spread on the table.

"See you all then," said Jackson, turning back to face the door with Wrightly before walking out. Hamilton waited for the other two to leave, shook his head as he stared at their backs. He grabbed his briefcase and wheeled it out the door. Gabriel scrutinized each one as they went out, wondering how much longer this ritual would play out.

Chapter 27: The Fighter

Miami, Florida: September 1981

Gabriel sat in his chair, shuffling papers and files from behind his desk. Rifling through labels and handwritten sticky notes, he did not raise his eyes from them as Susana walked in.

"Yes, Susana?"

"Mr. Mirabal is here to see you."

"Father or son?"

"Son," she answered.

"That's odd. Franco never comes to visit the office without calling me first. Is he in the waiting room?"

"Restroom, right now, but should be finished in a moment. Do you want me to have him wait or send him in?"

Gabriel peeked at his watch and calculated. Humming to himself for a moment, he processed his morning and afternoon schedule.

"I'll come and grab him when I'm finished up. I just completed the billing for a few of my cases and have at least an hour or so before I must make my next phone call, so I'll take care of it."

"Okay then," replied Susana, taking the handle of the door and beginning to close it.

"Susana, one more thing," began Gabriel, still staring at the files. "Good morning, and you look very nice today."

"I observed you the whole time, and your eyes were entirely on the documents. Not once did you raise them or your head to know what I was wearing."

"I saw you in my periphery, and that's all that it took."

"When did you learn to do that?"

"Grade school. Easiest way to pass notes without drawing too much attention from my teachers. I wasn't fond of being disciplined and it came in handy on the basketball court."

"I see. Well, thank you for the compliment. I will let Franco know that you will be with him in a moment."

As Susana turned and left, Gabriel surveyed his desk and began prioritizing his files. As he did so, he pulled his rolled sleeves back down, buttoned his top button, and tightened his tie.

"Franco, how are you?" he asked as he held the door open with one hand. Franco smiled and answered.

"Gabriel, I'm good. How are you?" replied the man.

"Good, thank you. God's been smiling on me recently."

"That's good to hear. I can't stay too long, but can we speak privately?"

"Yeah, just through here," explained Gabriel, allowing Franco entry from the open area to his office.

"Look, I want to make this quick and don't want to take too much of your time, but I need your help."

"What is it?" asked Gabriel after closing the door, "Do you want to sit?"

"I'd rather stand."

"So, this *is* serious."

"Very serious. My old man messed up."

"How bad?"

"Bad, *very* bad. Look, we've been struggling for a while. This recession has been tough on us like any other furniture store." Gabriel nodded, thinking of the clients that had asked to pay on an extended schedule. "We've had the store and have been getting imports from the Mediterranean since I was twelve, but our business model was always just selling retail to people who walked in through the door. When Carter took over the Presidency, we started looking to expand into other markets because people weren't coming through the door. Carter needed to get the economy moving for the election, so he just started printing money. That move ended up creating inflation on top of stagnation."

"Yeah, stagflation is killing everyone," agreed Gabriel.

"What matters is that my dad and I started branching out. When he entrusted outside sales to me, I began using my expertise as an interior decorator to look at furnishing hotel and resort properties."

"Well done. When did you start those?"

"We have a series of contracts signed." Franco tilted his head to the side and ran a hand through his ebony hair before tightening the hair tie in his ponytail.

"Are you ever going to cut that mane?"

"What, my hair? No way. It's like Samson's, the source of my strength." He lifted his left hand up to his hair and Gabriel could see the lighter scar that ran across the top of his olive skin hand.

"Just giving you a hard time, Franco."

"I know, my dad asks me that all the time, but my wife likes it. Anyway, these contracts are with a Venezuelan investment firm that wants us to furnish three of their hotels. The payout is big, and if we're successful, then they're going to give us a few of their other properties."

"Wow, Franco. Good job. That's an awesome contract. So, why are they updating in the middle of a recession?"

"Hotel standards. They are obligated to do that so the hotel will keep its rating."

"I understand."

"I had to work pretty hard to get those, and there was a lot of competition. The problem is that they're a foreign investor and given the problems with their currency and recent political history, the banks are skeptical about lending on those contracts. We only need money until we start getting paid for the work, but no bank is willing to work with us."

"Which banks have you gone to see?"

"Everyone in town, Gabriel. We've pretty much been surviving on savings and the occasional big sale, but we won't make the mortgage on the building beyond next month."

"How much do you need?" asked Gabriel, walking from the door over to his desk and taking a seat.

"Seventy grand," he admitted, staring Gabriel in the eye and raising his eyebrows.

"That bad, huh?"

"Yeah, that bad."

"So, how does this involve your dad?" Franco closed his eyes for a moment and rubbed his eyelids, squeezing around his nose and pulling up on the skin around his eyebrows before opening his eyes again and taking the seat in front of Gabriel.

"My dad is the best guy that I've ever known, but these have been desperate times, and he made a desperate decision. An old classmate of mine, Fulgencio, went to our store, not too long ago, to drop off some mangoes for my mom and dad from his parents. He got to talking with my dad about the store, and my dad, who is too trusting, told him about it. So, he offered my dad twenty-five hundred dollars to hold a stash of grass for a night."

"Are you serious?"

"Yeah, Gabriel, the guy's a low-level dealer."

"Please tell me that he didn't accept."

"He told him that his usual places were too hot to handle this load, and he was looking for a place that no one would suspect. So, my dad, in desperation, said okay. They dropped it off and picked it up the next day. Easy as one, two, three, and my dad got paid."

"And, of course, it didn't end there."

"No, that's not the way it works," the words came out as he shook his head, "A week later, he shows up and asks my dad if he can do it again, but this time, the payout was ten thousand for a lot more grass. My Dad accepted and, of course, again didn't tell me anything about it Since. Ángel was born, my wife works a lot less hours, I've been slammed, and my dad wanted me to focus just on the contracts, so I neglected the store's management. He should have said something to me, Gabriel, but he didn't want to add anything more to the feast on my plate. Now, we're closer to famine."

"Alright, so what else happened?"

"They did the same thing except that this time he was offered five thousand because there was more grass in this shipment, and someone broke into the store and stole all the grass. All seventy-five thousand dollars' worth."

Gabriel didn't know how to respond. Franco tried not to meet his gaze and instead just sighed.

"So, you need the money to pay that off?"

"When my dad told me about what happened, I got in my car, drove to Hialeah, knocked on Fulgencio's door, and knocked him out when he answered."

"I take it that you came to an agreement?"

"Yeah, those shitheads all operate the same. I know that he and his cronies stole the grass and broke into the store. That's what they do. They give you simple, good, and profitable deals, then steal the merchandise and make you pay for it. It's not like you can run to the cops and explain what happened."

"How much did it cost you?"

"Thirty-five thousand to buy him off, which I got by putting a second mortgage on the house."

"Marisel went for it?"

"Marisel supported me through and through, especially when I told her that I broke Fulgencio's nose."

"You broke his nose?" laughed Gabriel, shaking his head slightly.

"He wanted me to pay for the whole thing, and his friends came in to help him when I was on top of him beating his face in, but when I got away from them and beat the shit out of them, he dropped the price," he finished as his honey eyes lit up and his boxer's nose widened with his grin.

"How many did you fight?"

"Including him, three, but I don't really count him. He didn't do much but yelled a lot. He thought that he had me, but when I broke from their grip and let them have it, he became much more agreeable."

"He came down that easily?"

"I had to hold him over the burner of his stove until he dropped the price."

"Why didn't you erase it?"

"Because I wasn't paying for him. I was paying for his bosses. The money will force them to leave my father and me alone. Like I said, these are small-time operators. They talk a lot but don't kill anyone. I broke Fulgencio's nose to show them that it's not worth it, and so he won't suggest us as a mark for anything ever again. I paid their bosses' cut to avoid problems with those guys because they actually do kill people."

"I didn't expect that, Franco, but I wish that I could have seen this guy's face."

"I didn't have a choice, Gabriel. I went to negotiate peacefully, but he was an asshole and threatened me when I told him that I couldn't pay the whole thing. The next thing you know, I was putting my blackbelt and my wrestling moves to use."

"Peacefully Franco? Before you said a single word, you punched the guy out. I remember seeing you compete for the championship when I was only twelve or so. Your dad came into the office and brought my dad newspaper clippings about how you had made it to the finals. Any punch from you cannot be defined as an opening to peace talks."

"I was eighteen and very different than I am now."

"Yeah, who would have thought that the ferocious Franco Mirabal would go from a fighter to an interior decorator?" said Gabriel with a wide grin.

"People change. What more can I tell you? But you know I still own the boxing gym. Rigo runs the day-to-day training, but I still make it there every day."

"Look, I'm glad that you took care of the drug issue, but the serious question is this: How will we get you the money?

"I have no idea, but I don't make much from the gym, so I need to keep the store open. I am afraid to lose the business and our building."

"I need to talk to my dad first and figure out a plan. Can you and your dad come and meet me here next week? Let's say Tuesday."

"Yeah, what time?"

"I've got meetings after twelve," Gabriel said, moving to his desk and glancing at his appointment book. "So…can you be here by ten?"

"What do you need from us?"

"Financials, liens, existing notes and mortgages on the building, liabilities of the business, inventory, and assets for the business and of course last three years of tax returns. We will need everything, Franco. Anything and everything that might help us convince the possible lender that the loan is worth it. Getting a loan for a business that is bleeding money won't be easy, but we'll give it a shot."

"My dad and I can get you all that by next week. It won't be easy, but I promise. Thank you, Gabriel. I'm sorry to rope you into this."

"I'm just sorry that you roped me into this too late. I will forever regret not seeing you in action fighting those scumbags."

Franco roared with laughter.

"You know, if you ever want to go a few rounds, our gym in Little Havana is still open for fight night every last Friday of the month."

"Maybe I'll take you up on that. If I do, it'll be a few months. Anyway, I'll see you tomorrow, Franco."

Franco nodded and walked out the door. Gabriel waited a moment, processing everything that Franco had told him, and envisioned what Yasser's nose must have looked like after Franco punched it. Gabriel snapped back to reality and walked from his desk over to the door. Opening it and listening for noise from his father's office, he heard none and made his way there. He knocked.

"Come in," said Thomas.

"Hey, Dad, I need your help with something for Alfonso and Franco Mirabal."

"Can it wait?"

"No. You're going to want to hear this."

Chapter 28: The Economics of Justice

Miami, Florida: September 1981

The morning that had not turned out well for him. Gabriel had lost a motion aimed at delaying discovery in the Sørloth case and would have to produce a series of documents within ten days. Judge Stone had seen right through his ploy and had not been very kind. He was hoping this meeting would change his day.

He saw Joaquín and Rosa coming toward him, and he smiled. Joaquín smiled right back, showing his thick black mustache and white teeth. Rosa had hooked his arm with hers in what seemed a romantic gesture, but Gabriel realized she was making sure he did not trip and fall on the cracked and uneven sidewalk. In his condition, with his arm still in a sling, he would have been defenseless against the cement sidewalk.

They turned toward the building and walked up the walkway. At some point, this building was a beautiful office building with a small office on each floor. Two signs hung next to the door, which was now a strong solid wood protector of the documents inside. Damián Juárez, with an arrow pointing down, and Saul Wilensky, with an arrow pointing up. He opened the door for them, and he followed them inside before leading them to the staircase moving down. They stepped attentively as they descended before arriving at the door to the Juárez office. Gabriel saw a figure rise from a table in a room to the left that appeared to be a conference room.

Gabriel waved and an elegant man strode across the gray carpet to open.

"Gabriel," said the salt-and-pepper-haired man, "good to see you again."

"How are you, Damián?"

"Doing well, thanks. Please come in. I am Damián Juárez. Welcome," said the scholarly looking man as he greeted Gabriel's clients. His mixed Native American and Spanish features shone as he smiled. Gabriel turned and introduced his clients.

"Damián, these are Joaquín and Rosa Pérez."

"It's a pleasure to meet you both," said Damián, signaling for them to enter the conference room. Gabriel looked around the room, seeing a long maple conference table along with several well-cushioned chairs with armrests. After a moment, everyone found a seat.

"It's been too long, Gabriel. How is your dad?"

"He sends his regards and said the same." Damián laughed. His long straight jet-black hair touched his shoulders as his head went back.

"You know your dad sent me a couple of important cases that were fundamental in getting my office started."

"I did not know."

"Well, I am sorry to drag you here on a such short notice, but I am in a four-week trial and would be unable to see you until next month." Turning to Gabriel, he said, "In your note, you stated that you would like my opinion a soon as possible, so I thought we best meet today."

"Thanks for that."

"I have reviewed your file. As you guys may be aware, last year, the police transposed a house number to an address and ended up invading the wrong home. Thinking these people were drug dealers and violent criminals, they held guns to their heads and beat them when they resisted. It cost the county more than two and a half million dollars."

"I remember that," said Joaquín.

"And that is the problem. There is a limitation on the liability of the county when they are acting in their official capacity of $150,000.00 dollars. In that case, they had no choice but to waive that limit, but since then, they instituted new policies to waiver. I'm afraid that even if you are found not guilty as to the assault charge or the State decides to drop it, there is no feasible lawsuit unless they waive the limitation. Because, even if we recover the complete $150,000.00 when you subtract the expert fees, the costs of the litigation, and my fees, you would have maybe ten thousand dollars left for you if we are completely successful in court. If we fail, you will not owe me anything for my fees, but you would owe the experts, and the court reporter, and the copy place, and so on."

"What you are saying is that even if we win outright and get him off on the charge, the county will not waive the limit, and it makes the lawsuit worthless," said Gabriel.

"And I get nothing in return for the injustice that I have received," commented Joaquín, raising his good arm in disbelief.

Both men remained silent and chose to nod their heads. Joaquín abruptly stood up and nodded his head toward Damián.

"Thank you for your time. I appreciate your effort very much. Rosa, let's go."

He spun around and disappeared through the door of the conference room. Rosa stood up, but before she could reach the entrance hall, they all heard the door close sharply. Gabriel turned to Damián and began to apologize, but Damián waved him off. Gabriel began to chase Joaquín down, but Rosa grabbed his forearm to stop Gabriel from rushing after Joaquín. "We can talk to him, but he needs to calm down a little first." A little smile emerged on her face. "He has a wonderful heart, loving and compassionate, but it contains an intense sense of justice which overpowers his mind at moments like this. We need his passion to recede before we speak with him."

Gabriel calmed down, "Okay." Turning he continued "Damián, I know the amount of time you put into this analysis, and I am grateful for your professionalism and expertise. Apologies for my client." Damián nodded.

"No need to apologize, it happens often." He grinned.

Gabriel looked over to Rosa, "Let's start making our way downstairs, this man has to prepare for trial." She moved toward the door, and he followed her out, heading out back out to the staircase and ascending back toward the street in search of the angered Joaquín.

They walked towards the street slowly finding Joaquín leaning against his automobile, kicking at a rock. The two-floor converted duplex was lost in the background behind them as passing traffic hummed and strolled by around them. Joaquín scowled and muttered something to himself that neither Rosa nor Gabriel could hear. As he and Rosa drew near, Joaquín noticed them and straightened up, trying to look less angry.

"Joaquín?" asked Gabriel before Rosa could scorn him. Joaquín paused for a moment and then unleashed.

"I thought that I would be able to get at least some money to hold me over until I was able to go to school and prepare for life after this case. Now, with my condition, I don't know if I will even have time to find a job before the little money I have left runs out. Rosa brings in a little, and the kids have gotten part-time work. Even my father-in-law, at his age, is packing groceries, but it's not enough to cover our expenses." Gabriel did not interrupt. "You know Gabriel, this is not justice, this is so wrong in so many ways... An innocent man gets injured by the police, and there is no, how do you say?

"Redress?" Offered Gabriel, meeting Joaquín's gaze.

"Yes, that's it." They stopped short of their automobiles, where Joaquín paused for a moment. "But there is nothing for me from the government because my case does not look as bad as someone else's. I am not saying that theirs was not bad. It was, but they were not physically injured and prevented from doing their job because of that injury.

It was a question of politics. There was an election coming, and the mayor needed the votes, so they got money. With me, there is no election, and no one needs my vote or my neighbor's votes right now, so no money. That is not justice of any kind." Gabriel remained silent. There was nothing that he could say to make it better at this moment. He just had to let Joaquín speak. "I am worried that I won't get a fair trial no matter what you do. That all the jurors will look at what the case seems like and not what it is. I am afraid that they will decide on innuendo and untruthful testimony and not the trust simply because someone must be found at fault."

"But you are not letting me give them an alternative," explained Gabriel. Joaquín squinted his eyes in defiance.

"Why does an innocent man have to point at someone else to prove his innocence?"

"You just said it yourself because a jury may declare you guilty not on what the case is but on what it seems to be." Joaquín was silent for a minute. Gabriel saw Rosa reach their car and begin to open it. He turned to Joaquín. "Let me do the right thing and go to the prosecutor and tell him the truth."

"You know that I can't let you do that. I promised Aunt Cárola, who loved me as her own when I had lost everything, that I would look out for Ciro. If not for her, I would have been homeless and ended up who knows where."

"She would not have wanted you to go to jail for her promise."

"No, but that's my choice." Gabriel reached for the car door. He opened it and, moving aside so Joaquín could get in, he waved at Rosa and mouthed *Adios*. He closed the door, and they drove off. He shook his head contemplating while Joaquín and Rosa continued down the road. Still shaking his head, Gabriel wondered if Joaquín's promise meant more to him than his family as he rounded the corner to find his vehicle. *In a way I understand him. I walked away from the prosecutor's office because the boss ordered me to break my promise. That was easy. Now Joaquín is deciding between keeping a promise that could cost him fifteen years in jail and telling the truth and walking away free. Still, after our meeting today, the best ending for this nightmare that he can hope for is having a permanent debilitating injury, a false arrest with no recourse, no job, no money, and an unknown future.* His eyes broke away from the disappearing car and he began dragging his feet toward his own automobile. When he extended his hand to open the door, Gabriel winced. He turned his hand palm up and saw the marks on where his fingernails had dug into his skin.

Chapter 29: The Fathers and the Sons

Miami, Florida: September 1981

Gabriel and Thomas sat across from Alfonso and Franco in the large conference room. Documents and notes littered the tabletop, and Thomas found himself using a magnifying glass to examine some of the financials.

"Listen, Alfonso," began Thomas in Spanish, "your situation isn't an easy one to resolve. Any money is a lot of money to lend a company in the red, and the deal that Franco had to make on your behalf took all your reserves. You've drained your savings by staying open without any real income for three years. No bank is going to approve any loan on your business now. You've got enough resources to last you this next month, but that's about it. Your contract begins in six months, but realistically, you probably won't get paid until seven, eight, or even nine months from now. I don't doubt that the hotel group will honor their word, but with the way that things have been going, these are very uncertain economic times for all of us."

"What about the building?" asked the man that looked like an older version of Franco but with a lot less hair.

"What about it?" inquired Thomas.

"Can we try to use the equity in the building to make a deal happen?"

"No matter what kind of equity you have in the building, the regulations won't let a bank lend on the building without the borrower having any income to pay the loan. Additionally, by regulations, the bank would have to pay off the current loan and take the first position increasing your total loan to well over the seventy thousand you need. Still, if you received enough in rent, that might happen, but it's doubtful. Let me see the appraisal on the building." Thomas looked at the property's valuation intensely, and as he turned the last pages, he asked, "Do you use the second floor?"

"Not really. We use the second floor to house some extra furniture, but that's it. Most of the second floor is empty."

"Have you thought about renting the space?"

"We need to build it out and then fix a couple of things in the building, and we can't afford to do any of that. We also don't want just anybody up there, and there's no one that we trust." Said the older man his arm resting on the table.

"I see," began Thomas.

"What are you thinking?" asked Franco in Spanish.

"I'd need to make a few phone calls, but I want to run through everything first. What about the truck? Do you need it? Can you sell it?"

"We do need it, and we can't sell it, especially with these hotel jobs."

"I take it that there are no jobs that need your services immediately?"

"Not any bids that we've won. We were finalists for three jobs but lost them all to larger stores."

"Not too many options," admitted Alfonso.

"No, not at all," sighed Thomas. "Still, if you are flexible, there are things we can use."

"What were you going to say before?" asked Franco.

"I just spoke with a client who wants to put his administrative offices for his business in a better place, and he's been looking for buildings around your location."

"We can't fix the building, so why would he be interested?" interrogated Alfonso. Franco put his hand on his father's arm and calmed him down.

"I don't know. Do you want me to call him or not?"

"Call him," answered Franco, squeezing his father's arm to silence him, "I don't know if it'll work, but it's worth a try."

"That's what I was thinking. May I keep these documents to make copies of the appraisal, the photos, and the plans?"

"Of course," affirmed Franco.

"Alright then, let me make some calls, and I'll get back to you by Thursday."

Chapter 30: The Deal

Miami, Florida: September 1981

Three days later, Alfonso and Franco were sitting in the conference room when Gabriel came into the secretarial area from the waiting room. He stuck his head into the room.

"I didn't expect to see you both here so soon."

"We decided to come a little early. Traffic is rough this time of day," laughed Franco and signaled towards one of the chairs around the table.

"Let me put down my files and take off my jacket, and I'll be back in a second," he pulled his head back into the hall, "Susana, is my father here?"

"Yes, he is on a phone call on a separate matter, but he will be with all of you as soon as he's finished."

"Thanks, Susana. Franco, Alfonso, would you like anything to drink while you wait?"

"No, we're fine. Thank you," answered Franco. Alfonso looked at the painting on the wall; his nerves wracked him. His heart and head pounded as the guilt of his deal weighed on him.

"I'm nervous about this meeting. He will probably ask for seventeen percent on any hard money loan that he offers, and we can't afford that. If we lose our business, then we lose our building. I got us both into this mess and then made it worse," he said. Franco responded to his father as they conversed in their native language.

"Or we will have to liquidate the business, lose all the contracts I worked so hard to obtain, and then we will have to sell our building at a reduced price, and then Angel won't have the life that I always wanted to give your grandson, and it'll be all your fault. Come on, dad. There's always an honest way out," commented Franco rubbing his thumbs on his temples and smiling at his father. He put his arm around his father and pulled him close. "No matter what, we do this together."

"You're right. We have done nothing but work hard, and we'll get through this together."

Franco smiled at his father's words and squeezed him close. As they ended their embrace, the door to the conference room opened.

"Hello," said Thomas in Spanish, walking towards them. He held out his hand and smiled. He sat down in the chair at the far end of the table.

"I want you to know that Santiago is very positive about doing business. I spoke to him this morning, and he gave me permission to tell you that."

"That's good to hear," responded Franco.

"We were just discussing the fact that if he gives us current rates for a hard money loan, it will be difficult for us to pay him back," added Alfonso.

"Don't be so quick to close the book. You never know how much the story can change in just a few pages." Alfonso smiled.

"I guess I already tried the easy way out, and it turned out to be a disaster. Maybe the hard way out is better in the end," admitted Alfonso.

Franco turned to him and placed his hand on his father's.

"All we need is a way for our business to stay alive and succeed by working hard. We know how to do that, so whatever the conditions are, we will study them, and if they are at all doable, we will move forward."

At that moment, Gabriel came in and sat across from Franco. Three seats remained open at the table, including the head of the table on the near side. As Gabriel took his seat, Susana stuck her head in the door.

"Mr. Santiago Alemán has arrived. Should I let him in?"

"Yes, please do, Susana."

"Bring some Cafecito?" Thomas grinned.

"I think everyone here would welcome some. Thank you again."

A few seconds later, she escorted a short man with malt colored hair into the conference room. Everyone stood and shook hands as Gabriel made the introductions.

"Susana will be in with the coffee in a minute, but maybe we should get started." Moving his arms, he signaled everyone to sit down. Santiago sat at the opposite end of the table, face to face with Thomas. Thomas turned, reached behind his back, and grabbed a file from the shelf. "As you know, everyone here is a client of this firm. Because of that, I have prepared these letters for all of you to sign before we get started. These are waivers of conflict. Because your individual interests may be in conflict during this negotiation, you are absolving us from any liability and responsibility from the outcome of this discussion and recognizing that we do not represent any of you in this negotiation."

He gave each one a set of papers. As the men read the document, Susana entered, holding a silver tray with five cups of coffee and their saucers. Thomas rose, took the tray from her, and placed it on the table, away from the papers. After each man signed, they handed the document to Thomas, who, in exchange for the paper, gave them the Cafecito.

"Did everyone understand what they read?"

"Yes," everyone murmured.

"Do all of you understand that Gabriel and I will not take sides or negotiate for any of you? We are here simply to facilitate a deal between you." The men shook their heads. "You are on your own and without our protection. We will make no assessment of the deal you make, understood?" Nods all around. "Okay, then let's get started."

Santiago looked over to Thomas. He took a sip of his cup and opened his mouth to speak, his eyes focused on Thomas and Gabriel.

"I understand the delicate position you and Gabriel are in, so let me take you out of that position. I am not going to lend these gentlemen any money." There was absolute silence in the room for a handful of seconds until Santiago continued, "but hopefully, we will do business."

Alfonso dropped his pessimism.

"What do you have in mind?" he asked, looking straight at Santiago.

Santiago reached under the table and lifted his briefcase. He opened the case and removed a series of files, laying them out before returning the briefcase to the floor. He spread them in what appeared to be a logical order known only to him.

He looked back at Alfonso.

"Through the years, I have passed in front of your building often, and I have relatives that live in the surrounding neighborhoods. On occasion, I have even accompanied my wife to purchase furniture at your store, and I believe she has some type of credit card that is related to a group of stores or associations to which your business belongs." Alfonso nodded his head in acknowledgement.

"I have always thought that the building has a superior location, and it is one that I would be interested in." Gabriel saw movement in the periphery of his eyes and immediately understood that Franco had probably just stopped his father from informing Santiago prematurely that the building was not for sale.

"In the last few years, I have noticed that the building has deteriorated and requires repair."

He turned to Thomas for a moment.

"I had one of my people go by the store and through the merchandise. The customer service is first class; the physical store does not match its merchandise and service."

Turning back to Alfonso, he continued.

"While I understand that this recession is not the time to spend money in updating and upkeep, the store isn't in any condition to compete when the recession is over. I think you would be well served to have funds to update the store unless you are planning to follow a different approach to your business, concentrating exclusively on hotels and commercial buildings, in which case, you would be better served selling this building and buying one in the warehouse district. That would be the less costly option for the store if you were to follow that alternative." Before Alfonso could utter a sound, Franco interjected.

"No plans to do that. We have added our lines for hotels and commercial buildings to take advantage of my interior design knowledge. The idea is to widen the client base and not to make a choice between one group or another."

"I am glad to hear that. It's not my plan to buy the whole building."

"What is your plan then, Santiago?" asked Alfonso the crow's feet around his eyes becoming more visible.

At the other end of the table, Santiago's malt eyes sparkled as he smiled.

"I don't understand why people that want to do business together have to place unnecessary obstacles in the way of an understanding. As all of you sit here, none of you has the complete answer. Perhaps, if you let ideas flow between you, without posturing, one of them, perhaps the least likely one, will be the solution for all of you," said Thomas in a very even but firm voice and looking around the table at the faces of his clients. "Both you, Alfonso, and you, Santiago, are preparing for the end of this recession. We may be a few months away, or we may be a couple of years away. The question is, are you better off preparing together or apart? Each one of you has assets that the other one needs or, at least, would like to take advantage of, so quit posturing and take this time to find common ground. Let's start over," said Thomas.

For the second time, he turned in his chair and brought down a yellow legal pad. Reaching into the inside pocket of his suit jacket, he took out a silver Parker pen. "What are your needs, Santiago?" Thomas caught him off guard by the directness of the question and did not respond. "Okay, what are your needs, Alfonso?" Alfonso looked back at Thomas with what could only be characterized as a dirty look.

"Fine, no need to answer now. I can wait until you are both ready to do a deal."

"Santiago has money and access to financing in banks. He knows we don't have the same resources," blurted Franco.

Alfonso looked at his son with a stern look.

"It's not a secret, Dad, we were looking for a loan, so it is obvious that we need money. On the other hand, he is not willing to give us a loan, so why is he here?"

"Because your building interests me," affirmed Santiago.

"Yes, but I won't sell it," countered Alfonso immediately.

"I want you to sell me the upper half of the building, which you aren't using. If that is legally possible."

Thomas looked at Alfonso, whose face grimaced. He composed himself and took another sip of his coffee.

"I'll listen to the option, although I am not inclined to sell any of the building."

"I need a good deal of office space for my administrative people that manage my present gas stations." Santiago leaned on the table, supporting his posture with his elbows, and giving Alfonso and Franco a stern gaze. "And I will need additional space for the people who will assist me in a series of investments that I plan to make, but I don't want to be paying rent to someone else."

"Without considering the purchase price, the payoff or assumption of the existing mortgage, the simplest way that we can accomplish this is for Santiago to buy half the shares of stock of the company that owns the building and each of you gets a lease for one dollar from the company for the part you occupy. In terms of taxes, insurance, and repairs, you simply split it in half since each of you will be occupying a different floor, and you split use of the parking spaces in half," clarified Thomas.

"What about the existing mortgage. Does that have to be paid off?" queried Franco.

"No, but according to the terms of the loan, as a new shareholder, Santiago would have to be approved by the bank, and he would have to be added as a guarantor for the loan."

"I have no problem with that," confirmed Santiago.

"Why should I let you buy half my building?" asked Alfonso opening his hands before him, palms exposed.

"Because it's a good deal for both of us, given the circumstances."

"I don't see it. I have been paying that building for over twenty years, and now you are going to come along and buy that building at a moment when the prices are low and take advantage of me and my work."

Santiago remained quiet. Gabriel saw his eyes become fierce for an instant as Santiago received the slight. He held the fire in them for a moment before letting it slide and responding in a soft voice.

"It's important that you understand that I am not here to rip you off but to do a deal that helps me and solves your problems at the same time. I didn't come to this meeting unprepared. I have had my realtor check the possible price of the building on the market right now. The interest rate you would have to pay on a hard money loan, which is the only type you are eligible for, is high and unreasonable for your margins. The rent that I would have to pay on a similarly located building is high, but I want to be in this part of town. Finally, I have an estimate of what it would take to update the building." He reached into the pile of papers before him and took out a four-page booklet stapled together in the upper right-hand corner. Counting out four copies, he slid them to Gabriel, who immediately passed them around. Thomas put down the papers.

"Is there any room in these figures?"

"Not much room," responded Santiago, "You asked me to come to the table with my best offer, Thomas, and I honored that request. This is also why I discarded the loan. Regular real estate loans are running between thirteen and a quarter percent and as high as seventeen percent. Hard money loans are running from eighteen percent to twenty percent for corporations. I could not offer this to Alfonso because that would be equal to taking his property. He would not be able to pay, so I am here to do business in good faith. Here is my proposal." Santiago lifted his hands off the table, placing his weight on his elbows, and held his left hand inside his right palm, "According to the appraisal of the building Alfonso supplied, it is worth three hundred and seventy-five thousand dollars. My people verified that value and said that at this point, it is worth five thousand dollars more, so again, as a sign of good faith, I will accept the three hundred and eighty thousand as its valuation." Santiago glanced at Thomas, who nodded his head in turn.

"The amount of the loan on the building is sixty thousand dollars, so I will pay Alfonso one hundred and sixty thousand dollars or one half of the purchase price, less the loan amount since we shall both pay that.

"As soon as the recession is over, the building will be worth fifty or sixty thousand more, but you aren't paying me that. The value and equity will rise, and so you will not have to worry about the difference. The deal is for how the building is and not what it will be."

Alfonso stared at Santiago intently. Franco looked weightless and relieved, but Alfonso remained skeptical.

"Why do this and give us a hand, Santiago? You know that we are cash-strapped and have no options. Why would you give us a deal like this?"

Santiago smiled and reached under the table. He retrieved his wallet from his pocket and held it in both hands but didn't open it.

"I look at you, Alfonso, and I see a hardworking and proud man. I see your son by your side, and I know that it's the two of you together against the world." Santiago opened his wallet and pulled a small black and white photograph from within. He handed it to Alfonso, who took it with an outstretched palm. "My father was my business partner when we opened the gas stations. We had a few bad years when no one would come to our neighborhood to fill up. Then one day, a man came along and got to know my father. They talked a lot about family and its importance. The man told my father that he had lost his son to a bad business deal, and they never reconciled, so when he saw how desperate my father and I were, he gave us a reasonable and fair loan. When my father died, he let me buy out the gas station from him, and I went on to own the twenty that I have now. I am just passing it forward. Doing for you what someone did for me, and the venture looks good."

Alfonso rose from the table and did not say a word. Silence filled the conference room for a moment before Alfonso put his hand forward.

"Mr. Alemán, my son, and I would be honored to make this deal with you."

Santiago rose from his chair, and they both shook hands.

"The honor is mine, Alfonso." Franco stood and outstretched his hand as well, and Santiago took it. Lowering his eyes, Alfonso looked over to Thomas. "How swiftly can you draft the documents?"

"I can do so by Monday morning," said Thomas, noting the time.

"Good, I'm hungry. If anyone else is hungry, I think that this deal calls for a celebration. My treat."

"I'll have a preliminary Letter of Intent completed by the time you all come back."

"You're coming with us," said Santiago. Thomas raised his eyebrows above his glasses. "Yes, you called me for this deal, and now three of your clients are happy. You're the hero here. Let him draft the papers; he's the junior partner." Santiago pointed to Gabriel. Gabriel did not know how to respond. "I'm just kidding, Gabriel. Come on, if it's only one hour, then it's not a big chunk of time. It's Friday, and even after lunch, we'll still be out of here by three."

The five of them collected their things and began to make their way out. As they did so, Thomas hung back and wrapped his arm around his son.

"It's deals like this that make me grateful to work with you every single day," said Gabriel.

Thomas lowered his head and chuckled as they made their way through the office door and into the parking lot.

Chapter 31: The Benefactor

Miami, Florida: October 1981

Walter paced behind his desk as the blinds swayed back and forth from the large windows of his office. The air conditioning blasted the cool air, and Gabriel heard the humming of circulating wind in the ceiling above him. As Walter paced, he weighed the consequences of the information that Gabriel relayed.

"So, is this what Hamilton has alleged?" asked Walter, holding up the manilla folder Gabriel had given him while taking heavier steps.

"Yes, the house has to be renovated so that it's livable for her."

"They need to add a bathroom, blow out the back wall, build a ramp suitable for her, redo some of the plumbing in the house, and take the blown-out wall and create a bedroom from the demolition?"

"That sums it up," said Gabriel, focused on Walter, who began to pace again. Walter raised his eyebrows and furrowed them as he paced. His eyes opened and squinted as he considered the timeline of the construction, its cost, and then his own balance sheets."

"You're sure that your plan is going to work with Hamilton, Jackson, and Wrightly."

"Yes, Walter. If my numbers are right and be assured that I've calculated everything. The meetings have gone as I estimated, and I know the hand that Hamilton is playing."

"You've played it before?"

"I have."

"How did that case turn out?"

"We won."

"And you assume that this will be the same?"

"I do. Hamilton needs it to work out as we expect, and I know that Wrightly will be the key in this. He's going to work the numbers, and if he agrees to them, Jackson will fold. If Jackson resists, then I have what I need to control him." Walter chuckled to himself.

"This is the first time in my life that I've ever wanted to pay more out of a settlement." A slight grin appeared at the corners of Gabriel's mouth.

"Well, Walter, you'd rather pay out more than go out of business, but you and I both know that you believe that this girl deserves something for the life of pain that she will have to endure."

"You're right," said Walter, stepping back from his pacing and turning to Gabriel, "the bodies still weigh on me, Gabriel. I see their scarred and blackened flesh in my dreams and even when I wake. Nothing will ever rid me of them, but I don't want Katerina to be there too."

"So that's why you want to cover the costs of the family's remodeling?"

"No," he said, finally, "I want to cover this because it is the right thing to do. Her life will never be the same, Gabriel, and if it were my daughter," he said, gesturing toward the picture of his kids, "I would hope for the same. Hope, Gabriel, it's the most powerful thing that a person can have. Sometimes it's even stronger than faith." Walter exhaled and paused for a moment. He pulled his chair from behind the desk and sat in it. As he raised his eyes, he invited Gabriel to sit in one of the chairs in front of the desk.

"I've asked God many times for guidance on what to do with this situation and have asked Him to take away all the visions and nightmares that I get from the first accident."

"Have they lessened?"

Walter shook his head.

"No, they haven't, and that worries me." I've confessed my sins, I've prayed, I've donated, I've tried everything that my faith tells me I need to do, but to no avail."

Gabriel measured Walter's words.

"Maybe that guilt is what weighs so heavily on you, and maybe that´s why this case does too."

"The worst part is that I feel guilty, and I wasn't the one who caused these accidents, Gabriel. The black car ruined this girl's life, not my truck, but because it rebounded off my truck, the company is guilty and gets hit hard with all this. I don't think that I'll ever be able to really get rid of this guilt, but maybe I can make this a little easier on them." He paused, and neither of them uttered a sound. Walter analyzed his words for a moment and spoke again. "Find out who is doing the work, the final cost, and give me an estimate of what her treatment is going to run the family. When you do and when you're finished with the insurance company, let me know, and we'll discuss the final number."

"Sure thing, Walter."

"Thank you, Gabriel. I appreciate the work that you're doing."

"It's my pleasure, Walter. You and your father have been very loyal to us, and my father and I appreciate it." Walter nodded, and Gabriel gathered his things, bid farewell, and left to return to the office.

Chapter 32: The Odds of Innocence

Miami, Florida: October 1981

Gabriel closed the umbrella, placed it against the wall, and wiped the rainwater from his suit coat. From under the overhang, he watched the afternoon sky darken. He turned and stepped inside the building. The elevator doors slid wide, and he entered, pressing the button that would take him to Rodrigo's office. When the elevator came to a halt, he walked to the end of the hallway, reacquainting himself with the receptionist he had seen many times before.

"Good afternoon, Mr. Lock. We've been expecting you. Would you please follow me?"

Gabriel followed her through the entranceway over to the conference room. She opened the door as he walked in. Rosa, Joaquín, and Rodrigo waited for him along the edges of the large conference table. Gabriel raised his hand to greet them all and noticed the neatly arranged file folders covering the expansive table.

"You're late," said Rodrigo, almost jokingly.

"I'm also wet."

They all laughed for a moment, easing a little of the tension in the room.

"I was just explaining today's mission to Rosa and Joaquín, telling them that we are going to explain the trial proceedings and then we will examine every piece of evidence, every possible witness, and go through the key points of the depositions. Gabriel, why don't you take us through the steps of the trial?"

"Okay," said Gabriel, choosing the seat next to Rosa on the near side of the table. He pulled his briefcase and opened it, taking out his legal pad.

"As you know, we are set for a jury trial next Monday. The trial should last no longer than two days, three at max." Rosa shifted in her chair and focused on him.

"May I ask questions now, or should I wait until the end?"

"No, feel free to ask questions whenever you have them."

"Okay, why are we going to trial with a jury and not just a judge?"

"Joaquín is presumed innocent. What that means is that he starts the trial as a man who is not guilty of what he has been accused. If we have a jury, then the judge decides the law, and the jury decides the facts. The prosecutor must convince the trier of facts that Joaquín is guilty beyond a reasonable doubt. If we go with a judge, he only has to convince one person but with a jury he has to convince six people."

Joaquín ruffled his shirt as he shifted in his chair. Rosa bore a curious expression, tensing the gentle wrinkles on her forehead. "Not twelve."

"In Florida the only time a jury of twelve is required is in a murder case."

"I thought it was twelve for every crime."

"Most people do." There was a moment of silence and Gabriel continued, "Once both sides and the judge are in the courtroom, the bailiff will go and retrieve the jury pool. "Once we select the jury," continued Gabriel, "the prosecutor will tell them how he sees the case and the evidence. Next, Rodrigo will tell the jury how the defense sees the case and how we evaluate the evidence. Then, there will be a recess, and afterward, the prosecution will present its evidence. That includes the bat, the photographs of the victim, the paper on which the witness wrote the tag number, and finally, the court will hear the testimony of all the witnesses that will be called by the prosecution."

"Do you think they will call my daughter to testify against me?" asked Joaquín. A pause lingered for a moment.

"I don't think that they will because she is too unpredictable as a witness. Her testimony may endear both you and her to the jury. Donovan wouldn't risk that," explained Rodrigo.

"We have these things in our favor: the bat did not have your fingerprints, and the pictures show the damage done to the victim, but do not tie you to the attack."

"What about the tag number?"

"It's against us, but the witness did not get a good look at the driver. What the tag number does without the identification of the driver is to ask the jury to assume that Joaquín was the driver. That jump is something we can attack." answered Rodrigo.

"What happens then?" continued Rosa. Gabriel carried on.

"We have an option to request dismissal on the grounds of them not proving their case. That is usually denied, but we request it to prevent denying ourselves the opportunity to appeal."

"And then we put on our case," urged Rosa with renewed vigor.

"Yes," claimed Rodrigo, "you are our defense."

"Me?"

"You are our only witness." Rosa paused for a moment, absorbing the gravity of Rodrigo's statement. Her fingers began to tremble as her upper lip quivered.

"But there were so many people at the picnic, they saw me leave with Joaquín. There should be plenty of other witnesses. How am I the only one?"

"Because you were the only one that was with him at the time the incident happened. All those people cannot testify because they weren't with him."

"Then why did you talk to everyone?"

"I had to know what they knew."

"Did you talk to Ciro?" Interrupted Joaquín.

"He told me he was at the picnic the whole afternoon."

"And that's all he said?!" exclaimed Rosa.

"Rosa," said Joaquín, softly commanding his wife to remain calm.

"What are our chances?" asked Rosa.

Rodrigo paused, trying to diffuse the situation.

"When we took the victim's deposition, he was unable to recognize Joaquín from a photo lineup. And the witness who saw the victim's attack and your car leaving the parking lot admitted that he was unable to see the driver well, but that it looked like the person who had attacked the victim."

"You see, Rosa?! Neither witness can say that it was me. I will be a free man!"

"I fully expect one of them to identify you as the attacker," said Gabriel in a hushed tone. Rosa rose from the table so fast that the chair shot out from behind her.

"You see, Joaquín, you're gambling with your life and our family to protect Ciro, who has always been trouble!!!"

"Rosa!" bellowed Joaquín, also rising from his chair. "You will sit down, and you will not take that tone with me. My word is final; I will not break my promise. Gabriel will make sure that I am declared an innocent man!"

Rosa panted as she glared at Joaquín. He refused to back down, and after a few moments, she lowered herself into her seat and cried. Watching her shoulders shake, Joaquín settled into his chair. Rodrigo looked from Rosa to Joaquín and back.

"I think that you both understand what is involved as well as our chances of success. Joaquín, I'm going to ask you one last time to let me use the truth. Your cousin is the best key to your freedom. You see..."

Joaquín interrupted Rodrigo before he could finish.

"We will never mention Ciro in that courtroom. Thank you, Gabriel, and Rodrigo, for your time. Rosa, grab your things. It's time to go."

Rodrigo and Gabriel watched them leave. They walked through the front door of the office and disappeared into the reception area on the other side. Rodrigo waited a few seconds to make sure that they were out of earshot before speaking.

"You know, the only good thing about this meeting is if I lose, it's your fault."

Chapter 33: The Promise

Miami, Florida, May 1975:

Joaquín walked through the double doors at Mercy Hospital. He crossed the dark shiny floor with rapid straight strides. This was the same way he had come to see her every day for the last few weeks, but tonight his steps were urgent. The call from Ciro had left no doubt in his mind that it might be a matter of hours before it happened. He pressed the lit button and waited.

When the doors slid open, he jumped in. The doors closed, and Joaquín cursed as the elevator delayed its climb. Joaquín was through the metal exit almost before the machine came to a stop. He ran down the hall until a nurse yelled at him. "What is going on?" he asked Ciro, who stood in the hall.

"She's having trouble breathing, and they may have to put her on a ventilator in an hour or two. She is talking to Dad now, then she wants to talk to me and then you."

"Alright." They stood together outside the door, in silence, not knowing what to say or even what to think. They had all dreaded this day. Three months ago, they notified her that the cancer had metastasized and was all over her body. Lately, her lungs have been taking the brunt of the malignancy.

The door behind him opened, and Uncle Osvaldo appeared. Pointing at Ciro, he said, "She would like to speak with you first." Ciro went in, the door closed, and then Uncle Osvaldo looked at him. "You know you were the second son she always wanted but could not have. Ciro's birth was so difficult that we couldn't have more kids. We thought that in the United States, medicine would be more advanced, and they would be able to help us conceive, but it wasn't to be. Still, fate gave us a second son when you left Cuba. She always believed that God helped you swim across Guantanamo Bay just so you could reach her, and you did. She's always been so grateful to Him that He protected you in that crossing and so proud of you for doing it at such a young age." Osvaldo finished with a slight tear in his eye. Joaquín put an arm on Osvaldo's shoulder and hugged his uncle.

They stood in silence again, and a few minutes later, Ciro opened the door and whispered, "Hurry Joaquín, she is losing her strength fast." Joaquín grabbed the door handle and delicately opened the door. Closing it just as gently, he crossed the room and stood beside her bed. She reached for his hand.

"There you are my son. I was wondering if you would get here in time from your trip to Texas." He realized she was losing it. He had been home from the Texas trip for four days and had come to see her every day, spending the night with her and sleeping on that uncomfortable brown armchair so his uncle could go home and rest. Ciro had come at 5:00 am to replace him until noon when he had to go to work before Uncle Osvaldo took his place. She pulled his hand and interrupted his thoughts. "I want you to know that Ciro is the son I had, but you are the son I wanted." He began to protest, but she said, "No one can doubt I love Ciro. I was told that it might be best for me to abort him, but I did not, and after I went through all the dangers in carrying him, I almost died giving birth. He is precious to me because from the moment of conception, he has been difficult to manage and care for. He's a happy boy but has a temper that not even God can control. God brought you to me to raise you, love you, and give you the care that your parents couldn't. I understood the gift and have loved you and cared for you as best I could, but my time is almost over." She coughed and jerked forward. Joaquín moved closer to her, trying to support her. As he looked down at the sheets, blood speckled them red. She coughed again but continued. "So, as my eldest son, I ask you to take care of your brother and protect him like I've protected you. You know how wild and careless he is, so be his shield and keep him out of trouble." Joaquín nodded. "Promise me, Joaquín."

"He doesn't need my protection."

"Promise me. Please, I need to go in peace." He looked into her dying face.

"I promise." She kissed his hand and held it to her heart. He felt the beating stop. One look at the monitor, and he ran toward the door. He swung the door open and screamed, "I need help here, please somebody come immediately." Nurses and doctors came from everywhere, but there was nothing they could do. His promise ended her suffering.

Chapter 34: The Drinks

Miami, Florida: November 1981

The minute hand rested five minutes before the hour and Gabriel realized that he and Rodrigo had spent the better part of the afternoon and early evening working. He raised his eyes from his watch to the papers before him and then around the conference room before focusing on Rodrigo.

"Rod, don't you think we are taking quite a chance in going to trial?" asked Gabriel, turning his chair in the conference room toward Rodrigo.

"Do you think you can persuade him to plea?" Gabriel considered Rodrigo's question.

"No, he seems to have this unmovable faith that he will be found not guilty, in spite of the way the evidence is stacking."

"There is actually not that much against him." Rodrigo closed his file and leaned back in his chair.

"It's not much for him, and what is for him doesn't count because it's Rosa giving him the alibi."

"Do you believe he is guilty?" asked Rodrigo, pushing the file from him.

"No. Actually, I'm sure he is not."

"Then we transmit that to the jury."

"Come on, Rod, you think that will work?"

"What else have we got?" We can argue what they don't have but then if they get two identifications of our client by the two witnesses, especially the victim, and we are done for."

They heard the door open behind them and saw that Thomas had entered the room.

"I have been hearing the arguments on and off all afternoon. You guys work for ten to twenty minutes and then argue for five to ten minutes. That is a very difficult model for a way to prepare for trial." Both younger men chuckled. Thomas sat down in one of the empty chairs.

"Thanks for the comic relief. We needed it," joked Gabriel. Thomas stared at his son with a grateful glance.

"You guys are working hard on the case. Why are you so worried? You are going to give him the best possible defense, and all the points of the controversy will have been covered by the time the jury gets the case. Besides, if I just heard right, the prosecution doesn't have much connecting the client to the incident."

"It doesn't have any evidence to speak of other than the eyewitnesses, at least one of which is weak, but it does have logic. All roads point to our guy," stated Rodrigo.

"How's that?" asked Thomas, taking a hand to his thick glasses, removing them and massaging the space between his eyes.

"Our client is at a family picnic at Tropical Park with his family. His daughter goes jogging. During that jog, the victim has a problem with our client's daughter, she returns to where they are picnicking, and shortly thereafter, a guy looking very much like our client starts beating on the victim with a wooden bat for no apparent reason. Later a person looking very much like the man that beat on the victim is seen driving out of the park in the client's car by the same person that witnessed the beating. Therefore, providing a belief that our client had motive and opportunity."

"So why aren't we taking a plea?"

"Because our guy is innocent."

"Of course, they all say that, but you've got to convince him that the plea is the best way for him."

"No, Dad," interjected Gabriel, "our guy really is innocent. We know it, and we know who really did it." Thomas's eyes grew.

"What? Are you serious?"

"Could not be any more so," responded Rodrigo.

"Why don't you point the finger at the real culprit?"

"Our client has prohibited us from mentioning the perpetrator."

"You can do it in many ways..."

"He made a death bed promise to his aunt who raised him when he came by himself from Cuba that he would always take care of her son."

"And her son did it," finished Thomas.

"Yeah."

"So, he took your only weapon from you other than the truth."

"What do you mean, Dad? He prohibited us from mentioning his cousin. The cousin did it, and we can't say anything. That's the truth."

"It's also true that your client did not do it. You going to have to ride into war with that, and that is going to have to be enough."

"It's not," said Rodrigo.

"Then know that you did what you could for your client. You can only do what your client allows."

"The problem is that everything comes down to the victim. The only benefit we have is that when he was presented with Joaquín's photo, he did not choose him. He lingered over the photo but did not say that it was him," explained Gabriel, recalling the facts.

"The mind is a curious thing, son. Just because he didn't choose your client's picture then doesn't mean that he hasn't received the suggestion that it was your client from various sources and suddenly realizes that he didn't recognize him from the photo then, but he does in person. It's been a long time since the line-up. He may remember differently in the courtroom.

"That's our fear," admitted Rodrigo, "We don't know what he'll say, remember, be guided to, we don't know, and it all comes down to that."

"Is there anything more that you need to look at for the evening?" asked Thomas. Gabriel and Rodrigo exchanged glances and then responded in unison.

"No. we have been looking at the same issues over and over and it all comes down to victim and witness identification versus the alibi of the wife."

"Then come on, we need a change of pace."

"Where are we going?"

"A spot just up the road. Do you have busy days tomorrow?"

"My earliest meeting is at noon," replied Rodrigo.

"My day is clear tomorrow," admitted Gabriel.

"Good, it's a short drive from here to there, you'll need that time just in case."

"Where are we going?"

"Centro Vasco," clarified Thomas to Rodrigo, "it's one of my favorites." Gabriel and Rodrigo grabbed their suit jackets and followed Thomas out of the conference room and to Centro Vasco.

They delayed twenty minutes on their journey to the restaurant equally known for its bar as it was for its food.

It was a neat building with a limestone-chunk exterior, and new awnings. "It's had quite a journey since its days as The Garden," said Thomas, examining the building.

"What was The Garden?" asked Rodrigo, taking in the scenery.

"An Austrian restaurant until '65. Juan bought it from them and turned it into what it is now. The interior used to have walls like the Black Forest and all kinds of Germanic memories and poor Juan didn't have enough money in those days to change it when he bought it, so Cubans and Spaniards ate Caldo Gallego to an Austrian theme." He chuckled as he finished the last words. "These days, Juan's got plenty of money, they expanded the parking lot, painted the interior a pale-yellow color, and removed every trace of the original Austrian décor."

"Is the food good?" asked Rodrigo. Thomas shot him an offended look.

"Eating is one of the pleasures of life. We only get three chances a day to enjoy it so why waste any of them." His eyebrows rose, and his eyes sharpened, leaving his older face free of wrinkles.

"I suppose not," admitted Rodrigo.

"Come on, they'll be open for another three hours or so. Let's get started." The three of them entered and found exactly what Thomas had described. Gabriel would have sworn that it had always been Basque Spanish between the music, the menu, and the decorations. "Juan Saizarbitoria is his name," added Thomas. "His son, Juan Jr., *Juanito*, primarily runs it with his brother, Iñaki, but, occasionally, the old man comes through.

"Do you see him here tonight?" asked Gabriel.

"Not at the moment. Table or bar, fellas?"

"Table," they answered.

"Done deal." They waited a moment before a young woman came towards them. She asked if there were more people coming, and when they said no, she pointed to an empty table near one of the yellow walls. Thomas led them and, circling the table, they removed their jackets, loosened their ties, and rolled up their sleeves.

Thomas signaled to the waiter who nodded back to him. "Well, boys, what are you in the mood for, Zurito, Patxaran, or Alavesa?" Rodrigo wasn't sure of what Thomas meant.

"Beer, liquor, or wine?" explained Gabriel.

"Beer," said Rodrigo.

"Same," added Gabriel.

"Sure, why not?" added Thomas. He leaned back in his seat, peering at the oncoming waiter from behind his glasses. "Any food?" he asked before the waiter arrived. Gabriel and Rodrigo nodded.

"Three Zuritos," said Thomas. The waiter acknowledged and turned away, heading in the opposite direction.

"This case is straightforward. Your hands are tied, and you can only do what your client allows. If you worry anymore about it, you'll drive yourselves mad."

"Gee, Dad, that's not the statement that I expected."

"No, it's not, but would you prefer that I tell you to keep bashing your heads into oblivion to control something that you have no control over?"

"He's got a point," said Rodrigo.

"He's been a client of ours for almost five years and he's a good man, but both of you should know this. We can only do what our clients allow us to do. We know that he didn't do it. We know that his cousin did from what other people have told us, but unless you saw it, you can't prove that it was the cousin and the evidence against the client is circumstantial. He has an alibi, a weak one, but an alibi. In the end, it's in God's hands."

"Yeah, it is," admitted Rodrigo, leaning back in his chair, and sighing at the truth that Thomas shared.

The waiter returned a moment later and placed three Zuritos on the table. The three men took their drinks, touched glasses, and drank, enjoying the ambiance of the tavern and escaping from their legal lives for a little while.

Chapter 35: The Bitter Bargain

Miami, Florida: November 1981

Gabriel watched the clouds hide the sun from behind the window. It offered a brief respite from the stress of the proceedings and of Joaquín's decision from the night before. Hamilton had arrived early and once again spread his exhibits on the table. Gabriel didn't need to see them again. He looked to the parking lot and noticed Jackson exiting the driver's seat of his wine-colored Lincoln Continental. There was no sign of Wrightly, and Gabriel presumed that Jackson's hesitation to enter the building came from waiting on the adjuster.

Between last night's conversation and this morning's, Walter had once again changed his mind, and once again, he kept him on course. He wanted the matter closed. A few moments later, a beige Ford Taurus pulled into the parking lot and parked a few spots down from Jackson's Lincoln.

"Did they arrive?" asked Hamilton, noticing Gabriel looking down.

"Jackson has been in the parking lot, waiting for Wrightly to arrive. They are both walking up now." Seizing the moment, he looked over to Hamilton, who had returned to his exhibits. "You know, Hamilton, you and Jackson have worked a lot to cement your positions and make them clear. Perhaps today, it's time to find common ground."

Hamilton raised his eyes from the exhibits and stared at Gabriel, raising his eyebrows and giving an inquisitive look.

"Are you going to help push Jackson into the compromise that you know that we have to make?" Gabriel smiled.

"My job is to make sure that my client's trucking company survives, and I haven't decided what it's going to take to save it."

Hamilton gave an amused look. He opened his mouth to continue, but at that moment, the door opened.

"Good afternoon," said Wrightly, "I'm sorry I am late and sorry for holding everyone up."

Jackson emerged from behind Wrightly and nodded to Hamilton and Gabriel as he passed through the doorway and moved toward the table. Setting their briefcases down and placing their jackets on the backs of their chairs, they took their seats.

Gabriel stood up and walked to the credenza on the rear wall and grabbed a glass, ice, and a Coca-Cola can. He had made up his mind and was ready to begin. When Hamilton rose to speak, Gabriel interrupted.

"I know I haven't said much until now, but do you mind if I go first?"

Hamilton, caught off guard, ceded to Gabriel's request.

"Go ahead, Lock," he said as he sat back down in his chair.

"Thank you, Hamilton. I have not been totally fair to you. While it's true that my client had no other insurance at the time of the accident involving your client, the reason they did not have any more insurance left on their other policy is that another truck belonging to Miami Trucking and Cargo was involved in an accident worse than this one earlier this year. My client has operated in the trucking business for seventeen years and has suffered only two major accidents. Both happened this year. The first in early January, and this one, as you all know, took place in May." Hamilton twisted in his chair completely and stared at Gabriel intently. "The reality is that in January, my client had a second policy of insurance. It was an umbrella policy for ten million dollars. As you know, when the umbrella policy pays up to the limit of the policy in any given year, the policy and the law say it pays no more for that year. My client's other accident used up that policy entirely. Your client's accident happened while my client was in the process of attaining a new umbrella policy. Therefore, they have only the coverage that you see here, which is for one million dollars. I did not disclose the other policy because it was maxed out and no longer in force." Hamilton's face bore no emotion.

"Can you send me the policy and the settlement agreement for the other accident?"

"I can send you the policy, but not the settlement agreement. The settlement was confidential, and there was no lawsuit. Jackson," he began, turning and gesturing to where Jackson sat, "is aware of that policy and is aware that there is no coverage because he was involved in the settlement of the previous accident."

Hamilton looked over to Jackson, whose reply came in the form of two nods. Processing the disclosure, Hamilton returned to his notes, read them, jotted something down with his pen, and spoke.

"Send me the policy."

Gabriel surveyed Hamilton. His dark pupils gave away the feeling hidden behind the expressionless and professional face, and Gabriel knew that in some way, this was personal to him.

"We all agree that your client had a head-on collision with the black car after it hit my client's truck. That car, which we all know is the cause of this accident, spun around and traveled south in the middle lane of a northbound highway. We also concur, including my client, that your client is permanently and tragically disabled. I have reviewed the records, and I could not count how many bones in your client's body suffered damage. I have reviewed your income projections of the money she would have earned in addition to the cost of medical and therapeutic care and assistance she will need and have found them accurate. One million dollars is not nearly enough for just the medical services and care that she must receive during her lifetime. Chances are that the one million we do have would not be enough to scratch the surface, but this money and her underinsured coverage is all there is going to be. We all believe that the people in the black car will never be found, and if they are found, they will either not have had insurance or had minimal coverage." He rose and walked toward the window with his back to the table and asked, "I know that you reduced your fee on this case, Hamilton. This is more than just a case to you, isn't it?"

"I did, by ninety percent. Aside from the overhead, this case is *pro-bono*. Katerina is the daughter of a long-time client and friend," he paused for a second, then looked down. "I was at her baptism, her first communion, and I had received the invitation to her wedding. The silver lining for me in this is not being a pallbearer at her funeral." Hamilton rose from his chair and, raising his head, he faced Gabriel. "Listen, I am no saint because I have made a lot of money from people's pain as a personal injury attorney. But every once in a little while, you get a case where all sense of business goes out the window, and the only thing that matters is the client. When I agreed to represent Katerina, I suspected that there would be the possibility of insufficient insurance coverage because of the extent of her injuries. Given her injuries and the reams of bills that you see here," said Hamilton pointing to the lines of medical expenses, "I knew that it was important to obtain the money promptly because her medical coverage is running out. I cannot believe the hesitation on the part of Northwestern in not offering the policy limits for something as obvious as this. And I also knew it would never be enough and that the little girl that played softball with my daughter and was constantly at my house would not have enough money from this settlement to fully cover her expenses as time passed. I knew we would get to this point rapidly, but I thought that Northwestern would be reasonable once we got here. I accepted this litigation to protect her in the best way that I could, and I see this as my obligation and the right thing to do, but we're not resolving this the way it should be resolved." Hamilton finished and paused.

He walked over to the credenza and grabbed a bottle of Perrier, removed the top, and downed it to the last drop. Gabriel waited for a moment to let him finish recovering. Jackson scribbled on his notepad, tore out the sheet, and gave it to Wrightly, who glanced at it, folded it, and put it in his file.

"What are your estimates on the monetary consequences of the accident for your client? What would you be coming into court with?" asked Gabriel to Hamilton, who still stood at the credenza. Hamilton turned back to face the table.

"Twelve million three hundred and fifty thousand," he replied.

"So, if I take your number and multiply it by the ten percent of culpability, which Jackson claims that my client will be assigned by a jury, the result is one million two hundred and thirty-five thousand dollars."

Hamilton shook his head and mumbled.

"No, that's not my final number."

"I see your problem," said Gabriel to Hamilton, "Hamilton, all the trucks have mortgages on them because of bank financing. The property on which the business is located not only has a mortgage with the bank but belongs to a different company that has nothing to do with the business. I have brought the paperwork for your inspection." Gabriel reached for the briefcase, and Aleman produced another folder. "If you go to trial and obtain the judgement your client deserves, you won't be able to collect a single penny. The bank will have no choice but to foreclose on the business, and you will force my client into bankruptcy. At that point, the judgement you will have worked so hard to obtain will disappear. No one will benefit except the insurance company. So, will you accept the policy limits if given?"

Hamilton took the documents and examined them. Accepting Gabriel's truth, he remained silent but nodded his assent. Gabriel turned to Jackson.

"What do you have this claim valued at?"

Jackson did not respond and instead deferred to Wrightly, who answered the unasked question.

"I can't tell you that in front of the plaintiff's attorney."

Gabriel stared at the adjuster for a moment and then looked at Jackson.

"Jackson, do you think that I am playing games?" inquired Gabriel, staring at the man intensely.

Jackson disregarded the question but shifted his attention toward Wrightly and nodded, giving him the go-ahead. Wrightly sighed.

"My number, considering the total damages and the expected allocation of responsibility, is roughly seven hundred and twenty-three thousand dollars."

"Jackson, your position is that a jury may consider the truck as ten percent responsible for the accident. Hamilton's number for the total damages is twelve million three hundred and fifty thousand dollars, and it's a solid number. If we go to court and what you and Hamilton predict comes true, the judgement against my client will be one million, two hundred, and thirty-five thousand dollars. Your policy will pay the first million, but my client will be responsible for two hundred and thirty-five thousand dollars, and the company will go bankrupt. Now, you saw Hamilton accept and settle for one million, so for your company to not act in bad faith, leaving my client on the hook when you don't settle this case, you need to offer the policy limits," said Gabriel with a smile.

"I can't exceed my number without authority from my manager," admitted Wrightly.

"Since you can't offer the policy limits, on Monday, I will be sending Northwestern a bad faith letter for not settling in good faith within the policy limits and thereby protecting their insured, Miami Trucking and Cargo. Northwestern will then be looking at a twelve-million-dollar exposure plus any losses my client may incur due to the legal difficulties. When you get that letter, Jackson, do you think that your client will pay the policy limits?" Jackson repositioned himself in his chair.

"Considering the exposure that it will have and Hamilton's agreement to drop the lawsuit against our insured, I will recommend it to Northwestern."

"If that's true, let's all agree on the offering of policy limits, and we're through. If you look through the material that Hamilton gave us, on page 5 of Doctor Johnson's report, you will find that he says that if she continues to receive therapy, she may yet walk almost normally. The problem is that her medical coverage is running out and that therapy may be interrupted," finished Gabriel. "My client has insisted that this payment be made now instead of later for Katerina's good and continued recovery. So, Jackson, tell Mr. Wrightly to get on the phone and get the approval he needs and let's settle this now."

Jackson turned to Wrightly and nodded his head. The adjuster grabbed his things and began to make his way out of the room.

"Oh, and Wrightly, tell your supervisor that if he thinks of keeping the money a little longer so the company can profit off the interest, I will make sure that all of that is eaten up by Jackson's attorney's fees responding to my requests and letters. I am quite sure Hamilton will do the same." Gabriel said to him.

Hamilton smiled.

Jackson followed Wrightly, leaving Gabriel and Hamilton in the conference room. The afternoon sun filtered in through the windows of the room. Hamilton rose from his chair and turned to Gabriel.

"Thank you, Lock. I'm glad that you decided to push it. I don't think that they would have paid in time for Katerina to pay for her therapy if you hadn't stepped in."

Gabriel nodded.

"I acted in the best interest of my client just as you did for yours. Luckily, those interests coincided."

Both attorneys chuckled before Jackson came back in for a moment, announcing that the company would officially offer the policy limits within the next two workdays. Hearing the news, Hamilton grabbed his things, walked over to Gabriel, shook his hand, and left.

Gabriel waited until he saw Hamilton and the others leave. He returned from the window and took a moment to reflect on all that had transpired. He looked down at his folder, saw Katerina's mangled body lying next to the jaws of life, and brushed his fingers over her face. He had won for Walter, had saved the livelihood of most of Walter's employees and their families, but felt as lifeless as Katerina looked on the road. Somewhere in the city, Hamilton was telling Katerina and her parents that the most that he could do was not enough.

Gabriel brought the photograph up to his face, staring at the black paint etched into Katerina's car. The other driver fled the scene, was never identified, was never caught, and he understood that only the guilty walked away from this tragedy unscathed. He slowly collected all the documents and returned them to his briefcase, lingering on her picture. Katerina had a passionate advocate. No one spoke against her cause, and yet, she still lost. Gabriel closed his eyes, gritted his teeth, and surrendered to the truth that, sometimes, there was no justice.

Chapter 36: The Farewell

Miami, Florida: May 1975

They held the funeral three days later. Joaquín, Ciro, and Uncle Osvaldo stood at the entrance of Saint Brendan Catholic church, thanking those that came to pay their respects. As the last of the mourners entered, Uncle Osvaldo took Joaquín aside.

"Thank you for the coffin and the arrangements, Joaquín. Ciro and I couldn't afford more than the plot and the tombstone."

"I know, Uncle, no one thought we would have to be ready for this." began Joaquín placing his hand on his uncle's shoulder, "It was the least that I could do; she was my second mother." A lone tear welled in his eye and slid down his cheek. Uncle Osvaldo embraced him.

"Come, let's meet Ciro inside," said Uncle Osvaldo, ushering him through the entrance to the pew in the front where Ciro waited for them.

The Priest entered and took his place behind the altar. Father Gámez began mass, explaining the proceeding and stating that the whole service would be in Spanish, honoring the life of Cárola Lorant de Marcos.

"Let us pray," began Father Gámez.

They all bowed their heads, and he led them in prayer.

The mass lasted half an hour and Joaquín found himself guiding the guests over to their cars and reminding them that the burial would be at Miami Memorial Park. The ride lasted a little over ten minutes. Joaquín held his breath as they exited the car. Ciro, Uncle Osvaldo, and their long-time neighbor, Orfeo, gathered around the trunk of the hearse. Joaquín and Uncle Osvaldo were the lead pallbearers while Ciro and Orfeo followed, as was Aunt Cárola's final wish. The box was simple and discrete, belying the treasure it carried. As they walked from the hearse to the burial plot, he swore he would keep his promise because of the love she had always given him.

They placed her down and Father Gámez spoke again, leading them through their grief. Shortly after, two of her friends reminisced about her life. People hugged and one by one they said goodbye to Uncle Osvaldo, Ciro, and Joaquín.

As they lowered the casket covered with tears and flowers from loved ones the mourners murmured their final goodbye. Joaquín and Ciro left last, knowing that all they had was each other and the promises they made to the lady and mother who loved them.

Chapter 37: The Boxers

Miami, Florida: Late November 1981

He grabbed his briefcase and closed the door firmly behind him. His feet sank further into his shoes as he stepped toward the small glass door at the back of the building, juggling his thoughts between Katerina's settlement, Walter's relief, and the frustration of Joaquín's case.

He opened the door and proceeded down a dark hallway with black walls. The small incandescent lights above him offered small hints of yellow light as he made his way to another door at the hallway's end, hearing the beating of mats, grunts, shouts, and atmosphere of a fighter's den.

Small beads of sweat trickled down from his scalp down to his temples and the tops of his ears as he remembered that Franco's gym didn't bother with AC, only ineffective fans that hummed like the thunder of an impending storm. The door opened in front of him, and he saw a short, muscular, and stubble-bearded man emerge from behind it. The man squinted for a moment before letting his aged voice speak.

"Gabriel?" he asked in Spanish, "It's been sometime since you were here." Gabriel nodded and allowed the corners of his mouth to curl into a slight smile.

"Since my last year of college; some five years ago now, Rigo," responded Gabriel, keeping the dialogue in Spanish.

"What are you doing here? Is the gym in trouble?" asked Rigo, nodding at Gabriel's briefcase. He had forgotten that he still wore his suit.

"No," answered Gabriel, chuckling, "the gym is fine, everything is okay, and I'm here because Franco invited me a few weeks back." Rigo's serious eyes shifted to a more relaxed tone and his voice followed.

"You came to work out?"

"Yes," Gabriel nodded.

"Get dressed and then meet me at the bag; I'll warm you up."

"Is Franco here?" Gabriel asked as he watched Rigo turn and extend an arm to open the door behind him. He stepped through the door and walked a few paces trying to take in the old scene.

The gym was the same as it had been five years earlier minus a new water cooler that sat next to the old one. In the far-left corner were three punching bags with the speed bags next to them. On the right sat a small area with weights and machines while close to him were the rings he used to practice on with Franco when they were kids. On the other side, the ropes that he used to climb next to the pullup bars didn't impose as much as they did before. AC/DC's Highway to Hell roared in the background and forced Gabriel to smile.

"It's bigger than I remembered it," said Gabriel twisting back to Rigo who looked down at his watch.

"How long do you want to be here?" he asked.

"As long as you'll let me."

"Then you'll have to earn your stay. Get dressed and meet me in front of the bags. Can you still do a full circuit?"

"If not, I'm sure that you'll let me know," affirmed Gabriel, wiping the sweat from his forehead.

"Let's test it out."

It took Gabriel five minutes to change from his suit to his gym clothes. He sported a set of black shorts, a black tank, black socks that rose to just above his ankles, and his old black boxing shoes. He removed his cross from around his neck and hung it in the locker alongside his clothes, but it wasn't deep enough for his briefcase. As he tried to see where else he could place it, Franco entered the locker room.

"Wild man!" yelled Franco in a playful tone while grinning.

"It's good to see you, Franco," greeted Gabriel, extending his hand to Franco. He took it and then pulled Gabriel in for a hug. "Out there, I'm your client, in here, I'm your friend, got it?"

"Got it."

"Here, let me take that," offered Franco, reaching for Gabriel's briefcase and for the clothes inside of the locker."

"Thanks."

"I'll put these in my office; I have a few clients who come in the mornings and carry some of these, so I've got some hangers and a rack for them, and it'll be easy for your things. Rigo told me that you plan on being here for as long as we'll let you, huh?"

"Yeah, if that's alright with you."

"Now, Let's put you to work and see what you got."

"You don't want me to fight someone, do you?"

"I've got a kid that needs to tune up, he's six feet, three inches tall and will be twenty in three weeks. You mind sparring with him?"

"I came here to work out, not die." Franco snorted as he laughed, his ponytail whipping up and down as he grabbed his ribs.

"You'll be fine! Besides, the kid is seventeen and learning, he's not even amateur ranked yet."

"Yet is the key word. Where will you be? Why aren't you training him? What about Rigo?" Gabriel exhaled for a few moments.

"Rigo's warming you up because it's been so long since he last saw you, but he's had tendonitis in his elbow for a little while now. My other trainer, Fito, is on vacation, and I've got some things to do. You may not have been here in a few years, but I know that you've still got something in the tank."

"I had it. An occasional game of racquetball is no preparation for this," corrected Gabriel. Franco raised his eyebrows and tucked his chin. Gabriel lingered on the decision for a few moments. "Okay but tell him to take it easy."

"I like it! I'll bring you a mouthpiece." Franco departed for his office with the items while Gabriel returned to the main room.

He met Rigo by the bags and they began stretching. Rigo led him through the stretches both static and dynamic for about fifteen minutes.

"Put on your gloves." Gabriel retrieved his gloves from the gym bag. Rigo waited for him holding both wraps and tapes in his hands to prepare him. It took Rigo a few minutes to wrap Gabriel's hands, but when he put the old gloves on, they felt snug, almost too snug. He tried to shift them a bit by stretching and contracting his fingers when he heard Rigo cackling lightly. "They'll loosen up when you hit the bag." Gabriel shrugged and stepped over to the bag. He saw its stillness, suspended above the ground by the chains hanging from the beam overhead like the others which hung on either side. His eyes moved from the beginning to the end of the row, and, when he felt comfortable in the setting, he advanced toward the bag, loosened his shoulders, raised his hands, placed a foot forward, and jabbed the bag. Thud, thud, crash, jab, jab, cross.

"Harder!" urged Rigo. Gabriel nodded. Thud, thud, crash. With each swing, Gabriel increased the intensity, used his hips more to drive home the cross, stepped forward as he jabbed into the bag. Rigo's face tensed as he held the bag. "Concentrate, hit the same exact spot, every time."

Gabriel focused, aiming for the same spots, feeling his gloves make contact, controlling his pace and isolating his muscles to drill into the same place over and over.

"Control your breathing," commanded Rigo. Gabriel did not take his eyes from the bag. He grimaced, controlling his pace to strengthen his breathing, he struck the bag fiercely, with an undiscovered anger that surprised him and landing a punch that forced Rigo to brace the bag. "Good. Harder, with tempo!"

Silence dominated the room. The thunder of the overhead fans vanished, AC/DC faded from his mind, and Rigo's words became inaudible as Gabriel saw the lips move but heard no sound. All he could hear was his own breathing. All he could see was the bag in front of him. All he felt was the impact of the gloves as his body moved through motions his instincts began to remember. Thud. Thud. Crash.

"Wild man! Looking good!" Rigo eased and Gabriel noticed the bag swayed more. He composed himself, not even sure of what he heard. He turned and saw Franco, smiling with his ponytailed hair and dark eyes in their usual stances. "That power is back, my friend. Your movements are rough, but your body has not forgotten the patterns. Your hips give good power so that's good. Are you ready for the tune up?" Gabriel looked around and wondered where the kid was.

"Where is he?" asked Gabriel.

"I assume on his way. He hasn't called, so he should be getting here."

"Sure thing," said Gabriel. He returned to the bag and tried to reclaim his focus. He stared down at the black material and tried to drown out everything else. AC/DC had changed to Led Zeppelin and Gabriel did his best to tune out the rest of the world. He drew breath, lowered his center of gravity, and began anew with renewed vigor, striving to catch the music's rhythm. Thud. Thud. Crash.

Gabriel hit the bag for another five minutes or so before moving to the speed bag where Rigo lined up next to him and watched him attempt to keep rhythm.

"You're trying too hard. Relax, tempo, not speed, not strength, timing." Gabriel panted and wiped pools of sweat from his forehead with the back of his glove. He shot Rigo a dissatisfied look and Rigo snickered before taking a callused hand to his stubbled chin. "Again!"

His triceps began to tingle as he hit the speed bag in repetitive motion. He hit and then hit again and again, rising in speed but maintaining the right tempo. He synchronized his breathing with the rhythm of the hits, and he found himself relieved. "Good. Not bad," encouraged Rigo. He glanced at his watch, then to the bag, and back to his watch.

"What?" pressed Gabriel.

"Silvio should have been here by now."

"The kid?" Rigo nodded and Gabriel stopped for a moment.

"Come on, let's get you to the ring. He'll probably be here any minute."

"He's only going to have time for a quick warm up." Rigo smiled.

"He doesn't need to warm up against you."

Gabriel's eyebrows furrowed and Rigo knew his cheap shot landed. "You always had a good sense of humor, old man."

"I've got to. I'm a 72-year-old man, displaced from his country, and divorced for nine years. What do you expect?"

"You're 72 now?!"

"73 in December."

"You look great."

"I'm old, Gabriel, not dead." Laughter roared from within them as they took a moment to gather their things and walk to the ring. "Let me get your headgear," said Rigo, "I've got to grab it from the closet." Rigo strolled over to the other side of the gym where he took a few moments to retrieve the headgear. Gabriel began to shuffle around the ring, trying to keep limber and circling around, changing directions as he did so. He could hear the door clang against the metal closet and turned to see Rigo returning, but next to him was Franco, gloved, dressed, and limber.

"Where's Silvio?" asked Gabriel.

"Can't make it, so you get to spar me."

"You're kidding?"

"Not at all," said Franco, defiance surging through his calm voice.

"You're going to kill me."

"Nah, you looked great on the bags. Don't worry about it. I'll go easy if you want."

Gabriel's face flushed at the thought of Franco going easy. A small tinge of fury escaped his control and forced his head to become very hot, steam emanating from his temples and the tops of his ears.

"There's no such thing as taking it easy among friends."

"That's the Gabriel I know!" yelled Franco, "Still the same fighter, different ring!"

Rigo handed Franco the headgear as he stepped into the ring.

"Where's mine?" asked Gabriel, rhetorically, with more steam released from his words than his sweating head.

"You're right," admitted Franco, realizing the unintended disrespect, "Rigo, get my headgear, please." Rigo nodded and headed toward Franco's office, leaving the two friends alone. "You're angry about something. You wouldn't have come otherwise."

"That's not true," said Gabriel.

"The last time you were here was when she left, and you beat your rage out with each blow on that bag and on every serious fighter that you could until the battle on the inside appeared on your skin. So, I'll ask you now, what are you angry about?"

"I'll tell you afterward if you still want to hear it."

"Yeah, you said the same thing last time too."

"Yeah?"

"Yeah. You didn't tell me what happened until three months after I asked, just before you returned to law school."

"I was a different guy then." Guilt ripped through Gabriel as he struggled to remember that time.

"Same guy, just more mature. Still carry her picture in your wallet?" pressed Franco. Gabriel nodded.

"But she's not why I'm angry now."

"Okay, first we'll punch and then we'll talk."

Gabriel couldn't stop the grin. Rigo returned to the ring and Franco knelt so that Rigo could place the headgear on him, careful to pull the famed ponytail through the opening in the back of the head. Rigo handed them both mouthpieces.

"Ready?" asked Franco.

"Till knockout," answered Gabriel. Franco smiled.

"Like old times," said Franco before inserting the mouthpiece. Gabriel followed suit.

The friends touched gloves, Rigo sounded the bell, and the fighters began.

The men circled around the ring for a few moments. The tingling in Gabriel's triceps vanished as he took deep breaths. He kept his hands up, ready and loose, searching for an opening against Franco's relaxed pose. Franco swayed his head back and forth, fluid as a swan on water and Gabriel knew Franco fought more like an artist than a brute.

Gabriel closed the distance and landed a jab into Franco's glove. He dared a second at Franco's raised glove, grazing his jaw.

"First blood to Lock," joked Franco. The friends circled a bit and Gabriel hit Franco with a quick jab. Growing confident, he aimed for a jab-cross combo, aiming high with the left and low with the cross. Franco let the jab in, blocked the cross, and nailed Gabriel with a deep cross of his own to Gabriel's ribs. Wind escaped Gabriel's body and he felt himself gasp for air.

"Okay there, Counselor?" joked Franco.

"Fine, fine. Let's go!" He shrugged off the pain and the shock and closed the distance again. Gabriel tried a five-punch combo, jab, low cross, jab, high cross, and low jab to the abdomen. Franco winced as the hit to the abdomen landed.

"Okay there, coach?" joked Gabriel. Franco laughed.

"All good, Counselor. Ready to teach a lesson."

Franco moved like a serpent, curling his body as he thrust his jabs forward. Gabriel turned his body and used his arms to block the cutting blows, lashing a jab out to Franco's cheek that hissed as he evaded it. Franco countered and landed a punch just below Gabriel's outstretched arm.

His opposite ribs swelled with pain and his breathing shallowed. Throbbing took him, constricting his air and his mind as he tucked in his elbows and dipped his head. Somewhere the bell sounded, and he knew the round was over.

"Not bad, wild man!" shouted Franco, "You're not as rusty as you said."

"Yeah, not half bad, I guess." Gabriel winced as he said it and his lungs burned. I'm out of shape, he thought. Franco took a swig of water from a bottle Rigo handed him.

"Water?" he mouthed. Gabriel nodded and Rigo tossed him a bottle from the side. He drank, sucking up through the straw. He walked over to the corner. Rigo had placed a towel on the post and Gabriel took it, wiping his head and face.

"Ten seconds!" shouted Rigo, staring at his watch. Gabriel turned back to Franco.

"Like old times?" checked Franco.

"Like old times," assured Gabriel.

The bell rang and the friends returned to the fray.

Franco's feet tapped lightly on the mat as he danced around Gabriel, searching for an opening. Gabriel shuffled, taking a defender's pose, giving nothing before settling into the rhythm from the bag. He made contact: thud, thud, crash. He continued with the combo as Franco seemed to dodge or block every blow: thud, thud, crash. Franco sent a few jabs in between, but Gabriel took them easily. The pair traded and evaded blows until Gabriel yelled out to him.

"Like old times, Franco! Like old times!" Franco nodded and the tempo rose. Franco jabbed, ducked crossed, swayed, juked, and landed every blow he wanted. Gabriel did his best to block what he could, but Franco still got through.

Like old times, thought Gabriel. As he remembered the words, a sense of calm rushed over him. Franco's blows no longer landed as Gabriel blocked them instinctively. His ribs no longer hurt or throbbed, they felt as strong as plate armor. Adrenaline took him, and he ceased to think, he just moved.

As they fought, memories flashed through his mind. *Thud*. He recalled the conversation with Drakos, forcing him to backtrack on his promise to the Adegboyes. *Block*. The photos of the blood on the floor of the convenience store played like motion pictures. *Thud, thud.* Mr. Adegboye Sr.'s limp body, lying on the floor, motionless. *Crash.* He remembered the rage he felt when Abuelo had been beaten while leaving his own store all those years ago. Anger surged through him. Rage found its way to his gloves and scorched every punch. The anger driven adrenalin drowned the pain his body felt.

Franco reeled backward, dodging Gabriel's blows less frequently than before, he jabbed and crossed aiming for Gabriel's ribs and abdomen, but they didn't slow him down.

"The wild man is back!" yelled Franco, but Gabriel barely heard him. Rigo stared, surprised by Gabriel's stamina and Franco's inability to land a haymaker.

Instinct engulfed him as his mind changed to Joaquín, Rosa, and the kids. Fury incensed him. Frustration ripped through him as he pondered Rosa and Joaquín sharing Sundays together through a pane of glass and two telephones. He imagined their kids walking home from school with their heads down, suffering through the words of their classmates calling them the spawn of an animal. He knew the cruelty of children. He envisioned Rodrigo pouring hours upon hours searching for a strategy, some way, any way to get Joaquín out of this mess; torn between his duty to his client and a favor to his best friend. Each emotion dominated a second in his mind as his body turned and twisted, his arms moved and blocked the incoming blows. Both mind and body were at war.

"ENOUGH!" yelled Gabriel. His mind finally heard the screams from his body. Rigo seemed to jump backward, and Franco smiled through his mouthpiece.

"There it is," whispered Franco to himself. Gabriel launched into fury, releasing every blow with a renewed vigor. They traded blows until Gabriel swung his arm toward Franco's temple.

He ducked and for a second, everything slowed, almost suspended in time. Gabriel knew he had overreached, missed the target, and left himself open.

Franco pounced and put all his power behind his fist, landing the blow on Gabriel's abs and lurched him backward. Gabriel staggered, his impervious ribs throbbed, burning from the inside. The wind left him, leaving him to choke for a moment. His feet lost their footing until his back hit the ropes. His eyes watered and blurred as his mind fired signals to places his body could not respond to. He stumbled to one knee and placed his gloves on the floor. Franco remained in his place but spoke softly to him. Rigo did not move but watched attentively.

"Breathe, Lock, just breathe. Focus on breathing." Gabriel struggled, but spit the mouthpiece out, doing his best to take deep breaths and recover. His lungs burned.

"Stand up, Lock," commanded Franco. His low voice echoed, and Gabriel dragged his foot until it replaced his knee on the mat. "Now the other." Gabriel repeated the step, until the soles of his shoes paralleled the floor. "Rise." Gabriel drew breath for a few moments, then rose until he stood upright. He did not wince through the pain as his bones ached from the contact. "Can you breathe normally?" asked Franco, who still hadn't moved.

"Yes," choked Gabriel as his airways expanded.

"Good. You did well."

"How long was the fight?"

"A little under two minutes."

"Longest two minutes of my life," said Gabriel, taking deeper breaths and taking off his gloves to massage his body.

"I'll let that one go," joked Franco. Gabriel shot him a reproaching look from behind raised eyebrows. Rigo handed him a water bottle and he took a few gulps.

"Better?" asked Rigo.

"Yes," answered Gabriel, taking another swig of water.

"Rigo, can you get the shower in my office ready so that Gabriel can clean up? Remember to turn on the water heater."

"You have a shower in your office now too?"

"We had it installed a few years ago so that I could prepare for my meetings."

"It amazes me that you are an interior decorator and still do this." Franco chuckled.

"Says the lawyer who sits at a desk all day."

"Tell me. What was that all about?"

"What?"

"ENOUGH," mouthed Franco, "what kind of outburst was that?"

"I didn't intend to yell it."

"No kidding. So, tell me what's going on."

"I can't really talk about it."

"No, you can talk about it, you just can't give me the who or the where, but you can give me the why and the what." Gabriel laughed at the truth he spoke.

"Okay," he began, "You remember my friend, Rodrigo, right?" Franco nodded. "Well, we have a client who's not letting us use all the available evidence to defend him."

"Go on," said Franco, walking over to the ropes and inviting Gabriel to walk through. Gabriel exited the ring and Franco followed. They sat in a pair of chairs before Gabriel continued.

"The worst part is that he has a wife and kids and he's willing to risk going to jail for a someone who's a hot head and is constantly in trouble."

"Does the relative have priors?" inquired Franco. He took his teeth to the gloves and used them to untie the string. Gabriel watched for a moment, then contemplated, trying to recall if Joaquín had mentioned that.

"No."

"If he had priors, maybe your client figured that he would get one strike while the other guy would be on his third or something and would go away for a lot longer." Franco placed the loosened glove under his arm and braced it on his side before wriggling his hand free.

"Possibly, but it's deeper than that. There's something that the client isn't really telling us other than he made a promise to always look out for the hothead."

"And while everyone thinks that he's making a mistake by not protecting himself, he sees it as equal to protecting his family."

"Yeah, that's it." Gabriel drank some more water.

"Yeah, but there's something more that's bothering you."

"When did you become a psychologist?" pressed Gabriel.

"In here, you see these guys who come from nothing and sacrifice who they are to become who they want to be. All of this is psychology; the drive, the discipline, and the desire to put yourself through this, to suffer through the pain and the training for just a chance at changing your life. To train these guys, Rigo and I have to make them believe in the things that only they can see, so yes, we get to know people well."

"I see." Gabriel paused, taking another drink of his water and extended his glove to Franco who, having removed his gloves, began untying Gabriel's. "You know that I left the State Attorney's Office earlier this year, but I didn't tell you why. I was working on a case for a family that dealt with a robbery. The victim was an older gentleman who owned a convenient store."

"Like your grandfather did," added Franco.

"Yeah, like my grandfather, a little older, but same idea. Anyway, the family wanted to push justice all the way so I promised them that I would. We had all the evidence to proceed, but my division chief forbade me to move the case forward and to convince my client to accept a plea deal."

"And you refused?"

"Yes, I requested that the State Attorney's Office accept my resignation and I promised to not share the decision with the other attorneys as a part of my NDA."

"What does that have to do with your client now?"

"Franco, I left the State Attorney's Office because I didn't want politics to limit the pursuit of justice for my client."

"But now your client is limiting that justice."

"Exactly," said Gabriel, his voice rising. Franco paused and thought about his words.

"You can't choose for your client. You can advise, you can guide him, you can get him to where he would see things in the clearest way, but the decision is his, so you must find a way to live with that."

"But his family–"

"–Is not on trial; he is, and, in the end, it's his decision."

"That's easy to say, but I have to do something about it."

"There's nothing to do. You defend him in the best way that you can, but if he's making you fight with one hand, then you use the one you've got and if you lose, then it's on him, not you."

"You sound like you say this from experience."

"What do you think I go through with my clients and my fighters? I spend a lot of time training both sets. I can't fight for my fighters and my clients can fire me at any time if they want.

"You're right."

"Prepare the best that you can, as creatively as you can, and let God take the rest."

"Not the jury?" joked Gabriel, straightening himself in his chair.

"If it were one person deciding, it would be that person; when it's more than one, it's God."

"How do you figure?"

"Because one sheep makes its own decisions; when it's a flock, the shepherd decides and there's only one shepherd."

Before Gabriel could respond, Rigo returned.

"Everything's ready for you."

"Go," said Franco, "we've talked enough, and you need to get out of here and I have other fighters coming in later."

"Thanks, Franco. I really needed this."

"Come back soon, just call next time."

"I did. I had Susana call you." Franco looked over to Rigo.

"I forgot to mention that," admitted Rigo. Franco laughed.

"Call twice next time."

"Sure thing," said Gabriel, shaking Franco's hand and following Rigo to the office.

Chapter 38: The Gerstein Building

Miami, Florida: Early December 1981

Allowing the brisk air of winter to cool him through the cracked window, he bowed his head between his hands and rested it on the steering wheel as he took in the crisp breeze. "Lord, I ask that you allow the truth to deliver Joaquín from a fate that he does not deserve. May you forgive his choices and help us save a man who is only trying to keep his word. In your name I pray. Amen." He lifted his head and set his feelings aside. *Time for battle*, he thought and concentrated on the work ahead.

Gabriel walked from the parking lot over to the sidewalk. He looked up at the Richard E. Gerstein building, the place where his career began, where he had chosen his values over his duty, and where politics got in the way of justice.

"The place I never wanted to return to," he said aloud, "my boss tied my hands last time and now it's my client." As he waited for cars to pass, he remembered what Mo had told him the day he left. *Well, at least it's my client this time*, he thought, *chin up*.

Gabriel crossed the street and climbed the steps to the Gerstein building at a quarter before nine, hoping to find Rodrigo inside. As he opened the glass door, he passed through the entrance and strode across the rouge and charcoal ceramic floor, stepping onto the escalator to the second floor. He found Rodrigo seated on a wooden bench outside of a courtroom, staring down at the floor.

"The floor hasn't changed, has it?" asked Gabriel as he approached Rodrigo.

Rodrigo kept his attention on the small tiles.

"No, but the opening statement is on its fourth version," admitted Rodrigo.

"Feels different when you know your client's innocent, doesn't it?"

"It raises the stakes just a little, yeah." Rodrigo brushed his hair back with his tan hand and massaged his head for a second. "I've had a splitting headache since this morning and having my motion at eight didn't really help."

"I was going to ask why you were here so early."

"Houseman decided that eight o'clock was the perfect time on a Monday to have a hearing on a motion to suppress."

"Was it granted?"

"Not a chance, but hope is eternal. I wouldn't have minded having it that early, but I didn't want that issue to pull my focus from this case. Joaquín and Rosa need my very best."

"They've got it, Rod. But every client knows that they're not the only ones and, luckily, no one knows that we handle as many cases as we do at the same time. If they did, every attorney would starve." Rodrigo snickered in his seat and moved to the side so that Gabriel could sit beside him. Gabriel planted himself next to his friend and continued. "So, what's bothering you about this case?"

"I honestly think that it's clear that he didn't do it. We've combed through the evidence several times. I've run the outcomes in my head repeatedly, and every time I look at it, I feel more confident that we are going to win, but it doesn't matter because nothing is ever one-hundred percent certain. There's always a wild card in every case."

"Tell me about it," agreed Gabriel, thinking about the photographs he had used in Ernesto's case earlier that year to grant the restraining order.

"You know, Lock, you brought me this case in May, and now we are two weeks from Thanksgiving. Joaquín and Rosa have dealt with this since the police ripped his arm from his socket until now. Think about all that he had to give up and sacrifice. Joaquín had to sell his truck and will never be able to work in trucking again."

"I know, Rod. My dad and I talked about that extensively the other day."

"It is nine o'clock." Rodrigo rose from the bench and pulled on the sleeves of his navy suit, making himself more comfortable.

"And what did he say?"

"That God knows better than we do, and that sooner or later, we all get our justice."

"What time do you think Joaquín and Rosa will arrive?"

"In a few minutes. Rosa's nerves are probably killing her right now, and Joaquín is doubtlessly occupied with calming her down."

"You would think that it was her trial."

"It's amazing how much grace Joaquín has shown through most of this process." Rodrigo smiled at Gabriel.

Rosa and Joaquín appeared from behind the far corridor. They moved toward the two attorneys, formally dressed and with calm demeanors. Rodrigo greeted both of them with an outstretched hand and a warm smile. Gabriel offered the same salutation and let Rodrigo take the lead.

"We'll be starting soon, so we should go ahead and take our places," he said, moving toward the elevator. As they waited, Gabriel noticed a small bead of sweat slide down Joaquín's temple before seeing the tremble in his hand. Gabriel slowly reached for Joaquín's arm and touched it slightly. Joaquín, feeling the contact, turned his head slightly to meet Gabriel's eyes. The attorney returned a nod and a confident smile easing Joaquín's nerves and making the tremor stop. The elevator doors parted, and they made their way to the courtroom.

Chapter 39: The Judge and the Jury

Miami, Florida: Early December 1981

They crossed the crimson and charcoal tile floor of the third level, walking toward the end of the hallway on their right. They neared the end of the hallway and faced the enclosure to the left when Rodrigo took the handle of the glass door and pushed it open. Gabriel felt the noise lessen as they entered. Rodrigo looked beyond the slight glass panel on the wooden door of the courtroom in front of them.

"We can enter," said Rodrigo, opening the courtroom door. They walked through, and Gabriel reached for the knot of his tie, loosening it as he took in the familiar setting. The muscles in his lower back tightened, and the nerves in his legs began to jolt pain down his leg. His heart quickened, and his body began to sweat slightly. He calmed himself as he followed Rodrigo, Joaquín, and Rosa down the open aisle, passing benches on either side before reaching the wooden half-wall that divided the onlookers from the petitioners. Rodrigo crossed the opening and beckoned Joaquín to find his seat at the defense table on the left-hand side. Rosa joined him while Rodrigo and Gabriel backed off, giving them a few minutes of privacy.

"How do you feel?" asked Gabriel, meeting Rodrigo's eyes.

Rodrigo glanced at Rosa and Joaquín whispering to each other and holding hands, choosing to linger his gaze on them in answering Gabriel.

"You know how you get spasms in your lower back and your legs when you feel tense?"

"Yeah."

"I've got mine now."

"Every litigation?"

"Every single one," affirmed Rodrigo, "but you know what, we're going to do well today. I know that the assault charge will be in our favor. There's too much evidence our way but getting the resisting arrest charge is going to take a miracle."

"I thought about that last night and the better part of this morning," agreed Gabriel.

He raised his hand and rested his palm on his neck.

"Your neck gets tense, too?" joked Rodrigo.

"I tend to do this when I think."

"How much time do you think that we have before we get company?" Gabriel checked his watch and turned to the door behind him.

"Five minutes maybe."

"Anything that you want to say to Rosa and Joaquín?" asked Rodrigo, shifting his weight onto his back leg and gesturing with his chin.

"No, let them enjoy these moments in peace before it all begins."

"You're so dramatic," scoffed Rodrigo.

Gabriel and Rodrigo rose from the bench as they heard the door swing open. Rosa and Joaquín looked up to see the bailiff enter the courtroom, followed closely by the prosecution, Brian Donovan. Gabriel muttered something to Rodrigo, and Rodrigo cracked a sly smile. Donovan chuckled as he passed by and found his seat at the prosecution table. Rosa took it as her cue and left the defense table, giving Joaquín a reassuring kiss, and walked behind them to sit in the first row.

As Rosa found her seat, the judge's clerk walked in from the hallway behind the dais and took her seat to the left of the judge's desk. The clerk brushed her dark hair and placed her files on the surface in front of her, leaving them closed. Her ebony face peered at the paperwork in front of her, and her right arm moved as she jotted something down.

Gabriel shifted in his desk as the muffled sound of footsteps on carpet drew near. The bailiff, a tall, middle-aged man with gray at his temples, trotted his way down the aisle. Gabriel surveyed him as he passed, and the light of the overhead lamps reflected off the gold star that shone on his left breast pocket. Crossing between the lawyers' tables, the bailiff strode to the right of the courtroom near the jury box, passing the clerk and disappearing behind the wooden divide that covered the hallway to the judge's chambers.

"Where is he going?" whispered Joaquín, his dark eyes inviting curiosity.

"To ask Judge Martindale when he'll be ready."

"Oh, okay."

Gabriel noticed a few beads of sweat slither down Joaquín's temples and bury themselves in the collar of his dress shirt. His voice hadn't broken when he spoke, but Gabriel noticed the tremor in his hand as it rested on the table. He slowly brought his hand to Joaquín's.

"I understand that you're nervous, Joaquín, but remember that witnesses, the jurors, the judge, and the prosecutor will observe you during the trial. Try to keep calm and focused. Be confident that you will be found not guilty and don't give anyone any reason to think differently."

A few moments later, the bailiff emerged into view, holding two large envelopes in his hands, and walked toward them.

"Counsel, the judge will be out in fifteen minutes," he said, placing one envelope in front of Rodrigo before placing the other in front of Donovan at the prosecution table. Rodrigo nodded his thanks and opened the envelope.

Retrieving the contents, Rodrigo divided the stack of papers in half and handed one half to Gabriel. Both lawyers grabbed their legal pads and began to read and scribble, selecting the crucial information from the answers to the questionnaires.

"Are those the questionnaires?" asked Joaquín, trying to see over Gabriel's shoulder.

Gabriel answered without shifting his eyes from the document.

"Yes, these answers and the potential jurors' answers to our verbal questions will give us a better idea of who we want to pick for our jury."

As Gabriel analyzed the questionnaires, he jotted notes on the legal pad, marking down professions, addresses, and characteristics that might determine their prejudices. Rodrigo tapped Gabriel on the arm a few moments later, holding his stack of papers and offering to trade. Gabriel accepted and shuffled the documents over to him. Joaquín's knee bounced beneath the desk, heel tapping as it rasped the leg of the chair. Gabriel touched Joaquín's arm again, and the tapping stopped.

"Sorry," he said, smiling weakly.

Rodrigo shuffled in his seat, took his stack, and placed it in front of him, revising the notes on his legal pad. Out of the corner of his eye, Gabriel saw the bailiff move from his post to the wall behind the dais. He frantically examined every line that he could, searching for any relevant clue that would help their selection. The second hand on his watch ticked its path around the roman numerals until the bailiff returned with Judge Martindale behind him.

"All rise! The Honorable Judge Montgomery Lee Martindale presiding," exclaimed the bailiff.

They all rose from their seats. Joaquín held one hand in the other and stood as tall as he could. A serious demeanor had replaced the nervous one.

Judge Martindale grinned as he nodded his thanks to the bailiff and strolled over to the dais. His thin white hair swayed as he ascended the steps to his desk, and his nostrils flared on his long and crooked nose as he breathed deeply. He raised his gaunt hand.

"You may be seated," he stated in a slight southern drawl, waving his hand to motion them down.

Muffled sounds originated from the rustling of chairs on the carpet as they returned to their seats. Gabriel stared up at the pale and weathered man. Beneath the thin skin of his face, blood spots and veins rested just below the surface, and the hard lines of hard years entrenched themselves in the expressions of the seasoned judge.

"Ladies and Gentlemen, we are here today for the case of State of Florida vs. Mr. Joaquín Pérez," he said, looking from the clerk to Donovan and then to Rodrigo and Gabriel before lingering on Joaquín. "Bailiff, would you please bring in the jury?"

The bailiff nodded and exited through the door near the jury box. Gabriel and Rodrigo took a moment to exchange notes on the jury pool, determining which candidates were to be struck with cause and which without cause, which candidates would be in their favor, and which would not be. Gabriel glanced over to Donovan, who sat casually with his fingers interlocked and a smug smile on his face. The odds were in his favor, and he knew it. Gabriel returned to Rodrigo, who turned away from Donovan.

"He's got a smug smile on, doesn't he?" asked Rodrigo.

"Yeah, how did you know?"

"Somehow, I always end up with the pricks on the other side, and for a while there, I saw this guy more than I saw Arlene."

Gabriel suppressed his laughter, and the tension eased. Rodrigo was ready, and his calm demeanor was his sigil before battle.

"I don't know how you do it," said Gabriel, handing Rodrigo his notes.

"Do what?"

"Remain calm." Rodrigo lowered his eyes and allowed a small grin to crease the corners of his mouth.

"I'm not calm. It's one thing when your client is guilty, but Joaquín's innocent. My stomach is in knots, and my heart is in my throat right now," he said, gesturing to Joaquín, who stared directly at Judge Martindale. "I need to play calm for him and for Rosa. If I'm not calm, then they won't be, and will the jury really think that he's innocent?"

Gabriel shook his head slightly.

"You're right."

"Let's pray that we get lucky today."

The door near the jury box began to open, and Gabriel turned to Joaquín.

"I'm sorry that I couldn't pay more attention to you when we were going through the questionnaires, but we had to get through those."

"No problem. Is this the big moment?" asked Joaquín, meeting Gabriel in the eyes.

The jury pool entered the courtroom following the bailiff who stood to the side of the door. The first six entered the jury box and took their places while the remaining candidates sat in the audience behind the defense and prosecution tables. They formed a single file line as they made their way to the benches and filled them evenly until the last candidate sat.

Judge Martindale watched as they shuffled into place and furrowed his brows before scratching the bridge of his angled nose. He cleared his throat and began his introduction.

"Ladies and gentlemen, I am Judge Montgomery Lee Martindale; my friends call me Marty, but, in this courtroom, my name is Your Honor." The audience chuckled a bit as he grinned. "I'll be presiding over this trial. To my left is Clerk Viola Gosens, who will keep track of the evidence presented to the court," he said as he pointed to her with his arm. "And the gentleman who escorted you in and wearing the gold star is Bailiff Gary Caulfield. He helps me keep order in the courtroom and keep in mind that if you have any problems or concerns, he is the person who will assist you." Judge Martindale gestured over to the bailiff, who smiled slightly. "In front of the witness stand is Mr. Mortimer Horowitz. He is the court reporter and will be writing down everything that we say in this courtroom today." Judge Martindale pointed to the balding and pudgy man whose hands continued to type even as he was introduced.

"The first order of business today is for me to give you certain instructions approved by the supreme court of Florida." He opened a gray-covered three-ring binder about seven inches long entitled *Florida Criminal Jury Instructions* and began to read. "In order to have a fair and lawful trial, there are rules that all jurors must follow. A basic rule is that jurors must decide the case only on the evidence presented in the courtroom. You must not communicate with anyone, including friends and family members, about this case, the people and places involved, or your jury service. You must not disclose your thoughts about this case or ask for advice on how to decide this case." Judge Martindale spoke for a few more minutes, reading the instructions and making sure that he was clear. He paused, looked at the six individuals in the jury box, and cleared his throat again before leaning forward in his chair to speak anew. "Now, ladies and gentlemen, Mr. Donovan, the prosecutor, and Mr. Vivar, for the defense, will be asking you a series of questions. From time to time, I may ask one of you to step down from the jury box. If that happens, you will be dismissed from this case and will be free to return home. At that point, another member of the jury pool will be called up to take your place. Do not take this personally or as a reflection of you or your character; this is merely the part of the process through which we select the appropriate jury for any trial." Judge Martindale waited a moment until the jury pool seemed to process the instructions. Once he was sure that they understood, he turned his head toward the prosecution. "Mr. Donovan, you may proceed."

"Thank you, Your Honor," said Donovan, buttoning his suit jacket as he rose from his seat and strode over to the podium, legal pad in hand. He placed it flush on the surface of the podium and adjusted his voice to project. "Good morning, ladies and gentlemen, I am Brian Donovan, and I represent the state of Florida in its prosecution of Mr. Joaquín Pérez. The court has given us copies of the questionnaire that you all answered upstairs. The court has given me the opportunity to ask additional questions of you. Now, by a show of hands, how many of you have served on a jury before?" A lone olive arm rose in the top right corner of the jury box where a young, dirty-blonde man with broad shoulders sat. "Rogelio Mantovani, correct?"

"Yes," said the man, nodding.

"And what type of a case was it?"

"Car accident."

"That was a civil case?"

"Yes."

"Did the jury arrive at a verdict?"

"Yes."

"Did you award money for damages?"

"Yes."

Rodrigo noted something on his yellow pad, and Gabriel waited on the next question as Donovan reviewed his own notes.

"Did you agree with the verdict?"

"Not at the beginning, but eventually, I was convinced by the others."

"Did you disagree on who was responsible, or did you disagree on the amount of money awarded?"

"On the amount of money awarded." Donovan nodded and lowered his eyes to the notes in front of him, dragging his index finger on the lines as he squinted to read the handwriting.

"I see that you work for Latin American Export and Import. What does that company do?"

"We buy and sell industrial sewing machines."

"The sewing machines that make products like my suit?"

"Yes."

"And what do you do there?"

"I am the manager of inside sales."

"And what are your responsibilities?"

"To supervise all sales made to clients and companies calling the office directly."

"Anything else?"

"Yes, I also keep the books and records of all sales and manage my team of three salesmen who help me make quota."

"That includes accounting work?"

"Yes, I graduated from Miami Dade Junior College with an Associate in Accounting."

"You have two children?"

"I do," replied Mantovani, his eyes beaming.

"Well, I can tell that you must be a proud papa judging from the smile that lit up from your face when I mentioned them."

"I am, very much so," agreed Mantovani, his cheeks rosing.

"Thank you, Mr. Mantovani." Donovan shifted his weight as he moved through his notes. "Has anyone ever been part of a legal case or other judicial proceedings?" another hand rose, but this time, from the center of the first row. The hand was small and slightly wrinkled, with a few brown spots and freckles. Gabriel tilted forward slightly in his seat to see around Rodrigo, who partially blocked his view.

"Chariya Suwan?" asked Donovan, looking over to her.

"Yes," answered the slight woman in an Asian accent.

"What type of case were you involved in?"

"My husband and I own a Thai restaurant on the beach. One late night, as we were closing, we saw two men break into the watch store next to us. We called the police, and the two men were arrested. It was very scary for us."

"Did you testify?"

"They took my deposition, but the men declared themselves guilty and did not go to trial."

Gabriel knew that Mrs. Suwan might have to be eliminated from the jury, so he jotted the word *possible strike* next to her name.

Donovan continued his questioning for another twenty minutes before reaching the final candidate. Sitting in the back row on the left, a burly man with a wrinkled face and ginger hair played with his thumbs as Donovan turned to him. The ginger man fidgeted, and Gabriel saw what looked like the bottom half of a generous heart tattoo slip from his short-sleeved shirt.

"This ought to be fun," whispered Rodrigo to Gabriel as the man gave Donovan a playful look.

"Lars Simensen?"

"Yes, that's me."

"It says here that you work at Swanky's Gentleman's Club on Biscayne boulevard."

"Yes, sir."

"Have you worked there for long?"

"It'll be five years next month."

"What do you do there?"

Simensen straightened himself in his chair as his eyes glinted and the corners of his mouth expanded to speak in a very serious tone.

"I am a full-time bartender at the establishment."

"Have you ever been involved in a legal case?"

"We have fights at the bar all the time, but it's usually the manager that testifies in court. Well, the bouncers have testified also."

"So, you don't participate in ejecting people from the bar."

"Only if the fight's really good and the bouncers need a hand. See this bruise here," he said, raising his fist to show two dark purple knuckles, "this is from last Friday night. Still stings."

"I see."

"It's no big deal. It's fairly routine."

Gabriel and Rodrigo contained themselves, and Gabriel drew several circles around Simensen's name. As he closed the fifth circle, Donovan turned to the judge, asking him to approach the bench. Judge Martindale turned to Rodrigo.

"Attorneys, approach the bench."

Rodrigo and Gabriel rose from their seats and walked toward Judge Martindale. The attorneys met the judge at his desk while the court reporter flanked them, waiting for the next words.

"Your Honor, I would like to strike Mr. Simensen for cause as it seems that he is completely desensitized to violence."

"There is no nexus to this case," the judge responded quickly. "Under your rationale, I would have to exclude anyone that works in a boxing gym, dojo, law enforcement, or any sport that has some measure of violence which may include football players. Therefore, your motion to strike for cause is denied." Donovan did not expect Judge Martindale to be so reticent but recovered.

"Then, Your Honor, I use one of my preemptory strikes to remove Mr. Simensen."

"That's fine, Counselor." Judge Martindale pushed back onto his chair while Gabriel, Rodrigo, Donovan, and Horowitz returned to their places. The judge turned to the jury box.

"Mr. Simensen, you have been gracious in coming here today and fulfilling your civic duty. At this time, I am excusing you from further service. Please, go upstairs and report that you are excused for the week."

"Thank you, Your Honor," responded Simensen, rising from his chair and shuffling by the seated candidates before exiting the box and meeting Bailiff Caulfield who escorted him from the courtroom. When Bailiff Caulfield returned, Judge Martindale asked him to call the next name in the jury pool.

"Mr. Jacob Tarkington, will you please approach the jury box?" A gruff man in his early fifties with tanned skin from the hard sun rose from his seat in the audience and walked down the aisle toward the jury box. He held a Dolphins cap in his hands, wore a green and white thin striped shirt with dark gray pants and black dress shoes. Bailiff Caulfield signaled for him to take the empty seat. Donovan waited for Mr. Tarkington to take his seat.

"Mr. Tarkington, I see here that you own a farm, is that correct?"

"Yes."

"What do you grow on that farm?"

"We grow avocados, mangoes, and tomatoes which we sell locally."

"Have you ever been involved in a legal dispute in any way?"

"Yes, I had a truck full of tomatoes stolen on its way to the wholesale produce market."

"And what happened?"

"The idiot who stole my tomatoes tried to sell them to a good friend of mine, so he called the police, and they caught him red-handed."

"Did you have to testify at the trial?"

"No, there he got smart, and he pled guilty, but I'll tell you something, I have all kinds of problems with thieves on the farm all the time."

"If you caught one of these thieves, what would you do?"

"Turn them into the police."

"Thank you, Mr. Tarkington. Your Honor," said Donovan, turning back to Judge Martindale, "I tender the jury."

The judge nodded and turned to Rodrigo.

"Mr. Vivar, you may begin your questioning."

"Thank you, Your Honor," said Rodrigo. He checked Gabriel's notes for a moment before rising and moving to the podium with his file tucked in his arm and his side. He spread his documents and the legal pad on the surface of the podium and began his introduction.

"Ladies and gentlemen, I am Rodrigo Vivar, and together with Mr. Gabriel Lock," he said, pointing to Gabriel behind him, "we are the attorneys for Mr. Joaquín Pérez, who is seated to Mr. Lock's left at the defense table. Mr. Donovan has already asked a series of questions that I will not ask you to answer again, but I do have some other questions for you."

Rodrigo smiled warmly before beginning.

"Mr. Mantovani, you were involved in a trial as a juror once before in a car accident, correct?"

"Yes," answered Mr. Mantovani.

"That was a civil case, as you explained earlier, and, in that case, you were asked to decide how the victim was damaged and how much money was needed to compensate that victim for those damages, correct?"

"Yes."

"In that case, the result favored the victim because the scales tipped in the victim's balance, correct?"

"That's exactly how one of the lawyers described it." Rodrigo waived his arm across the podium, indicating that he was asking the entire group.

"This case is not about money, but instead about a man's freedom, do you all understand that?" The jurors nodded their heads. "Therefore, our constitution demands that the prosecution prove its case to the exclusion of each and every reasonable doubt. Today you will hear witnesses talking, you will see pieces of evidence that will give you reason to believe one thing and question another, and you will hear closing statements that will attempt to solidify your thoughts toward their sway, but I wish to communicate one solemn idea. In cases pertaining to a man's freedom, there can be no decision based on sway. Any and all decisions of conviction must be made beyond a reasonable doubt, and if there is any doubt in your mind that my client, Mr. Joaquín Pérez, is not guilty of this crime, then you must find him not guilty. You must follow the fundamental instruction of our constitution; can you all do that?"

Gabriel saw all the jurors nod their heads and knew that Rodrigo had them following him.

"Mrs. Suwan, you saw the people who stole from your neighbor. Correct?

"Yes."

"And you were sure, beyond any doubt, that it was them?"

"Oh, yes."

"Would you have testified against them if you had any doubt?"

"No."

"Would any of you testify against someone unless you were absolutely sure that what you are testifying to is the truth?" And again, Rodrigo waived his arm across the podium, and all the jurors shook their heads.

"Can you apply that to this trial today?"

All the jurors nodded.

"You would not condemn a person and take away his liberty unless you were sure beyond and to the exclusion of any reasonable doubt, would you?" All jurors shook their heads, and some even uttered the word.

"No."

"Do you realize that this is all we are asking of you today, not to take a man's freedom without being absolutely sure he is responsible for having broken the law?"

All jurors nodded their heads. Walking briskly toward Joaquín and pointing at him, he said,

"This man depends on you, do you understand?"

All jurors nodded their heads.

Rodrigo stepped away from the podium and turned to the judge.

"I tender this jury."

The judge looking out at the courtroom.

"We have a jury. Mr. Bailiff, will you escort the remaining members of the pool back upstairs? Let's take a brief recess, and then we will get started with opening statements."

Chapter 40: The Incident in the Park

Miami, Florida: Early December 1981

Everyone filed back into the courtroom and found their places as the recess ended. Bailiff Caulfield's deep voice boomed across the room.

"All rise," he said as Judge Martindale entered the courtroom.

Gabriel looked up from his documents over to Rodrigo, who winked before rearing his head back toward Judge Martindale's dais.

"Are you ready to begin, Mr. Donovan?" asked Judge Martindale.

"Ready, Your Honor."

"Good, then let's please get started."

Donovan rose from his chair and walked in front of the Prosecution table. His leather shoes tapped slightly as the carpeted floor muffled their sound.

"Ladies and gentlemen, I am Brian Donovan, and today I represent the great state of Florida and her people. We have before us a simple but grave case about a man who simply cannot control his anger. During a fit of his uncontrollable anger, he grabbed a baseball bat and bludgeoned a young man named Rafael Delgado. He hit him so hard and so continuously that Rafael spent eight weeks in both the hospital and a rehabilitation center with broken bones, a punctured lung, a ruptured spleen, and severe contusions. During that fateful day at Tropical Park, Rafael met a young woman, and that young woman was Mr. Pérez's daughter. While both were running on one of the many trails that cross the park. Rafael had cut her off, causing them both to fall to the ground. Understandably, she called him a dumb shit." A few of the jurors tried to remain professional by muffling their laughter with their hands. "It is true that he responded in a manner not befitting a gentleman. Could he have behaved better? Probably. But he did not touch the young lady, he did not threaten her, and they both walked away at the end of the conversation. It was the defendant that was the sole violent person on that sunny afternoon. Rafael was not violent, the young lady was not violent, and the two people that had the initial conflict knew to walk away. This man," said Donovan pointing to Joaquín, "the defendant, Joaquín Pérez, did not walk away that day. He was arrogant, he was angry, and he was relentless as he hit the defenseless young man, Rafael, over and over. The evidence in this case is clear. You will hear testimony from the victim; you will hear testimony from an impartial witness that saw the defendant drive out of the park in his car and so took down his tag. The evidence will show that the police were able to track down the defendant from his tag numbers. And the evidence will show that once they found him at his home, in line with his previous behavior, he made the arrest difficult, which cost him a broken shoulder. There will be some testimony that the defendant was not there at the time of the incident, that he was with his wife at Walgreens. You will see a time-stamped receipt that purports to be proof of payment for the merchandise being bought. You will also see that the merchandise was paid for with the defendant's credit card, but that receipt is no proof at all. She could have paid with that card all on her own. It simply boils down to the word of a loving wife protecting her husband versus the words of the victim and an independent witness. Once all the evidence is in, I know that your minds and hearts will have no problem finding the defendant guilty of the crime of battery."

Donovan eyed the jurors for a few moments before he picked up his papers from the podium and, nodding his head toward the judge, found his way back to the Prosecution table.

Rodrigo watched Donovan sit down, and, giving the jury a moment to get settled, he rose from his seat and walked towards the podium.

"Ladies and gentlemen, as the trial moves forward, you will see that the evidence the prosecutor calls *clear* is not clear at all but full of inconsistencies and inaccuracies." Rodrigo turned from the jury and strode over to where Joaquín and Gabriel sat, pointing at Joaquín with his index finger. "My client, Joaquín Pérez, was not at Tropical Park at the time that the prosecution claims he was..." Rodrigo, having humanized Joaquín for the jury, slowly made his way over to the jury box. "My client's wife, Rosa, who you will meet later, will testify that she was shopping with Joaquín at the time this incident occurred. We will show you the charges on his credit card. And time-stamped receipt with the same time as that of the incident. The independent witness that the prosecution claims saw everything saw my client's car driving out of the park but could not make out the driver." Rodrigo paused for a moment and drew closer to the jury. "The arresting officers did not investigate this incident fully and, as a result, they arrested an innocent man, shattering his shoulder, as you can see." Rodrigo pointed to Joaquín, whose slung arm hung cradled for the jurors to see. "The officers claimed the defendant tried to flee, but Joaquín never fled. He simply turned to make a phone call to the lawyer sitting right next to him today, Mr. Gabriel Lock. He wanted what any innocent man would want in the face of great injustice, to call his lawyer. Please listen to the witnesses fully. Evaluate every detail with precise care and an open mind. And if you do, then I know that you will find Joaquín not guilty, and you will allow justice to prevail today."

Judge Martindale allowed Rodrigo the same time that he had allowed Donovan before speaking. After prudently waiting, he cleared his throat to speak.

"Ladies and gentlemen, you will now retire to the jury room where your lunch shall be served. I want to caution you again not to discuss the case with anyone or permit anyone to say anything to you or in your presence about the case. If any of this happens, please advise the bailiff as soon as possible. We will return to the courtroom by half-past one this afternoon."

Everyone stood up and, after the jury had left the courtroom, they too began leaving for lunch.

"It's already 12:20 and we have only until 1:30, so we'll have to go somewhere quick," said Rodrigo, turning to Gabriel but really informing Joaquín.

"Should we eat here then?" asked Gabriel.

"The cafeteria?"

"That should suffice. It should be quick enough."

"Can Rosa join us?" asked Joaquín.

"Yes, you just can't talk to her about the case," replied Gabriel.

"That's the last thing that I'd want to talk about."

"Alright, we're fine then. She's likely just outside of the courtroom.

Lunch lasted just under an hour as they tried to keep it light. Rosa took her seat on the bench next to the door and gave her husband a reassuring smile, touching his hand for an instant before he walked into the courtroom, where Gabriel and Rodrigo followed. They took their places, sitting in silence and waiting for Judge Martindale to recommence the trial. Rodrigo concentrated and prepared himself for the cross-examination. Gabriel leaned over to him and whispered in his ear.

"Firm but direct questions." Rodrigo smiled.

"You've got the notes, right?"

"I'll take as many notes as I can," answered Gabriel.

"We need to poke as many holes as possible to stand a chance."

"No, we don't. We just need one big one." Rodrigo grimaced.

"You better start praying then. All exculpatory evidence is off the board, remember?" Rodrigo nodded slightly to Joaquín, who held his head down with his laced fingers beneath the desk.

Gabriel knew that Joaquín was too focused on praying. Gabriel sensed Rodrigo rise from the chair next to him and automatically rose. Bailiff Caulfield and Judge Martindale entered the courtroom. Judge Martindale took his seat.

"Please bring in the jury," requested the judge.

The bailiff disappeared, and shortly afterward, the jurors began filing out into the courtroom and finding their seats. Once the jurors were seated, Judge Martindale addressed the jury.

"We will now start the examination of witnesses and the presentation of evidence. Questions asked and comments made by the attorneys are not evidence. Only the statements by the witnesses or physical and documentary evidence are to be considered by you in appraising the guilt of the defendant in this matter. Mr. Donovan, please call your first witness."

"I call Rafael Delgado, Your Honor."

Judge Martindale nodded his head, and the bailiff quickly stepped out of the courtroom.

"This is it," whispered Rodrigo to Gabriel. The veins in Gabriel's temple pulsated, and the muscles in his lower back knotted themselves. To his left, Joaquín's leg tapped and jittered.

The door opened, and Bailiff Caulfield returned with a lanky, skinny young man dressed in dark blue jeans, a linen shirt, and brand new black athletic shoes. His face bore the scars and renewed skin of healed wounds. He limped as he stepped, and his walk seemed almost crooked.

Clerk Gosens got up from her chair and met Delgado. She offered the court bible, placing it before him.

"Do you solemnly swear or affirm, to tell the truth, the whole truth, and nothing but the truth?"

Rafael placed a damaged hand on the bible.

"I do."

From his seat, Gabriel could see the splinted fingers resting on the bible. Rafael took the witness stand on the right side of the judge.

"Would you please state your name and address for the record?" asked Donovan.

"Rafael Delgado, 7731 SW 32nd Street, Miami, Florida 33155."

"Do you remember where you were on February 22nd of this year?"

"Yes, I was at Tropical Park. First, I was hitting the ball with a baseball bat, and then I was thrown to the ground and beaten. I did my best to defend myself, but after a while, I blacked out."

Gabriel saw some of the jurors cover their eyes. Others stared at Joaquín, unable to comprehend his actions. Others tried to meet his eyes with questioning anger.

"It always starts like this when you're the accused," explained Gabriel, whispering loud enough for only Joaquín to hear, "our turn will come next."

Joaquín's leg stopped jittering.

Donovan walked across the room to the clerk and whispered something. The clerk reached down and handed the prosecutor a wooden bat. He raised the bat over his head as he walked toward Rafael, who grimaced at the bat.

"Do you recognize this bat, Rafael?"

"I do," he replied, "it's my bat."

"Is this also the bat that was used to beat you?"

"Yes."

"Let's back up a little bit, then, if you don't mind," said Donovan. "Why were you at the park?"

"I play in a softball league there on Saturdays, and I had a game at three. So, I go there a little early to get ready for the game."

"What did that entail?"

"Excuse me?" asked Rafael, confused by the question.

"What did you do to get ready?" rephrased Donovan.

"Mostly, I stretched, jogged a little, and then did a few arm and leg exercises."

"Do you normally arrive early and stretch before all your games?"

"That is my typical routine."

"Did anything disturb your routine that day?"

"Yes, I bumped into a girl, and we got into it."

Donovan paused, lowered the bat from above his head, and allowed it to hang by his side.

"What do you mean?"

"I went running before the game. She was also running, and when we bumped, she said I cut her off and made her fall. I told her she was crazy, and she called me a dumb shit."

The jurors all focused on Rafael's testimony, and Gabriel felt Joaquín tense up next to him. He moved his foot to Joaquín's, tapping it lightly. Joaquín eased, remembering the instructions.

"Did you do anything?" pressed Donovan, walking over to the clerk's desk and giving the bat back to her.

Gabriel jotted down a line on his legal pad before sliding it to Rodrigo. Rodrigo saw the handwriting.

Smart stipulating to the bat.

"Unfortunately, I reacted. I said that if she did not have such a wide ass, there would have been more than enough room for the two of us."

"Then what happened?"

"We both stopped. She had a few more choice words for me. I laughed and wished her a good day."

"Did you see her again?"

"No."

"Did you wear any piece of clothing that made you recognizable?"

"I wore the shirt and the cap with my team's name. I always wear a white sweat band around the wrist of my throwing arm."

"Did you have those on when you went running?"

"Not the cap."

"What did you do then?"

"I went back to my stuff, put on my spikes, and played in the game."

"Did you win?"

"We got beat four to two. I lost the fly ball in the sun that let them score two extra runs."

Two jurors smiled.

"What did you do then?"

"I got my stuff, said goodbye to everyone. I walked toward my car at the end of the parking lot."

"Did you make it to your car?"

"No."

"Why?"

"I got jumped from behind and knocked to the floor."

"Did you see who did it?"

"Not then."

"Did anything else happen after you got knocked to the floor?"

"He put me on my back, grabbed my bat, and began to hit me with it."

Again, Donovan walked across the room to the clerk. For the second time, Clerk Gosens reached down and handed Donovan the wooden bat. Donovan took it and raised it over his head as he walked toward the victim.

"He hit you with this bat?"

"Yes."

"Where did he hit you?"

"All over."

"Did you see who hit you?"

"Yes. He then got close to me and told me that I was a *stupid and rude son of a bitch* and that I had to learn to *treat women better*. Then he punched me and punched me until I passed out."

Rafael lowered his head and tried to hide his face. A long silence filled the room as the jury envisioned the brutality of the account. The clock ticked above them with each passing second, and Donovan allowed it to tick for as long as he could before he slowly walked back to the clerk's desk and surrendered the bat for the final time.

"What happened when you regained your senses?" questioned Donovan, returning to the podium.

"I was in the hospital emergency room in a bed covered in tubes and hooked up to monitors."

"How long did you stay in the hospital?"

"Three weeks after the surgery and a month in a rehabilitation center."

Rodrigo and Gabriel's expressions did not change. Donovan put on a commiserating expression and walked slowly toward the witness stand.

"Would you recognize the man that attacked you if you saw him again?"

"Of course."

"You are absolutely sure?"

"I am."

Walking halfway between the witness stand and the jury box, and, looking at the defense table, Donovan stared straight at Joaquín.

"Do you see your attacker in the courtroom today?" he asked, not removing his eyes from Joaquín. Rafael looked at the defense table and then to the jury box.

"No."

Gabriel stopped writing, trying to comprehend what had just been said as the clock ticked louder than before. He raised his head and stared at Rafael, who did not move or say anything else. From the corner of his eye, Gabriel saw the jurors bearing puzzled faces and blank expressions as no one spoke. Donovan tried to recover.

"What other injuries did you have, Rafael?"

"Well, I had a severe bruising and a black eye."

"Any heart problems?"

"No. At least not yet."

Donovan turned once more to the defense table before asking Rafael once more.

"So, do you see the man who hit you so savagely on February 22nd in the courtroom today?" Once more, Rafael surveyed the defense table, then the audience, and then the jury box.

"No, I don't."

The original silence returned as Donovan's face remained impassive.

Judge Martindale interjected, surprised by the answer.

"You mean you don't recognize him because you don't remember what he looked like after the beating, right?"

Rafael turned in his seat to face the judge, raising his hand in the air about a foot and a half away from his face.

"No, Your Honor, he put his face eighteen inches away from mine as he screamed at me each time. I will *never* forget that face."

"Any further questions, counsel?" asked Judge Martindale, hastily moving on.

"Not at this time, Your Honor, but I would like to reserve and recall the witness later."

Judge Martindale accepted and turned to the defense.

"Any questions of this witness, Mr. Vivar?"

Rodrigo looked at Gabriel, then back.

"Your Honor, I'd like to consult with my co-counsel."

Judge Martindale nodded. Rodrigo pretended to gather his documents, rising from the desk with his back to the jury, shielding the conversation before whispering to Gabriel.

"Should I ask any questions?" he muttered under his breath.

"Absolutely not."

"I didn't think so." Rodrigo turned back to the judge. "No, Your Honor, not at this time."

Judge Martindale, trying not to emphasize the testimony, looked back at Rafael.

"Your testimony is completed here today; you may leave the courtroom."

Rafael descended the witness stand and, walking between the lawyers' tables, exited through the main door. Judge Martindale watched him leave before looking up at the clock and addressing Bailiff Caulfield who stood ready.

"Oh, my goodness, we have blown right past our break time. Bailiff Caulfield, would you please escort the jury to the jury room and make sure that they have whatever they need?"

Bailiff Caulfield nodded and moved toward the jury box, escorting the jury from the courtroom and into the deliberation room.

Judge Martindale watched the jury file out of the courtroom and waited until the door snapped shut behind them before turning to the prosecution.

"You've got a problem."

"Well, Your Honor, I do have other evidence," responded Donovan, "I have the...."

"Don't tell me you think you can convict this man when he has been definitively ruled out by the victim, do you, Mr. Donovan?" interrupted Judge Martindale. Spinning around and pointing at the sign above him, he challenged the prosecutor. "Does that ring a bell as to what we are doing here?"

Gabriel looked up at the sign with a smile. *We who labor here seek only truth*, it read.

"What I meant, Your Honor...," fumbled Donovan.

Rodrigo jumped in.

"Your Honor, not only have Mr. Lock and I been telling Mr. Donovan that he had the wrong guy, but now that we know he is innocent, is it fair to allow Mr. Donovan to prolong this?"

"I am dismissing the case now, Mr. Donovan. There is no need for us to be here," decided Judge Martindale.

Donovan nodded his head, and the judge called to the bailiff, who had reentered the room.

"Please bring in the jury."

Within seconds the bailiff was leading the jury into the jury box.

"Well, it seems that your participation has come to an end. I want to thank you for your service, your time, and your attention to this case. This court is very grateful that folks like you make up our juries in this county. You are all dismissed and do not have to return until the next time you receive a notice to come and visit us sometime down the road."

As the jury was about to stand, Bailiff Caulfield called out.

"All rise!"

Everyone in the courtroom rose as the jurors stood up and began filing out of the courtroom. After everyone else stood and watched them leave, Judge Martindale rose and left the court room followed by the clerk. Donovan begrudgingly grabbed his files and briefcase before walking down the aisle and leaving.

Gabriel, Rodrigo, and Joaquín congregated at the defense table, congratulating each other.

"What happened? Please tell me what happened."

Gabriel rotated to see Rosa, very pale, walking towards them from the aisle.

"It was good; it's alright. The accusation against Joaquín for the attack was dismissed by the judge," he said as he gently grabbed her by the shoulders.

"Oh, thank God. I became so worried from the parts of the conversations that I overheard between the members of the jury. I didn't understand what was going on. Then I saw the prosecutor walk out, and then I really had no idea about what was going on. I got so nervous. I thought

Joaquín lost it in the courtroom and thought he'd go to jail again!"

"Rosa!" shouted Joaquín, his eyes bright.

"Well, I didn't know what to think. I just freaked out."

"You're a free man, Joaquín," said Gabriel.

"I knew it the whole time! God rewarded me like I told you He would!"

Gabriel and Rodrigo decided against arguing. After a moment, Rodrigo grabbed his briefcase.

"Let's go home. My shoulder is starting to hurt badly. I need to take my painkiller," said Joaquín.

The four of them exited the courtroom and walked down the hallway toward the elevators. Some of the fellow attorneys and bailiffs waved and nodded their heads. Some smiled. The elevator doors parted, and they entered, riding the car down to the main lobby.

"Drive carefully; we will talk as soon as we get the judge's final order," said Gabriel to Joaquín and Rosa as they got into their automobile.

Rodrigo waved goodbye to them while he and Gabriel walked silently toward his car.

"I want you to know that in all these years, I have never had a defendant reach trial that was actually innocent," said Rodrigo to Gabriel. "We need to enjoy this one. Come on, I'll buy."

Chapter 41: The Debt

Miami, Florida: Early December 1981

The stone angels above the entrance to Miami Memorial Park Cemetery loomed over Gabriel as drove through the gate. Joaquín was due to meet him at a quarter after three and Gabriel was curious to know what the free man wanted from him at a graveyard. As he parked the Regal, he straightened his tie and brushed the wrinkles from his suit before walking onto the hallowed ground. The scents of freshly mowed grass and incense greeted him as he stared at the tombstones, seeing the names of those who came before him and knowing that one day he would rest alongside them.

"Gabriel?" called Joaquín's voice. Gabriel turned to see Joaquín, dressed in his finest suit, hair combed, and wearing his best watch. The sling was gone.

"You didn't look this nice in court," joked Gabriel. Joaquín smiled warmly.

"This is a bigger occasion than that was. Thank you for meeting me here. I know that you are busy working on other cases, so this really means a lot to me."

"I have other work, but it's also December. Most of it is delayed because holidays."

"I suppose. This was always the busiest time of the year for me. I worked hard driving freight around the country. I barely had time to see Rosa or the kids and almost always spent Christmas on the road."

"Well, I guess God blesses us in ways we don't expect," added Gabriel, smiling. "So, what did you want to discuss?"

"Do you mind a short walk?" asked Joaquín.

"Only if it's short, I went to the boxing gym three weeks ago and it still hurts." Joaquín laughed and they departed down the aisles of loved ones, careful not to tread on the markers.

"I know that I put you and Rodrigo through a lot. I stopped you from doing your jobs to the fullest degree and I'm sorry, but when I came, I lost my childhood friend when the Cuban army shot him as we swam across Guantanamo Bay to the American base, The Fidelistas sentenced my father to thirty years in jail, and I lost my mother and my sister because they were trapped on the island. The family of political prisoners were not permitted to leave the country. I lost everything that was dear to me as a child." He paused, taking his thumb to quell the swelling from his eyes. Gabriel did not speak and allowed Joaquín to continue uninterrupted. "My aunt, Cárola, became my new mother. Uncle Osvaldo is not my blood but raised me like his own. She struggled so hard when Ciro was born that she couldn't ever conceive again, and she always wanted Ciro to have a brother, so God gave her the son she wanted and gave me the mother I lost." His face puffed with red as he battled the emotions. "Sorry, Gabriel, it's this way," he said, pointing forward. They walked a few paces until they came to a section with humbler stones. Joaquín moved to the side, and Gabriel stood across. Joaquín gestured with his chin and Gabriel saw the name before him.

CÁROLA LORANT DE MARCOS

QUERIDA ESPOSA Y MADRE

18 DE ABRIL DE 1919 - 28 DE MAYO DE 1975

"This is all that we could afford in those days," said Joaquín, a tinge of shame lined his voice.

"I'm sure that she didn't care," countered Gabriel, "she was happy to see that you were there in her last moments and she's happy that you still care about her."

"Before she died, she made me promise to take care of Ciro and to be there for him. When I tried to protest, she made me swear. When I did, she left this world. How else could I repay the debt of what she did for me?"

"And what about the promise you made to Rosa and your kids?" Gabriel asked softly. The question surprised Joaquín whose face flushed, and he sharpened his eyes. "Joaquín, I understand the promise you made to Cárola, but your family needs you too. What would you have done if they had lost?"

"I would have fulfilled my promise," he barked in defiance.

"Would you? How exactly were you going to do that?

"You know Gabriel in life we are trapped between duties, continuously!"

"But you took your duty too far don't you think? You promised to look after him and to protect him, but not to trade places with him," continued the attorney without ever raising his voice. "Do you think that Cárola wanted you to go to jail for something you didn't do?"

"You don't understand, Gabriel. You sit there pretending to be some savior when in the end you have nothing to lose."

"You're right, Joaquín, I had nothing to lose in that courtroom, except my client and my friend." Joaquín glared at Gabriel, but he kept a steady voice. "Joaquín, you could have been sentenced to jail for assaulting a young kid, and especially with a bat!"

"He was fifteen, that's a man for Christ's sake," yelled Joaquín.

"In this country, fifteen is still a minor, not only in the eyes of the law but in society." Joaquín's defiance receded. "Who am I to argue with a lawyer about the law?

"I can guarantee that if she were alive, she would have never wanted you to take that kind of a risk." Joaquín nodded his head in agreement. Gabriel eased off, realizing that the message had gotten through to him and choosing not to restoke the fire. "I had come here hoping to show you why I made you and Rodrigo suffer, to better understand the reason, but you do not understand."

"No Joaquin, I understand, but I do not agree." Joaquín paused as he processed Gabriel's response. The corners of his mouth curled, and an understanding smile followed.

"Come on, Rosa I'm sure is waiting for you at home."

"She is. Now that this is over, I must find a new job."

"How's that going?" asked Gabriel.

"Terribly. There seems to be nothing out there for a guy like me. I can't drive anymore, and becoming an instructor would take longer than I can afford."

"How long?"

"Too long. Let's go."

The two men left the tomb behind, following the same route that they travelled earlier. Arriving at their cars, they shook hands, and drove their separate ways, one to his office and the other to his home.

Chapter 42: The Christmas Party

Miami, Florida: December 1981

Gabriel merged onto the side street next to the major highway as cars, trucks, and cargo honked and roared on by. He drove for a few moments, accelerating and braking as traffic required. As he neared Miami Truck and Cargo, his briefcase slid and jumped in the passenger seat on the road, eaten away by the weight of the constantly passing trucks. Looking ahead, he saw the frontage street bend, and so he began to turn. When he finished turning, he witnessed the familiar older trucks to his left while the office building sat no more than a hundred paces ahead. Beyond the eighteen-wheelers lay the full car park. He struggled to find a spot and squeezed into a space.

Music sounded from beyond the office building, and he could hear the lyrics of *Caballo Viejo* from what he imagined was a local band. Gabriel reached for his briefcase before exiting the Buick and walked toward the loudening music. When he rounded the corner, he saw the band atop the flatbed of an eighteen-wheeler. Behind them, he saw the crowd of employees and their families gathered around them, dancing, talking, and eating. On top of the cab of the flatbed stood a Christmas tree, decorated with garland, ornaments, and an enormous angel that resembled Walter at its top. Among the crowd of people, he saw long sleeve guayaberas, dress shirts, and colorful party dresses. He saw cigars, cocktails, laughter and heard jokes that only adults should hear. Gabriel entered the crowd, searching for Walter. Along the way, different employees greeted him and complimented him, calling him *Doctor* in their native Spanish. Gabriel thanked them, exchanging hugs, and shaking hands until Walter reached out to him from among the crowd.

"You made it," said Walter in Spanish, offering Gabriel his hand.

"There was no way that I was going to miss it."

"Have you had anything to eat?"

"I wanted to try some of your famous Argentine barbecue."

"Then follow me."

Walter led him through the sea of employees, leaving the blacktop and reaching a patch of earth and grass at the edge of the property. As they approached, the smell of smoked pork and beef filtered through the air. He savored the aroma as he took it in.

"We have two types of barbecue," said Walter, pointing at the two stations where middle-aged men guarded and tended to the food. On one side, there was a large pig stuck on a spit surrounded by four walls of cinderblocks. The flame had turned the pink skin to various shades of blue, golden, and dark orange. "This is Cuban pork with mojo," continued Walter, gesturing toward the surrounded pig. "And this is Argentine barbecue."

The two men moved toward a huge cylindrical grill, and a wide grin spread itself across Walter's proud face.

"Asado," he said, putting on an oven mitt and reaching for the handle. He pulled the handle upward, raising it enough so that the aroma of wood-smoked pig wafted from the grill. Gabriel could not contain his smile as the corners of his mouth stretched. "You won't want any other type of pork after this."

Gabriel pulled himself back from the grill and removed his smile.

"American barbecue, my friend, I'll just say Kansas City and leave it at that."

"We'll see. Come on, let me introduce you to my family."

They left the stations to head back through the crowd, where more people danced than before. Walter moved about halfway through the crowd when he stopped and tapped on a dark-haired woman's shoulder.

"Vittoria, Love, I want to introduce you to Gabriel, the lawyer, and friend that I've told you so much about."

Vittoria turned her head.

"It's a pleasure to meet you, at last, Gabriel. Walter has told me so much about you. Thank you for helping us through this past year."

Her dimples splayed as she thanked him, and Gabriel nodded his appreciation.

"It was my pleasure to help. The truth is that Walter is a fantastic client and a better man. I'm sure his best capacity is as a husband and father to you and your kids."

"Most days, but there are some that are really tough." She joked, putting her arm around his back and under his own outreaching arm. "No, thank you, Gabriel. He is a good man, and your company only validates it."

Gabriel nodded his thanks and waited for Walter to continue.

"Vittoria, I need you to keep an eye on things for a moment. Gabriel and I need to speak in the office for a minute. Can you keep everyone entertained?"

Vittoria looked around at the rest of the party.

"I'll do all I can," she answered, smiling.

"Come on, Gabriel, let's go meet my kids and then talk."

"They're over by the band," affirmed Vittoria, pointing near the flatbed truck.

"Thanks, Love."

Walter and Gabriel cut through the crowd, heading toward the band, when they spotted Antonella and Luciano clapping their hands together and standing directly in front of the band. They approached the kids, and when they got close, Walter tapped them both on the shoulders.

They turned around, staring up at their father. "Hey, Daddy."

"Hey, kids. How's the band?"

"It's great!" they beamed.

"I'm glad to hear. I have someone that I'd like you both to meet," he said, opening his body up so that they could see Gabriel from behind them. "This is Daddy's friend, Gabriel."

"It's nice to meet you both," he said, shifting his eyes from Antonella to Luciano and outstretching his hand to both.

"Alright, kids, Gabriel and I need to go to the office and talk for a bit. We'll be back in time for food."

"Okay, Daddy, we'll see you later," replied Luciano.

"Bye, Gabriel!" shouted Antonella, turning her attention back to the band. Gabriel and Walter set off toward the office. A few moments passed before Walter opened the front door of the office building, and they disappeared.

Climbing the stairs to the second floor. They reached the second level and moved toward Walter's office. Gabriel heard the band's music muffled by the thick walls and saw the swirl of colored shirts, fire, and lights from the party below. He loosened the grip on his briefcase as they reached the door of Walter's office.

Walter walked over to his desk and pulled out his chair. Gabriel followed and sat in one of the chairs opposite Walter.

"I know that this situation put a bit of pressure on you...."

"Don't sweat it, Walter. It's really nothing."

"I know, but I appreciate your taking the time to get this summary for me."

"Were you really that stressed about the situations?" asked Gabriel, changing the tone of the conversation.

"More for the second one than the first since the insurance policy had ended. I know that you explained what the outcomes could be and the worst-case scenarios, but yes, I was nervous, to say the least."

"I meant what I said."

"So, how much do I owe?"

Gabriel nodded and popped his briefcase up onto the desk, retrieving the invoice summary that Walter had asked for.

"Thank you, Gabriel," said Walter, reading the final numbers and filling out the check. "This should help with the repairs. Make sure that she reads it all," said Walter, placing the check and folded piece of paper inside a white envelope.

"I'll make sure to get it to Hamilton in the morning," declared Gabriel, reaching for the check.

"Thank you. Please tell him and Katerina's family that I wish them a Merry Christmas."

"I will."

"Anything else, Gabriel?" Gabriel paused for a moment.

"Yes," he answered, standing a little straighter, "I wanted to speak to you about employment."

"Your cases can't be going that badly for you, right?" joked Walter. Gabriel laughed it off.

"I'm referring to a client of mine, Joaquín Pérez."

"Go on."

"He's no longer able to operate his eighteen-wheeler and is looking for work."

"What's he looking to do?"

"Anything, really." Walter looked outside for a moment, staring through the window.

"How long has he been around trucks?"

"At least fifteen years, maybe more."

"Would you say that he's a bright man?"

"Bright, honest, and keeps his word." Walter changed his view back to Gabriel.

"You trust him?"

"Yes."

"Okay, I'm in need of a new operations manager. The last one I had moved to Los Angeles about three weeks ago. If you trust him and if he knows his stuff, then he's got the job."

"Do you want to call him, or should I?"

"I'll call him," answered Walter, thinking better about it. "Leave me his number, and I'll call him next week. If the interview goes well, he'll start in January."

"Thank you."

"You got it."

Gabriel and Walter rose from their seats. Gabriel walked over to the large window overlooking the parking lot while Walter arranged his desk. Bright lights, colorful clothing, and flags representing every employee surrounded the band while the long tables with Christmas-colored tablecloths occupied the quadrant just behind them. The soft orange of the lechón spit glowed off the cinderblocks while the Argentine barbecue shone from its wooden fire.

"Looks different, doesn't it?" Gabriel answered, not taking his eyes off the scene.

"It looks so different with so many people here. I'm not used to seeing the space occupied."

"You're used to seeing it empty. Well, all these people are here, and a lot of it is thanks to you."

"Thank you, Walter."

"So, are you going to stay for the food, or do you have to go?"

Gabriel glanced at his client inquisitively.

"Are you kidding me? Do you really think that I'm going to miss that Argentine barbecue of yours?"

Chapter 43: The Old Timer

Miami, Florida: December 1981

The next morning the Buick cruised down Sunset Drive, passing the array of homes on either side, surrounded by palm trees, bushes, and the remaining oak trees of an earlier time. The sun lay in the east, and a light breeze streamed down the road.

Hamilton's office looked more like an old house than an office. He approached the front of the stucco building and pressed the doorbell. A woman's voice sounded from the other side welcoming him in. He reached for the handle to open the door. Beyond it sat a middle-aged blonde woman with brown eyes and freckles.

"Good morning. How may I help you?"

"Good morning to you as well, I'm Gabriel Lock, and I'm here to see Mr. Hamilton."

She nodded.

"Do you have an appointment?"

"I wanted to deliver this to him."

Gabriel reached inside of his breast pocket to retrieve the envelope for her to see.

"Wait, are you the attorney on Katerina's case?

"I am."

"I can take that to him," she said briskly.

"I'd prefer to deliver it in person if you don't mind."

Gabriel raised his eyebrows slightly as he spoke, and she realized that it was for something other than Hamilton's services.

"Just a moment, Mr. Lock, let me see if he is available."

The woman departed from view, walking to a small hallway behind her and turning right. Gabriel examined the entranceway around him. The secretary's desk sat in front of the door, just a few feet from it, while the small hallway lay behind her. He looked at the surface of the desk, moving from the pencil holder to the notepads and post-it notes. As he scanned, he found a small nameplate almost concealed by the objects on her desk. *Rita McClintock*, it read.

A door closing at the end of the hallway pulled Gabriel from his visual exploration and, emerging in a white dress shirt, navy slacks, and matching suspenders was Hamilton.

"Good morning, Gabriel. How are you today?"

"Good, thank you, Hamilton."

"Please, call me Julius." As he finished, his secretary walked next to him, moving back toward her desk. "Thank you, Rita. I'll take Mr. Lock back now."

Rita acknowledged and found her seat, then Gabriel followed Hamilton.

"It's just down here," he said, pointing toward the end of the hall.

They walked down to the end and hooked right, entering the same place where Hamilton and Rita had emerged earlier.

"So, what brings you in?" Hamilton opened his hand, gesturing toward the comfy leather seats in front of Hamilton's desk. Classical decorations to a taupe-painted office. Cherry Board and Batten lined the walls touching and opposite the door, while the wall to his right harbored floor-to-ceiling cherry bookcases. On either side were two paintings of what Gabriel assumed to be Newcastle.

"Is this Newcastle?" he asked, delaying Hamilton's query and piquing his interest.

"Newcastle-upon-Tyne," affirmed Hamilton, "My family is originally from there. My brother and I took a trip a few years ago to visit Newcastle and see our roots. My great-grandfather used to tell us stories about it when we were kids."

"Great-grandfather?"

"Yes, he lived to be very old, and he lived with my mother and father. The Northern English can be very hardy people. My family's been in the Americas since the 1830s, and we made it to Miami thanks to Mary Brickell in the late 1930s. You've got English blood, don't you?"

"Some, the Lock name is from England, but my father's maternal side is from Ireland as well, while my mother's family is entirely from Asturias, Spain."

"You and I are from the same tribe."

"Come again?"

"Celtic blood. The Asturians of Northern Spain are Celts, with a small group of Iberians and some Visigoths. My family's blood is Celtic. We changed our name to Hamilton from something else before we came to the States, but the rumors in my family were that we had Celtic blood from Scotland."

"Quite the historian."

"My passion throughout life, but law paid better and was a little more personal. I wanted to serve others, and this was the better fit."

Gabriel took in the history lesson and returned to Hamilton's previous question.

"Sorry, I'm here because I wanted to talk to you about Katerina and her family."

Hamilton shot him a confused look.

"I'm a bit surprised, Gabriel. Is there pushback from the insurance company?"

"Not at all," answered Gabriel, dismissing the suggestion, "I'm here because my client, Mr. Buendía, wanted me to bring this personally." He retrieved the envelope from his breast pocket and handed it to Hamilton, who, still perplexed, accepted it in his fingers. "We know that things aren't easy, and while we had no fault in Katerina's accident, Mr. Buendía and his family wanted to help."

Hamilton opened the envelope. His lines folded as the wrinkles in his pale face moved. He took a hand to his clean-shaven chin, and his blue eyes opened. In Hamilton's face, Gabriel saw a likeness similar to his father's.

"You have to deliver this to her."

"What do you mean?" asked Gabriel, now the one shocked.

"I can't deliver this. This needs to come from your client. She needs to see you deliver this, so she can feel that there are people out there who care. That it is not a check to clear the conscience but genuine compassion and a willingness to help."

"Isn't it better if you deliver it?

"You'll know it when you see it. Come on, we've got to go. I'll drive."

Hamilton grabbed his coat from the standing hook next to the bay window, tidied up his desk nimbly, and ushered Gabriel out of his office. He almost jogged out of his office, passing Rita with alarming speed for a man his age.

"Rita, I'm going out with Mr. Lock. I'll be back in an hour or so. Keep everybody out of here until I get back!"

"Okay," agreed Rita, bewildered.

Hamilton and Gabriel exited the office building and walked toward Hamilton's car. The white Cadillac shone in the sunlight. Gabriel entered and fastened his seatbelt, unusually leaving his coat on.

"It's a short drive from here to there."

Gabriel nodded and watched Hamilton put on his seat belt. His speed lessened as he ignited the engine and settled into his seat. The air conditioning blew the cold air at full blast, and a country music station blasted Johnny Lee's *Bet Your Heart on Me*.

"You don't mind country music, do you?"

"Not at all. This song is oddly fitting."

Hamilton laughed and put the Cadillac in reverse. They moved onto Sunset Drive and set off toward Katerina's house.

They drove down the road for a few minutes, passing blocks of businesses and houses that flanked both sides. Hedges, bushes, and palms lined Sunset Drive until they turned onto 72nd Avenue. Hamilton lowered the volume on the radio and turned slightly to Gabriel, making sure to keep his eyes on the route.

"This is going to mean a lot to Kat and her family."

"It was all Walter's idea."

"Professionally speaking, of course, it is, but you also helped me secure the most that I could from the insurance."

"It's not like the company paid out everything that she needed, but I never thought I would get that much in such a short time." The light changed to green, and the car lurched as it buckled forward. "Sorry about that; I'm getting older quicker than I thought." Hamilton laughed at his joke, and Gabriel offered a slight grin. "You know, I've been in this profession a long time. I've seen clients of all kinds, performed hard work, easy work, and long work. This one hit a little harder to home because I see Kat like my own daughter. I will always see Kat as the little girl that used to sleep over my house in Jennifer's bed, right next to her. When it's your kid, you want the best for them, but I couldn't get Kat all she needs. I could only give her the best of what was available. "You," he turned his head to face Gabriel, "you made sure that I got her the best of what the law and policy allowed. You did that, and she wasn't even your client." Hamilton's eyes returned to the road as a car passed to their right. Gabriel did not speak, he wasn't sure of what to say other than give his thanks, but Hamilton sensed something more. "So, what's still bothering you about all of this?"

"What kills me is that the people who caused this accident walked away unscathed. They never answered for their transgressions, and our clients never got to face them."

Hamilton leaned back in his chair.

"You were at the State Attorney's Office before joining your father, right?"

"Yes."

"In the State Attorney's Office, you represented the state of Florida. Your client wasn't a person. It was a concept and is an institution that doesn't directly suffer the consequences of loss. In most of your cases, you were going to do justice by punishing the criminal for breaking the law. Welcome to the other side, where your client is a person and where they select you because they trust you. You represent the clients who have suffered the loss or the ones who have created the loss. The world that you knew as black and white now has infinite hues of gray. It's no longer clean and easy, and that's the hardest part to get used to."

Gabriel sighed, taking it all in. Hamilton gave him a stern look as he calculated his next words.

"Since February, I've handled probably somewhere between fifty to sixty cases, some were routine, and a few were extraordinary. Of those extraordinary eight in total, I only found true justice in two of them. I found justice for one client being ripped off by her neighbors and justice for a single mother and her two kids when the police put her husband away. I achieved the best results that I could for all these clients, but I have felt many times that there were restraints on my work, and you never knew where those limits would come from, the circumstances, the client, or the law. However, I still feel like I should have accomplished more."

Hamilton slowed the car as they approached a speed bump at the entrance of a residential neighborhood.

"A good lawyer always feels like he should have done better. A great lawyer knows when he can't."

"What makes you say that?"

"A lawyer becomes great when he wins the best result that he or she can under the circumstances. Limits, barriers, and constraints exist in every case. Sometimes you have evidence that will help your client, but you bring it before the court and the judge rules that the jury will never see it. In your case, your client decided no one would ever see it. There is no difference because the result is the same, the jury never knew it. You can't always win, but if you can get the best possible result for your clients and keep them afloat, then you can stay in the game, and that's what your dad and I have done. At some point, you have the potential to become great, but most lawyers burn out, become dysfunctional, become alcoholics, forget their families, and are plagued by insomnia about what could have and should have been. Have you given everything that you can to attain the best realistic result that you could have for your clients?"

"I have," answered Gabriel, slightly begrudged.

"Then? You left everything on the table and that's all you can do. Don't you think that I heard about your client, Joaquín Pérez? It was the talk of the courthouse when the victim turned to Judge Martindale and told him that his attacker was not in the courtroom that day. Judge Martindale was so surprised that he asked the victim a question on the stand for clarification. I mean, come on, Gabriel. You don't think that Joaquín and his family have better lives because of what you and Vivar did for him?"

"But I didn't make a difference in Joaquín's life. The police shattered his arm in an arrest they should never have made. He then had to sell his truck to pay our fees and his hospital bills, leaving him to find a new job in his forties. And then, to top it all off, Joaquín didn't go to jail because we got lucky."

"I can tell that you're still a little green. You and Vivar put Joaquín, and his defense, in a position to get lucky. You both busted your tails for him, did not give up on him, and conducted his defense to the highest level possible. They are not all going to turn out like Joaquín's case. You will lose your share like the rest of us and how you will learn to deal with those losses will determine where your professional life and personal one will go."

"That's what my dad keeps telling me," answered Gabriel, turning his head as the car slowed.

"Now, come on," said Hamilton, bringing the car to a halt, and stepping out in front of a house with a beautiful white porch, "we've got a gift to deliver."

Chapter 44: The Christmas Gifts

Miami, Florida: Late December 1981

Hamilton and Gabriel exited the car and walked across the front lawn toward the house. As they reached the front door, Hamilton knocked once. A scuffle from chairs sounded beyond the wall, and footsteps grew louder. The peephole in the door darkened for a moment, and then the door swung half open with a tall, dark-haired man standing behind it.

"Julius, I wasn't expecting you today. How are you?"

"Good, Miloš, good, thank you. How are you?"

"Great, thank you. Just trying to finalize Christmas decorations now that all the renovations are finished." Miloš looked over to Gabriel. "Who's your friend, Julius?"

"This is Gabriel Lock, Miloš, the lawyer that I told you about."

"The one who forced Northwestern to pay their share?"

"Yes, he's the one," finished Hamilton, pushing Gabriel slightly toward Miloš.

Miloš closed the door behind him as he exited the house. He outstretched his hand. His eyes widened and a slight tear formed in his eye.

"You have all of our thanks. As you can imagine, this hasn't been easy on our family and especially for our Kat, but the money that we recovered has been great to cover the repairs of our house, some of Kat's medicines, and all the equipment necessary to help her through this." Miloš's grip tightened on Gabriel's, and he could feel the fervor of the man's thanks.

"You don't have to thank me, Mr. Danek. I did what I could to help my client, and in doing so, I was able to help your family."

"He's much too humble, Miloš. Thomas Lock raised him right."

"That is your father?" asked Miloš.

"Yes," affirmed Gabriel.

"Then give him my thanks too." Gabriel nodded in appreciation but didn't know what else to say.

"Miloš, Gabriel has come here to deliver something for Kat. Do you mind if we speak with her?"

"Sure. She's just in the family room, staring at the ducks near the lake. You can come in if you'd like."

"That would be great."

The three men entered the house walked toward the family room.

"Darja!" shouted Miloš to the open house, "we have guests. Julius and his friend, Gabriel, are here."

"Be right there," she replied as they crossed the foyer and entered the family room. The kitchen lay across. There, in a rocking chair, with a slight blanket hanging over the side, sat a young brunette facing the shimmering lake laden with ducks and sunshine.

"Hey, Sweetheart, Uncle Julius and his friend, Gabriel, are here to talk to you."

Gabriel noticed a set of crutches leaning against a wheelchair to the side of the rocking chair. She did not respond but made an effort to turn the rocker toward them.

"Here, let me help you," offered Miloš.

"I've got it, Daddy," responded the brunette, denying his help. Katerina Danek strained in her chair, using the windowsill and all the strength in her arms to turn herself toward them. When she finished, her eyes darted from Gabriel to Hamilton.

"It's nice to see you, Uncle Julius."

"Good to see you too, Kat."

Before she could say anything to Gabriel, a blonde-haired and blue-eyed woman in her fifties joined them from the direction of the kitchen.

"Julius," she said, wrapping an arm around him and giving him a quick hug.

"You are Gabriel?" she asked, surveying him from head to toe.

"You must be Mrs. Danek."

"Please, call me Darja. Mrs. Danek makes me sound so old."

"Thank you, Darja."

"So, what brings you here, Julius?" she asked, turning her attention to Hamilton.

"This young man did. May we sit?"

"Of course," ushered Miloš, "would you like anything to drink?"

Hamilton and Gabriel both shook their heads in refusal. Darja and Miloš sat down on the couch opposite Katerina's rocking chair while Gabriel walked toward her.

"It's nice to meet you, Katerina," he said, outstretching his hand to hers. She smiled softly and reached for his hand, groaning slightly.

"Katerina, Darja, and Miloš, I understand that you all have been through a lot this year. I can only imagine the strength, endurance, and courage that it has taken to get past all this. When I say these words, I do so on behalf of my client, Mr. Walter Buendía, and all his family, who, despite having no culpability from his company, wanted help in some way." Gabriel reached into his breast pocket and retrieved the envelope that he had shown Hamilton earlier. "This, Katerina, is for you."

She grasped it between her thin fingers. She slid her index finger in the space and, with calm dexterity, tore the top of the envelope. Gabriel smiled, and Katerina's eyes met his for a moment, allowing a mischievous grin to appear from the corners of her mouth.

She opened the envelope and pulled out the check from within. Behind it lay a handwritten note from Walter. She lowered the check onto her lap and took the letter, allowing the folds to fall down as she read.

Tears formed at the base of her eyes, and she tried her best to hold them back.

"That was very sweet of him to write that, Gabriel. Please give him my thanks and wish him a Merry Christmas."

No one said a word as she stared at Gabriel through puffed eyes.

"I will, I promise," answered Gabriel, shattering the silence. Gabriel shot Hamilton a glance, and Hamilton understood. They rose from the couch. Mr. and Mrs. Danek thought about protesting, but Hamilton waved them down.

"We can let ourselves out, Miloš, don't worry."

Hamilton led the way, and as Gabriel turned to follow, he stopped, stared at Darja, Miloš, and Katerina one last time.

"Merry Christmas, and Happy New Year."

He followed Hamilton through the foyer and out the front door.

As Gabriel opened the door to the Cadillac, he heard a man shout with excitement before hearing tears of joy.

"Still think that you didn't make a difference?" asked Hamilton.

Gabriel pondered but chose not to answer. They entered the car, and Hamilton began to drive.

By the time he arrived at the office on Coral Way. Thomas's car was gone, and only Susana's remained. He recalled Hamilton's advice in the car and felt the advice his father had given him earlier in the spring, but something wasn't right.

He walked through the glass door, crossing the carpeted hallway. As he approached the door, the glass window slid, and Susana's face emerged from behind it.

"You know, your sense of timing is always a little off during the holidays."

Gabriel shot a look of surprise.

"How so?"

"You just missed Rosa Pérez; she was looking for you."

"Is everything alright?"

They are going on vacation for a few weeks to the Dominican Republic, and she wanted to see you before her flight took off. She wanted to wish you a Merry Christmas."

"Did she need anything else?"

"No, she came to speak with you and left some stuff, and I placed it on your desk."

"I hope that it's not a request to defend Ciro," joked Gabriel.

Susana laughed, and Gabriel stepped through the door. On the other side, he crossed the secretarial area and entered his office, leaving the door ajar.

"Susana, is my father coming back?" he asked, turning back to face her.

"No, he is helping your mother with some things, but he did ask me to tell you that your grandmother is making dinner for all of you tonight and would like for you to join them."

"Did he leave a time?"

"Six o'clock sharp."

"Spanish time or American time?"

"Cuban time!"

"Eight o'clock it is then." She winked at him, and he thanked her for letting him know. "Susana, why don't you go ahead and take the rest of the day off. I'll take care of things here."

"Are you sure?" she asked, giving him a quizzical look.

"Friday afternoon, just before Christmas, positive."

"Alright."

She grabbed her things, delaying just a few moments. As she went to leave, she gave him a quick smile and wished him both a Merry Christmas and a Happy New Year.

Gabriel waited a moment before turning on his heels and walking toward his desk. He removed his coat and hung it on the back of his chair before sitting down and staring at the small cube wrapped in red wrapping paper with gold ribbon. He opened it, making sure not to rip it. Beneath the paper was a small box with a lid. He lifted the lid to find a small statue of Don Quixote and Sancho Panza. Amused, he retrieved it from the desk and saw a folded piece of paper at the bottom. He pulled it out and unfolded it. Something fell from between the folds back into the box,

Dear Gabriel,

Thank you for always being loyal. Your efforts gave us the greatest gift of all this season.

Merry Christmas,

Rosa

Gabriel placed the note to the side and grabbed the fallen item from the box. He turned it to find a photograph of Rosa, Josué, and Esmeralda, all smiling and posing with an unamused Santa Claus who held a bemused Joaquín across his lap. He stared at the photo for a moment while laughing, then realized the wisdom of Hamilton's words. He and Rodrigo had made the difference even against the odds.

Gabriel placed the photo inside his desk drawer along with the note, rose from his chair, and checked his watch. There was only one place to be, and for the first time, he would arrive early for Abuela's dinner. He departed the office, got back inside the Regal, and took off on Coral Way, leaving for Abuela's house and the family that waited for him.

About the Authors

Humberto was born in Cuba in 1953 but immigrated to the US at 6. At 12 he moved to Spain where he attended the American School of Madrid for six years. Upon his return to the states, he graduated from Duke University with a BA in Political Science and Public Policy Studies. He attended the University of Florida obtaining a JD. He has practiced law for over 40 years in Miami Florida representing multicultural civil and family law clients and is AV rated pre-eminent. Humberto is married with four grown children and two grandchildren.

David, co-author and son, was born in 1991 and has lived in both Florida and North Carolina, graduating from NC State with a major in Spanish. Additionally, he is native in English, fluent in French, and can communicate in Portuguese, German, and Italian. On his way to being a writer, he has made his living through training, sales, and client success. Among other things, David is 33, a practicing Catholic, and a Knight of Columbus.

Acknowledgements

This work would have never been possible without the belief and efforts of our friend, Luís Felipe Díaz Galeano, our publishers from Atlas Elite Publishing, Dar Dowling and Michael Beas, and our proofreader and editor, Angela Schutz as well as the wonderful people who read, critiqued, or supported our work along the way. They are honored alphabetically below:

1. Adam Nathan
2. Alex Rabre
3. Amanda Cancio
4. Amar Brkić
5. Amélie Meppiel
6. Andrew (Drew) Rice
7. Anna Shope (Dr.)
8. Anne Van der Giessen
9. Beth O'Lear
10. Brennen Edwards
11. Brittney Leggett
12. Cabe Akers
13. Carter McDine
14. Cathalyn Van Deusen
15. Cecilia Bikkal
16. Charles Suaris
17. Chel Cartmill
18. Chiekezi (CK) Akagha
19. Cindy Le Guel
20. Cory McDine
21. Danielle Villarán
22. Darla Stuckey
23. Dragica Dodevska
24. Elegear Primus
25. Eliécer Ávila
26. Ellen Sadovy
27. Fran H. Hudson
28. Hayley Vatcher (Dr.)
29. Iván Sánchez Gómez
30. Jamie Snider
31. Jonathan Shinholtz
32. Joyce Horowitz
33. Judie Dellis
34. Julie Fairman
35. Karen Tharrington (Dr.)
36. Kemjika (KC) Akagha
37. Kevin Javor
38. Krithika Ramesh Kuhn
39. Leo Sadovy
40. Liam Shearin
41. Lisa Ivey
42. Lourdes Avino
43. Luly Avino
44. Luís Fernández, Esq.
45. Marcus Pauling
46. Mark Mullauer
47. Mary Claire Lachiewicz
48. Moriah Ruthford
49. Nathan Kuhn
50. Nicholas (Nick) Solovieff
51. Nicolás Sánchez Cuerda
52. Raphael Chanis
53. Rick Rosenberger
54. Rodrigo Villarán
55. Sean Isabel
56. Sean Witty
57. Thomas Stafford (Dr.)
58. Tom Minton
59. Ty Prentice
60. Verónica Cancio De Grandy
61. Xavier Primus
62. Zeta Yarwood

Made in the USA
Las Vegas, NV
28 September 2024

bc87535f-461e-48a6-bef9-e910015f6f73R01